Centerville Library
Washington-Centerville Public Library
Centerville, Ohio

DISCARD

America's Gun Wars

America's Gun Wars

A Cultural History of Gun Control in the United States

Donald J. Campbell

 PRAEGER™

An Imprint of ABC-CLIO, LLC

Santa Barbara, California • Denver, Colorado

Copyright © 2019 by Donald J. Campbell

All rights reserved. No part of this publication may be reproduced, stored in a retrieval system, or transmitted, in any form or by any means, electronic, mechanical, photocopying, recording, or otherwise, except for the inclusion of brief quotations in a review, without prior permission in writing from the publisher.

Library of Congress Cataloging-in-Publication Data

Names: Campbell, Donald J., 1948- author.
Title: America's gun wars : a cultural history of gun control in the United
   States / Donald J. Campbell.
Description: Santa Barbara, CA : Praeger, [2019] | Includes bibliographical
   references and index.
Identifiers: LCCN 2018055623 (print) | LCCN 2019000279 (ebook) | ISBN
   9781440870309 (eBook) | ISBN 9781440870293 (hardcopy : alk. paper)
Subjects: LCSH: Gun control—United States—History. | Firearms
   ownership—United States—History.
Classification: LCC HV7436 (ebook) | LCC HV7436 .C35 2019 (print) | DDC
   363.330973—dc23
LC record available at https://lccn.loc.gov/2018055623

ISBN: 978-1-4408-7029-3 (print)
        978-1-4408-7030-9 (ebook)

23 22 21 20 19   1 2 3 4 5

This book is also available as an eBook.

Praeger
An Imprint of ABC-CLIO, LLC

ABC-CLIO, LLC
147 Castilian Drive
Santa Barbara, California 93117
www.abc-clio.com

This book is printed on acid-free paper ∞

Manufactured in the United States of America

In sweet memory of
Kathleen Riggin Campbell, PhD
Wife, Mother, Lover
Forever my delight in work and play

Contents

CHAPTER ONE

Introduction:
An American Controversy

Anyone having even a passing familiarity with the history of the United States knows the iconic place the gun occupies in American culture. Even before America's independence, firearms were an integral part of the country. For the many European groups who explored, colonized, and eventually tamed the great North American wilderness with hatchets, plows, and rifles, guns were an essential tool of daily life. Firearms ensured protection against the unpredictable dangers of unfriendly inhabitants and savage animals, and they secured much of the game that supplied the newcomers' supper tables. As one commentator observed, America was born gripping a rifle in her hands[1]—and with that rifle, she went on to establish a legacy of unparalleled achievement and accomplishment.

The Europeans who came to America brought with them the best small arms available in their homelands and then improved them to meet the peculiar challenges of their new world. Beginning in the 1700s, when immigrant gunsmiths transformed the Old Country's Jaeger rifle into the quintessentially American Kentucky rifle, through the development in the 1800s of the "guns that won the West"—Samuel Colt's renowned Peacemaker revolvers and Oliver Winchester's repeating rifles—and the classic firearms designed by John Browning in the 1900s, spanning hand-guns, rifles, and machine guns,[2] firearms have always been a prominent feature of the American landscape. Accepted as indispensable instruments in dangerous times and as useful skill-building recreational implements in more relaxed times, firearms shaped the American experience in essential ways.[3]

For instance, the innovative designs and superior manufacturing of high-quality, mass-produced firearms helped propel American commercial activity into the international spotlight. American entrepreneurs and inventors, grappling with the limitations that custom gunsmithing placed on the production of arms, created new techniques and approaches that achieved worldwide adoption. Custom firearms were not only exceedingly expensive to make but also required individualized hand-fitted parts, which restrained the number of weapons a competent smith could produce in a given period. In addition, because they were not standardized, if a weapon part broke or needed repair, the owner could not simply swap out the part with an equivalent from another weapon. It was the American inventor Eli Whitney who radically reshaped arms manufacturing with the simple expedient of parts interchangeability; in 1801, he demonstrated the value of this leap by creating a workable musket from the randomly selected parts of 10 other muskets that he had machined earlier. Through his efforts and those occurring in the factories of Colt, Winchester, Remington, and others, 19th-century America led the world in the development of pioneering arms and the machines essential for their manufacture.[4] The cataclysmic War Between the States only intensified these efforts. Inventors and engineers filed over 500 arms-related patents between 1860 and 1871,[5] and by 1900, the United States had both the most advanced military arms in the world and the most advanced production processes for arms manufacturing—a position it has never relinquished.

Similarly, hunting and its commercialization not only helped bind Americans to firearms but also spurred early Americans into preeminence as the best marksmen in the world. Throughout much of the country's early history, game animals were plentiful—seemingly inexhaustible—and hunting for profit provided a livelihood for any individual having the weapons and wherewithal to harvest such public bounty. Many individuals did. Hunting prompted legions of Americans to become intimately familiar with the firearms of their age. Reflecting on hunting in the 1800s and 1900s, one observer noted, "There is not a man born in America that does not understand the use of firearms. . . . It is almost the first thing they purchase . . . and in the cities you can scarcely find a lad of 12 years that [does not] go a gunning."[6] These common experiences revolving around hunting, comradery, and firearms forged in individuals a shared American outlook and a shared American identity, with firearms prominently centered.

However, this short summary of the gun's pivotal impact on the nation's self-identity is not a complete evaluation of its cultural legacy. The full story of the gun's imprint on America is a Janus-faced narrative, having a second theme that is much darker and more sinister. This second theme centers on the inherent lethality and misuse of firearms. It emphasizes their facilitation of violent disputes, their power to provoke terror in peaceable citizens, their capacity for creating civil chaos, and their frightful ability to magnify the consequences of evildoing in the hands of evil individuals. Anyone with a passing familiarity of American history also knows of Al Capone and gun-toting big-city mobsters, of the St. Valentine's Day tommy-gun massacre, of inner-city drug shoot-outs, and of crazed teenagers using AR-15 rifles to kill schoolchildren. They also know of other senseless mass shootings of nightclub patrons, concertgoers, and Sunday service worshippers, and they know that Americans with firearms caused such carnage. This disturbing theme is also an integral part of America's gun legacy.

As Americans who have traveled abroad in Asia or Europe can likely testify, America's gun culture both bewilders and fascinates the rest of the world. A casual exchange of any length with a friendly foreigner familiar with American ways will eventually focus on America's seeming love affair with firearms, with the stranger asking questions along the lines of, "Do you own a gun? Doesn't everyone in the States have a gun? American cities must be pretty dangerous, right?" Perhaps easily dismissed as a bit of cultural teasing by someone slyly imputing the superiority of his own gun-free culture, the questions in themselves are nonetheless provocative—in that, they highlight core issues in America's gun controversy. What does gun ownership imply about a person? What does being "pro-gun" or "anti-gun" reveal about the individual? What does the prevalence of large quantities of pistols, rifles, and shotguns in a society imply about that society: is it a "free" society or simply a "mad" society? Does access to these weapons enhance personal safety and reduce danger, or does such access increase an individual's peril? Is the net benefit to society greater when firearms are freely available or when they are highly restricted? Questions like these underlie the gun controversy in America, and answering these questions is surprisingly difficult because substantive answers require a complicated mix of rational consideration, empirical evidence, and philosophical preference; in encountering these elements in discussion or debate, reasonable individuals often disagree on the basic validity of one or more of the components.

A Cultural Perspective

This examination of America's gun controversy assumes that a true appreciation of the Janus-like nature of the country's gun legacy—and any hope of arriving at answers to the questions posed above—requires more than a familiarity with the ongoing political and legal wrangling that characterize current evaluations of the topic. A number of insightful observers[7] have maintained that, at its core, America's gun controversy is a cultural controversy, and the present examination firmly subscribes to that contention. Without knowledge of the historical and cultural roots of the "gun question," current discussions will primarily appear to revolve around the efficacy of gun restrictions for reducing crime and improving public safety. These are important empirical questions, and with little effort, the interested individual will discover in popular media outlets a host of contradictory claims, with one list of research findings and statistical studies purporting to demonstrate that gun control is indeed effective and another list of studies and research purporting to show (just as convincingly) that it is not.

Even under the best of circumstances, attempts to use empirical evidence to evaluate the gun question and firearms' impact on the nation are intellectually hazardous. An examination of America's first rigorous attempt to regulate pistols and revolvers—New York's Sullivan Act—provides an illustration of the dangers involved. Supporters touted the 1911 law as a major bulwark against New York City's rampant gun crimes and violence. A year after passage, however, an evaluation of its effectiveness using the number of homicides as a metric showed an *increase* in the city's shooting homicides: 114 in 1912 compared to 93 in 1911. The *New York Times*, which had vigorously championed the Sullivan Act during its legislative passage, concluded that it had not proven effective. But this judgment was possibly premature, because by 1919 gun homicides across the city were distinctly treading downward, while before the act they had trended upward. But then again, although gun homicides were certainly on the decrease, homicides by other means had also decreased![8] Given these empirical results, was the Sullivan Act effective? It seems apparent that the varying results and confounding factors make an unambiguous interpretation of the data impossible. As alternative readings of the findings are available, individuals are free to see in the numbers whatever they prefer to see. Such equivocal results and confounding factors beleaguer virtually all attempts to evaluate gun control legislation empirically.

Similarly, gun control assessments centered on just logical argument also suffer the same limitations of ambiguity. For instance, advocates of gun control, believing that extensive handgun ownership results in greater violent crime, frequently argue that additional restrictions on firearms can only result in a safer community. In response, pro-gun advocates note that armed citizens commonly deter lawbreakers from committing violent crimes to begin with, and they further assert that hindering the access of law-abiding individuals to firearms will doubtless increase crime.[9] Both arguments are reasonable, and the choice of one over the other reveals more about the orientation of the individual than about the likely effectiveness of gun control. All this is not to say that empirical investigation or logical analysis does not constitute worthwhile pursuits; it merely means that empirical efforts or logic alone are unlikely to yield satisfactory answers to controversial gun control questions.

In contrast, the cultural orientation adopted in this examination approaches these questions not as empirical issues but as an encounter—often a bruising and bitter encounter—between contesting cultural values. Seen as such, the confusing and contradictory evidence regarding gun control efficacy becomes less bewildering. If cultural values are at the heart of the debate, these values unsurprisingly operate as filters, guiding the selection, interpretation, and assessment of the available empirical evidence. These filters work in ways that ensure that gun control proponents and opponents are unlikely to agree on what even constitutes credible evidence, much less on evidence compelling enough to warrant switching sides. Thus, individuals expecting present gun control discussions to provide convincing, empirically justified answers to the "gun problem" will only find disappointment. Current exchanges between champions on either side of the issue are better understood not so much as analyses aimed at identifying workable social policies, but as advocacy opportunities designed to bring uncommitted individuals over to their position. For many of these individuals and groups, the actual effectiveness of gun control is usually a secondary concern to the value-affirming significance of the position being championed. As one commentator has observed, "The gun control debate has been conducted at a level of propaganda more appropriate to social warfare than to democratic discourse."[10]

A cultural orientation toward America's gun controversy—viewing gun control as a "culture clash"[11] rather than as a debate about whether gun restrictions "work"—offers a more sophisticated understanding of the forces creating the controversy and a deeper appreciation of its divisiveness. The controversy is not about one side or the other selfishly refusing to see what is plainly evident to all reasonable individuals; it is about surrendering worldviews and self-identities that few are willing to abandon. At its heart, the dispute centers on how we as Americans want to see ourselves and, as importantly, how we want the rest of the world to see us. As one gun control analyst put it, "Gun control is really a question about what kind of a country America wants to be. One that has guns and is willing to use them given the chaotic nature of the world; or one that believes throwing them away can bring us closer to peace because change is possible."[12]

In exploring this gun-centered dichotomy, some observers have argued that its roots exist in a more fundamental separation of American society, one that divides the country along individualistic and collectivistic lines.[13] This argument proposes that all societies have to wrestle with the many tensions that arise in maintaining the rights of the individual while providing for the needs of the community. Different societies strike different balances, and in America, the balance has traditionally tilted toward individualism, stressing self-reliance, autonomy, and personal accomplishment. Because individualism puts only limited emphasis on the collectivity, citizens in this type of society primarily focus on their own self-interests. In societal contests for achievement and resources, they expect to compete in an environment open to all, with special treatment for no one. Also, because only weak ties bind the individual to the collective, society's ability to regulate the individual is also lessened, with citizens typically skeptical of government, suspicious of attempts at regulation, and willing to challenge institutional controls.

In collectivistic societies, individuals place more emphasis on sharing resources, and they frequently look to the government to ensure an equitable distribution of common goods. Citizens are more tightly bound to the community and are more accepting of putting the group's interests above their own. Individuals endorse cooperation and working with others to accomplish common goals, and they share a sense of collective responsibility to aid less-favored members in need of help.[14] Of course, no society is completely individualistic or collectivistic, and within any large populace, some members (based on personal experiences and individual backgrounds) may gravitate to an individualistic orientation, while others hold a collectivistic orientation. This is certainly the case within American society, and investigators exploring gun control issues have found these two orientations (or similar ones) useful for understanding why gun regulation questions create such divisiveness.

For instance, pro-gun proponents are more likely to have an individualistic orientation and have less faith in the collective's institutionalized structures. Reluctant to rely solely on institutionalized law enforcement for individual and family protection, they instead marshal private firearms for personal security—even if doing so diminishes the overall good of the community. Anti-gun individuals are more likely to have a collectivistic orientation and a greater willingness to rely on the community's structural institutions. They are more willing to forgo whatever additional personal security a firearm might provide, if doing so enhances the community's collective safety. To understand the decision making in both cases, an observer must center less on the gun and more on the person's general societal orientation.

Two Opposed Cultures

The individualism/collectivism distinction effectively captures two broad cultural orientations relevant for appreciating an array of societal problems in America. On the issue of firearms specifically, other observers have generated a similar cultural dichotomy, categorizing American society into "Bedrock America," reflecting a more individualistic orientation, and "Cosmopolitan America,"[15] having a more collectivistic orientation. Within this separation, the gun is a stand-in for two particular worldviews. For the proponents of Bedrock America, the worldview represented is one of self-sufficiency and individual independence; for the proponents of Cosmopolitan America, it is one of violence and conflict. Importantly, the gun itself has not created these worldviews; it has merely come to represent them. Much larger social and institutional events created these orientations.

In adopting these two categorizations, this book differs from many other "gun-culture" studies whose main goal is to identify and examine the specific psychological and demographic characteristics of individuals having pro-gun orientations. These studies use "culture" in a more general way, primarily as a classification variable that gauges an individual's standing on some type of gun-culture continuum. Those regarded as gun advocates are then treated as a distinctive subgroup within the larger society, and the key objective of the ensuing examination is to uncover the individual-level characteristics (for example, a person's religiosity, family upbringing, or beliefs about masculinity) that make firearms especially attractive to this subgroup, probing how these characteristics determine gun attitudes and gun control beliefs.[16]

These studies are important in their own right for understanding the role of guns in American society, but their focus differs from the cultural perspective adopted here. In this narrative, the gun is merely a symbol for a host of values that define Bedrock America, and the book treats Bedrock America itself not as a gun-oriented American subculture but as the country's dominant culture—at least initially. The focus is on cultural-level factors (such as the prevalence of violent crime in a period or the entertainment themes dominant in an era) that nurtured the minority views of Cosmopolitan America and grew this group's values into a societal force capable of challenging the country's dominant culture. Consequently, the book excludes individual psychological dynamics and demographic considerations to concentrate on the societal-level events that have influenced America's gun debate.

Cultural values are principles and beliefs that are broadly endorsed within a society, and they are significant because they encapsulate the worldview of the typical member. Central to members' concepts of what is right and wrong, proper and improper, fair and unfair, these values shape attitudes and behavior unthinkingly. Different societies often have different cultural values (giving rise to the cultural uniqueness of each society), and judgments regarding what is fitting, just, and appropriate can vary radically from one society to another. It is also possible for groups within a society to develop their own particular set of values, ones that may stand in stark contrast with (or even in opposition to) the cultural values of the larger society of which they are a part.

In the context of the gun controversy, Bedrock America has championed those cultural values that have defined American society for much of its history. A nonexhaustive list of these values would include a belief in independence; personal accomplishment; self-reliance; justice; and the rightness of democracy, equality, and freedom—values captured in the ideal of "rugged individualism." Given these values, it is easy to imagine how Americans could also develop exceedingly strong beliefs about the appropriate place of firearms in their society. After all, in the larger history of the country and in the personal histories of individuals, the gun was often a pivotal instrument in gaining or ensuring such values. These traditional values still shape the beliefs and attitudes of pro-gun proponents and form the cultural basis of Bedrock America.

In contrast, members of Cosmopolitan America have endorsed a distinctive new set of shared values. Responding to a changing and evolving world—the end of Frontier America, explosive escalations in city crime and violence, and the growing professionalization of urban police forces—these individuals are distrustful of firearms, seeing the gun's place in American society as appropriate in earlier days perhaps, but no longer. Believing the country has long moved beyond its frontier past, they view what they regard as America's "gun culture" as an anachronism and an embarrassment, not worthy of a nation whose peers on the world stage have severely curtailed or banned gun ownership by private citizens. Typically situated in the urban enclaves of politically liberal, college-degreed, upper-middle-class America,[17] these anti-gun advocates of Cosmopolitan America see little necessity for firearms in modern society, and they fervently desire to end the centrality of the gun in American life.

The values of Cosmopolitan America are communitarian in orientation, and they emphasize civil cooperation, reciprocal obligation, interdependency, inclusiveness, and trust in government for solving social ills. While not wholly rejecting Bedrock America's more individualistic values, members of Cosmopolitan America view this individualistic orientation as ill-fitting and no longer applicable to the complex social environment that has developed. Within this cultural perspective, far from being a symbol of all that was right with society, the gun represents all that is wrong with society. These are the values shaping the beliefs and attitudes of those individuals inhabiting Cosmopolitan America.

In the 1900s, Cosmopolitan America's emerging orientation toward firearms somewhat uneasily coexisted with Bedrock America's traditional orientation. Cosmopolitan America emphasized the need to keep guns out of the hands of criminals and individuals of questionable character, and the reasonableness of these arguments—the first glimmers of widespread, serious gun control—were accepted, although not fully endorsed, by Bedrock America. Over time, as Cosmopolitan America continued its calls for additional and stricter regulations of firearms—such as greater limitations on who may own a gun and on the conditions under which firearms can be purchased and used—the gun advocates of Bedrock America became increasingly convinced that the gun control advocacy of Cosmopolitan America was, at its core and despite its seemingly benign facade, an insidious attempt to destroy America's time-honored acceptance and celebration of firearms.

If the struggle that has emerged between the proponents of these two cultures reflects a much larger battle, pitting two philosophically and politically opposed camps against each another, with each determined to define the cultural values shaping a future America, a disconcerting implication emerges. If the gun controversy is actually just an ongoing skirmish in a larger cultural battle, then the resolution to the major social ills gun control hopes to provide—lessened crime, violence, and suicide—is unlikely to emerge regardless of how America's gun controversy progresses. Indeed, as these ills were never truly the primary issue, by holding out the hope of eventually offering some solution to these societal problems, the continuing controversy may merely distract the country from pursuing more fruitful avenues of resolution.[18]

Dimensions of Gun Control

Up to this point, our discussion has treated gun control and gun restrictions as relatively straightforward and intuitively obvious terms. In reality, this is not the case. *Gun control* is a generic term that has varying meanings in social discourse and in the restrictions one legislative bill imposes relative to another. Because of the generic nature of the label, misunderstandings and confusion often abound in common discussions of the subject, with one individual assuming one type of gun restriction and the other imagining an entirely different restriction. For example, gun control restrictions may take a multitude of forms, including marketing prohibitions, required registration schemes, permissive or restrictive licensing, or complete gun bans and prohibitions.[19] Even more concretely, all of the following are gun control methods of varying severity: (1) denying an individual the right to own or carry a firearm or handgun, (2) requiring a permit to purchase or own a firearm or handgun, (3) requiring testimonies of good character to obtain a firearms license, (4) restricting the kind of firearms an individual can purchase or own, (5) requiring in-person purchases of firearms, (6) restricting places where a firearm may legally be carried, (7) imposing waiting periods before taking possession of a purchased firearm, (8) imposing firearms training of specified lengths and content, (9) imposing specific firearm storage and safekeeping requirements, (10) imposing licensing and administrative restrictions on individuals wishing to sell firearms, and so forth.

From a cultural perspective, most proponents of Bedrock America sees gun control as encompassing *any* rule, regulation, or legislative action that limits a private citizen's use of, access to, or ownership of firearms. Depending on a restriction's reach and severity, members are likely to consider any specific restriction a major or minor infringement of the Second Amendment. In contrast, proponents of Cosmopolitan America, while perhaps acknowledging the draconian nature of *some* of the above restrictions, see many of the listed controls as simply "commonsense" measures demanded by America's high-density society. These differing assessments of specific gun control measures are not surprising, in that they reflect Bedrock America's individualistic orientation relative to Cosmopolitan America's communitarian perspective. However, the differing evaluations highlight a fundamental issue dividing the two cultures: what ultimately determines "enough" restriction? If Bedrock America accepted Cosmopolitan America's commonsense measures as justified and unavoidable infringements, would that suffice to resolve the gun controversy? Or might Cosmopolitan America encounter later circumstances that required still further restrictions, reopening the battle? Such concerns influence the assessment of otherwise seemingly reasonable restrictions in Bedrock America and account for its intransigence on even minor concessions.

Further, such concerns are not speculative. In 1967, New York City, under Mayor John Lindsay, enacted a rifle and shotgun registration law that required city dwellers to register their rifles and shotguns by make, model, and serial number. They were to pay a nominal fee for each of their long guns and receive a permit to keep them in the city. Mayor Lindsay assured gun owners that registration was simply to keep track of these potentially dangerous firearms and was not in any way geared to prohibition. With the exception of substantial fee increases, Mayor Lindsay kept his word.

However, in 1991, New York City had a different mayor, David Dinkins, and this mayor signed into law a new gun control bill that banned certain rifles and shotguns that had been allowed previously. Using the city's rifle registration records, the Dinkins administration notified more than 2,300 city residents owning such rifles and shotguns that they either had to surrender the now banned long guns to the police, make them inoperable, or remove them from the city. Owners were also mandated to return a sworn statement indicating the actions they had taken to comply with the ban.[20] Obviously, the earlier gun registration under Lindsay strongly facilitated the later gun prohibition under Dinkins. This and other examples of seemingly innocuous gun regulations having morphed into more serious restrictions alarm Bedrock America.

Additionally, the example above imputes no deceptive intentions or disreputable motivations to Mayor Lindsay's assurances. He may truly have intended to limit his gun control efforts to registration rather than prohibition, but events a quarter century later simply thwarted his intentions. However, because so little trust characterizes the gun controversy, Bedrock America would likely reject this interpretation as naive, assuming instead that Lindsay anticipated that his registration law would eventually result in more severe gun restrictions.

Proponents on both sides believe that the gun controversy involves not only publicly espoused stated goals but also privately held unstated goals. These unstated goals are sometimes more significant in determining attitudes than stated goals. The existence (or *perceived* existence) of unspoken agendas has been a major contributor to the intractability of the gun debate. Bedrock America is unconvinced that the stated intentions of Cosmopolitan America are its actual intentions and instead believes its ultimate, long-term objective is more radical: the eventual prohibition of *all* firearms in civilian hands.

Illustrating this issue is the controversy in the pro-gun community surrounding the interpretation of Senator Diane Feinstein's well-known gun ban quote taken from her 1995 interview on the news program *60 Minutes*: "If I could have gotten 51 votes in the Senate of the United States, for an outright ban, picking up every one of them—Mr. and Mrs. America, turn them all in—I would have done it." Her stated goal was just the banning and prohibition of rifles she considered assault weapons. However, many pro-gun advocates have interpreted the statement as inadvertently signaling an unstated goal of collecting and prohibiting all guns. This ambiguity surrounding espoused and actual goals makes it difficult to determine whether a particular gun control dispute is over the espoused goal of a proposed new gun regulation or over the perceived goal believed to underlie it. A sensitivity to likely unstated goals is helpful for understanding the gun controversy, as assumed intentions appear to strongly affect the attitudes and reactions of Bedrock America.[21]

Organization and Approach

This book explores America's gun controversy by dividing the time line of the United States into seven temporal intervals, noting the important social and historical developments relevant to each interval's orientation toward firearms. By tracing the attitudinal shifts that occurred in each period, and by examining the influences creating those shifts, the book attempts to show how the roots of the controversy are more cultural than pragmatic in nature and what this implies for today's debates about guns and gun restrictions.

Specifically, the exploration reviews evolving attitudes toward firearms as found in a reasonable cross section of societal mechanisms involved in cultural and values transmission: legislative and judicial bodies; popular media (newspapers, television, magazines, literary digests, etc.); professional and educational associations; family and religious organizations; and so forth. This examination confers a familiarity with the social forces that shaped the ideas and arguments prominently encountered in this controversial arena. What was the zeitgeist surrounding these ideas and arguments, and what historical events formed Bedrock America's culture? What events triggered reactions to this traditional culture, creating anti-gun individuals fiercely opposed to the long-held gun values knitted into the country's cultural fabric and coalescing them into Cosmopolitan America? What events moved the pro-gun adherents of Bedrock America to judge the cultural changes taking place not as societal improvements but as ominous threats to a cherished way of life? What cultural forces continue to fuel this controversy, and what strategies have the two factions cultivated in attempting to capture the uncommitted to their way of thinking about guns?

In exploring these questions, the cultural analysis attempts to provide a deeper understanding of America's gun controversy, but it does not offer any resolution to the controversy—offering a resolution is not its goal. On the other hand, a better cultural understanding of the gun issue permits a more incisive assessment of the pragmatic and philosophical arguments underpinning the two positions, as those arguments embody their differing cultural orientations. Thus, in the concluding chapter, the book assesses the various actions the two cultures propose for addressing gun-related violence, the impact these actions have had or are likely to have, and their probability for minimizing the value clashes underlying the pro- and anti-gun stances. As it is impossible to do extensive reading in this area and not form a judgment about the relative persuasiveness of pro-gun and anti-gun arguments, this judgment has undoubtedly influenced the assessments the chapter presents. Thus, this final chapter is necessarily subjective. However, regarding the material presented in earlier sections, I have tried to minimize the impact of my personal conclusions on that material and have striven to present a balanced, nonpartisan account of the gun controversy when exploring the social and cultural forces that led to and shaped it. The reader must determine my degree of success in accomplishing this.

CHAPTER TWO

Origins of American Gun Culture

The roots of American gun culture began even prior to the United States becoming a country, when it was just a scattered group of settlements and colonies. Whether seeking a better place in the world or just seeking excitement and a challenge, the explorers and settlers from Europe and elsewhere brought the customs and norms of their mother countries with them, and these customs frequently included a high regard for firearms.

Foundational Events: The English Experience[1]

The English colonists in particular brought with them an affection for firearms. Reliant on firearms to put food on the table and to defend against both animal and human threats, they had consequently developed a long tradition of battling the Crown for the right to own and use weapons, long guns, and pistols. In her analysis of the English origins of the right to keep and bear arms, noted constitutional scholar Joyce Lee Malcolm observed that although the English Bill of Rights of 1689 *formally* established this right for Englishmen, English citizens had a tradition of possessing and bearing weapons much earlier than this, dating back as far as King Alfred in the ninth century, when Saxon law gave every man the right to keep and bear arms.[2] In later centuries, when the Crown pragmatically desired to avoid the expense of financing and maintaining a professional army that both commoners and aristocrats would have regarded with dark suspicion, the country's long reliance on citizens' militias to help keep the peace and defend the kingdom reinforced this basic right. To save the Crown money, militia members (which generally included all males between ages 16 and 60) were responsible for furnishing their own arms and weaponry, which were brought from home and typically kept there.

This is not to imply that the average militia member saw the carrying of arms as either a sacred right or a check against tyranny. Judging by the records of the many petitioners asking to be excused from it, militia duty for most members was frequently undertaken only as a burdensome obligation. Nonetheless, because the king's use of the militia required the cooperation of the local gentry, who actually commanded and led the citizen soldiers, the militia approach to the common defense had the practical benefit of giving both aristocrats and common citizens some influence over the Crown's use of military force. This curb on royal power created by the government's dependence on an armed civilian militia was not lost on English monarchs, and over the centuries, they periodically attempted to contain this latent threat to royal authority.

During the 1500s, as firearms became increasingly available, the monarchy acted to impose controls on their use. In 1541, King Henry VIII restricted the ownership of crossbows and handguns to only select individuals (i.e., those having a certain annual income derived from property rights), and a dozen years later, the regent representing Henry's son, King Edward VI, ordered all individuals with guns to register with their local justices. Similarly, in 1569, Queen Elizabeth's Privy Council recommended that the government store the militia's firearms rather than leaving them in the hands of the members themselves.[3] This proposed regulation generated much local opposition and strong resistance, and it was withdrawn. Nonetheless, these efforts to curtail the availability of firearms reveal the government's (and the ruling aristocracy's) mixed feelings regarding an armed militia predominantly composed of commoners. As a result, the Crown continued to seek ways to limit the circumstances in which commoners might go armed.

Hunting provided a frequent justification for groups of commoners to go about armed, and in the following century, the Crown tried to control firearms primarily through edicts restricting hunting. Early in his reign, King James I passed three such edicts between 1604 and 1609. His edicts put additional property restrictions on those who might hunt, added constraints on the weapons they could use, and appointed as gamekeepers local aristocrats who were given wide latitude to interpret and execute the new rules. His son, King Charles I, similarly viewed armed commoners as a potential threat, and when he assumed the throne, he extended and expanded the game laws, both to raise revenue and to control weapons.

However, Charles's policies gravely alarmed the population and had the effect of linking peasants and landowners together in fierce resistance to these new laws. Counties across England experienced extensive rioting and disorder, including armed confrontations with sheriffs and other authorities attempting to restore order.[4] For the Crown, these disturbances confirmed the dangers associated with having a large number of English commoners armed with handguns, muskets, and pikes, and for commoners, the despised forest and game laws confirmed the usefulness of firearms for ensuring their ability to resist a king's unpopular or unfair policies.

Not surprisingly, then, when Charles needed war funds in 1640 and had to call a parliament—the famous Long Parliament—to grant approval, those suspicious of Charles's motives saw an opportunity to wrest concessions from the king, and they attacked the Crown's long-standing monopoly on the manufacture of gunpowder. Understanding the practical implications of the monopoly for effectively disarming the kingdom's people, the king's opponents passionately argued for ending this royal prerogative. In 1641, Charles conceded the gunpowder monopoly, closing this potential method of firearms control. Not long after this concession, Charles clashed again with Parliament, this time over control of the militia, which had been called up to put down a rebellion in Catholic Ireland. Fearful that Charles might later turn his armed forces against his opponents in England, Parliament demanded command of the militia. Charles's refusal and his subsequent seizure of militia weapons for the creation of a field army independent of traditional militia limitations eventually sparked the English Civil War in 1642. This conflict culminated in the defeat of Charles at Naseby in 1645 by Oliver Cromwell and his forces.

Unlike the Royalists, Cromwell and the Parliamentarians had generally allowed the militia to keep their arms during this period, and Malcolm suggests that the private ownership of firearms was common and widespread.[5] However, after executing Charles in 1649 and setting up a republican government, the "victors found they had to deny the rights they had meant to protect."[6] Worried about insurrections and a counterrevolution internally and foreign incursions and invasions externally, Cromwell was determined to maintain his New Model Army (the parliamentary field army that had defeated Charles at Naseby) and to disarm those deemed as enemies, untrustworthy, or papist. In addition to its customary duties as a home defense force, the militia was also granted a new policing role to focus on seeking out conspiracies and subversion and the arrest and imprisonment of individuals thought to be dangerous to the new order. When Cromwell died in 1658, his legacy included a population of

Englishmen intimately familiar with the capricious ways in which arms, political power, and self-determination might link together.

With the death of Cromwell, the Commonwealth did not last, and the great English flirtation with republicanism ended. In 1660, England again became a monarchy with the ascension of Charles's son to the British throne. While the Restoration represented a major realignment of the political levers of power and influence for the aristocracy, governmental attitudes and policies regarding weapons and firearms for the common Englishman remained remarkably similar to the attitudes and policies of past regimes. Where Cromwell and his followers worried about and attempted to disarm Royalist sympathizers, malcontents, and dangerous subversives, so also did Charles II—only now the potential treachery resided in former Roundheads, army veterans, and radical religious sects. Acutely aware of the precarious hold he had on power—a parliament had made him king, and a parliament might as easily unmake him king— Charles II found it prudent to follow the course charted by Cromwell, extending the militia's policing powers to control those judged troublesome and to disarm individuals suspected of disloyalty.[7] Recognizing the danger posed to his regime by a well-armed but fickle public, Charles II also passed regulations banning weapons in London and ordering gunsmiths to maintain lists of the weapons they manufactured, with the names of the customers who obtained them. Around the same time, using rumors of insurrection plots as a justification, Charles II ordered the militia to conduct house searches of his political opponents, seeking to confiscate arms and ammunition found in "excessive amounts." Somewhat later, pointing to the danger of plots not yet uncovered, he amended this order to cover *all* arms and ammunition.

King Charles II continued to secure his hold on power by using increasingly severe measures. To avoid the traditional limitations placed on the militia, he established a volunteer militia completely under his control. Despite the country's long-standing antipathy to a standing professional peacetime army, he created one using particularly trustworthy regiments of the disbanded New Model Army. He maneuvered the first parliament after the Restoration—the Cavalier Parliament—to pass measures broadening the definition of treason, increasing censorship, and limiting petition. Under the guise of supporting English gunsmiths, he banned the importation of firearms and gun parts, giving the Crown de facto control of the manufacture and distribution of firearms.

In 1662, suspicious of army veterans who fought with Cromwell, Charles II ordered them banned from London for six months. He also forbade them to wear, use, carry, or ride with pistols, swords, or other weapons. Right before the ban was to expire, he renewed it for another six months. He later issued similar bans in 1664, 1665, and 1670.[8] In 1666, he attempted to regain control of the kingdom's gunpowder supply by instituting a seller's licensing requirement, but Parliament refused to act on this bill.

This ongoing skirmish between the Crown and the English commoner over weapons and firearms peaked in 1671. Having had a decade to restore England to absolute monarchy, King Charles II passed the Game Act, which went further than any previous game act in English history. This act did not just prohibit most English commoners from hunting with firearms and other instruments (as past game acts had) but actually barred prohibited individuals from *owning* guns, bows, and other weapons used in hunting. The act in effect deprived about 90 percent of the population of a legal right to even possess firearms.[9] This prohibition on firearm ownership remained in effect until 1689, when Parliament included a clause affirming a "true, ancient and indubitable right" to keep and bear arms in the English Bill of Rights.[10]

Malcolm has argued that, practically speaking, this historical tussle between the Crown, commoners, and country gentry over the right to possess firearms is probably less significant than it appears. Evidence indicates that many Englishmen, accustomed to using weapons during years of strife and determined to protect themselves, their families, and their neighbors, retained their personal arms, albeit illegally.[11] The real impact of the continuing contests over firearms was its influence on English political thought and in shaping cultural attitudes central to the notions of self-government and armed civilians. Luminaries such as Thomas Hobbes would argue in *Leviathan* (1651) that individuals by nature have a right to protect themselves by all means available, and laws abrogating that right are simply void. Similarly, John Locke would assert in *Two Treatises of Government* (1689) that self-defense is a natural law that even the king cannot take from the community. Less renowned writers, such as political theorist James Harrington, would portray the armed and independent agrarian warrior in a popular 1656 publication.[12]

In the following centuries, other eminent English jurists, historians, and philosophers echoed similar sentiments. In his *Commentaries on the Laws of England*, William Blackstone (1765) asserted that constitutional guarantees unsupported by citizens' private firearms are guarantees in name only, and in the 19th century, the Whig historian Thomas Macaulay argued that the right to private arms was precisely the right that secured all other rights of a free citizen.

Building a Culture: The American Experience

For understanding American attitudes toward guns, the English politi-cal and philosophical analyses upholding the place of arms in a free soci-ety are the substantive outcomes of the Crown's ongoing attempts to disarm the English population. The shared struggles of Englishmen, and their implications for a free citizenry distilled in the writings of notable English intellectuals, shaped the English orientation toward firearms. English emigrants coming to the New World, intimately familiar with the political struggles undergone by their forebears and themselves, brought that cultural orientation with them, valuing the gun not just as a tool nec-essary for physical survival but as a weapon for securing individual rights and political freedom as well.[13]

From an American perspective, the English struggle over firearms highlighted the difference between simply *having* firearms and having the *right* to have firearms. For the most part, English villagers had always had and owned firearms, but as their right to own them was always at the pleasure of the king, the government could forbid ownership to any group out of favor with the Crown with minimal justification. This recognition of the need for an unambiguous right to keep and bear arms culminated with James Madison's decision to include an explicit statement of such a right in the U.S. Constitution. Familiar with the potential shortcomings of the "bearing arms" statement found in the English Bill of Rights, which limited the keeping of arms to Protestants, Madison's version was broader and more ecumenical: "A well-regulated militia, being necessary to the security of a free state, the right of the people to keep and bear arms shall not be infringed."

Contemporaneously, four states—Pennsylvania, Vermont, North Caro-lina, and Kentucky—also incorporated an explicit statement of a right to keep and bear arms in their state constitutions.[14] Other states soon fol-lowed their example.[15] Of course, as noted previously, the beginnings of America's gun culture had emerged long before these official statements. But these constitutional declarations gave a formal legal nod to more informal attitudes and cultural understandings.

More generally, the English struggle over the right to bear arms and the citizen's relation to the state produced a wealth of legal documents and philosophical arguments that profoundly influenced the thinking of the American political class. The writings and public statements of promin-ent Americans during this period reveal the results of this thinking, and a brief sampling of their remarks provides sharp insight into the similar conclusions they reached regarding the role of arms in a free society. For example, Patrick Henry asserted during the Constitutional Convention that "the great object is that every man be armed. Everyone who is able may have a gun."[16] George Washington, who later quoted Henry's assertion, approvingly, also declared during his first Annual Message to Congress that "a free people . . . ought to be armed."[17] Even John Adams, the second president of the United States, who harbored some personal reservations about arms in the hands of private citizens, acknowledged that, in America, "every private person is authorized to arm himself"[18] for self-defense and that "arms in the hands of individual citizens may be used at individual discretion in private self-defense."[19]

His cousin Samuel Adams even more strongly championed the individual's right to own firearms, seeing it as a natural right stemming from a God-given right to freedom: "Among the natural rights of the Colonists are these: First, a right to life; Secondly, to liberty; Thirdly, to property; together with the right to support and defend them in the best manner they can."[20] In another later argument, he stated that the Constitution shall never be construed to "prevent the people of the United States, who are peaceable citizens, from keeping their own arms."[21]

Insight into Thomas Jefferson's views on firearms can be gleaned from a passage in his *Commonplace Book*, where he translated and copied a passage from Cesare Beccaria, an Enlightenment philosopher: "The laws that forbid the carrying of arms . . . disarm only those who are neither inclined nor determined to commit crimes. . . . Such laws make things worse for the assaulted and better for the assailants, they serve rather to encourage than prevent homicides, for an unarmed man may be attacked with greater confidence than an armed man."[22] This sentiment in altered form appears again in Jefferson's draft constitution for Virginia, where he writes, "No freeman shall be debarred the use of arms."[23]

In many cases, individuals championing the right of arms ownership did so in the context of an important contemporary necessity: the country's need for an armed and prepared militia to defend the new nation from outside threats and to minimize the internal threat of an overreaching central government. Thus, Richard Henry Lee, a signer of the Declaration of Independence and later a senator from Virginia, stated, "To preserve liberty, it is essential that the whole body of the people always possess arms and be taught alike, especially when young, how to use them."[24] Similarly, Noah Webster argued, "Before a standing army can rule, the people must be disarmed. . . . The supreme power in America cannot enforce unjust laws by the sword, because the whole body of the people are armed and constitute a force superior to any band of regular troops."[25] This juxtaposition of a citizen's right to keep and bear arms with the need for a citizens' militia (as seen in the Second Amendment) has led some scholars and jurists in the 20th century to conclude that the citizen's right to arms is constrained to military service. The writings of Tench Coxe, a well-known Pennsylvanian delegate to the Continental Congress, suggest that he and his contemporaries would likely reject such a conclusion: "Who are the militia? Are they not ourselves? . . . Congress have no power to disarm the militia. . . . The unlimited power of the sword is not in the hands of either the federal or state governments but . . . in the hands of the people."[26]

As with their English forebears, Americans of this period saw the citizens' militia as a viable alternative to a professional standing army and as a formidable check against the possible rise of a tyrannical central authority. With a guaranteed right to keep and bear arms, the citizen-comprised local militias could ensure both the protection of the state and the preservation of individual liberties—and could do so at a cost far cheaper than a standing army. Implicit in this reasoning is the idea that the protection of freedom invariably requires the presence of local citizens acting as an armed force and united by a common cause. Even in the absence of a local militia, the individual possession of arms remains necessary to ensure the citizens' ability to revolt and to protect their liberties.

Not only did the political zeitgeist of this period elevate the armed citizen in American society but also the well-known exploits and notable successes of American marksmen during the Revolutionary War shaped the popular view of firearms' appropriate place in this society. The skill and effectiveness of these rough-hewn backwoodsmen with firearms made them the equal of the best-trained English infantryman. Their exploits also helped to mold the American belief in the independent, rugged individual, utterly at ease with arms and quite comfortable with self-protection.[27]

All these developments laid the cultural foundation for Bedrock America in the 19th century. American political leaders of the 1700s believed in the inherent right of individuals to protect their freedoms using arms, and so self-evident was this right that it went unquestioned, "lying outside the Constitution and requiring Constitutional endorsement only."[28] Thus, going into the new century, encouraged by the provisions of their state and federal constitutions, supported by the writings of eminent political philosophers, and having experienced firsthand the good wrought by skilled firearms usage, Americans not only believed in their right to keep and bear arms but also made this right an essential and defining characteristic of their new society.

The Cultural Growth of Bedrock America: 19th-Century Developments

Not long into the new century, America was again at war with England and soon after also with Mexico. If nothing else, these wars served to confirm Americans' belief in the practical utility of arms and in the benefits accruing to those who could produce and distribute them more efficiently. War fosters discovery and experimentation, and, as previously noted, entrepreneurs such as Colt, Winchester, Smith and Wesson, and others discovered new techniques and designed new machines to speed up the manufacturing of small arms, making them not only cheaper but also more powerful, reliable, and accurate. As importantly, these same entrepreneurs also began to use early mass media to sell their merchandise to an enthusiastic public. Firearms manufacturers prominently advertised their wares in the many new mass-oriented newspapers and magazines made possible by the development of the linotype machine and pulp paper processes.[29] Large and small advertisements for Smith & Wesson revolvers, Savage rifles, and other small arms shared space on the pages of popular periodicals with ads for soap, cigarettes, and health tonics. Such advertisements enticed readers to drop into local retailers stocking the touted firearms to personally feel the heft and balance of the new weapons and perhaps acquire some.

With the introduction of mail-order catalogs by Montgomery Ward and Sears in the last quarter of the 19th century and the rapid development of railroads and other transportation infrastructure, Americans almost anywhere in the country now had mail access to all the latest offerings of the firearms industry, but particularly to inexpensive revolvers and pistols light enough to mail. Indeed, the mail-order firms often used firearms as "loss-leaders" and disregarded the manufacturers' factory-set retail price. This practice, plus the flood of anonymously made, cheaper imitations that always hit the market when the patents of a prestigious manufacturer expired, made gun ownership affordable for all and ensured that pricing ceased being a barrier to firearms possession. In 1892, a survey undertaken by the *New York Daily Tribune* indicated that gun production was impressive and gun sales were booming—findings that confirmed (albeit indirectly) the continuing widespread, enthusiastic acceptance of firearms in mainstream American culture.[30] As Professors Lee Kennett and James Anderson have declared, "Throughout the nineteenth century, the small arms industry possessed a staid respectability. . . . Its dominant figures enjoyed generally unimpeachable reputations; . . . But their public image was honorable chiefly because the American public attached no more opprobrium to their products than it did to sewing machines and typewriters."[31] This lack of any disapproval associated with firearms is all the more remarkable considering the human carnage wrought by firearms in the American Civil War, and it stands in sharp contrast to the contempt and condemnation that firearms will evoke in some sectors of 21st-century American society. The war generated no systematic calls for personal disarmament, no general movements to restrict guns, and no national legislative attempts to control their use. The war did, however, familiarize enormous numbers of men with various models of rifles, pistols, and shotguns.[32]

Restrictions and Limitations in Bedrock America

Although gun acceptance (if not gun fervor) generally characterized 19th-century America, some regions of the country passed significant gun control laws and regulations. These measures put limitations on the right to keep arms for particular classes of individuals and for bearing arms in specified designated areas. The most notable of these limitations occurred in the Southern slaveholding states, where fears of slave rebellions were ever present in the minds of their masters. Prohibitions on the possession of any weapon, let alone firearms, kept guns out of the hands of slaves, servants, and blacks in general, at least from the middle of the 17th century until well into the third quarter of the 19th century. As early as 1640, Virginia had passed legislation denying blacks the right to own guns,[33] and such restrictive laws commonly existed throughout the South until well after the end of the Civil War. Similarly, desultory attempts to limit the access of Native Americans to rifles and pistols also occurred prior to and during the 19th century, but the substantial profits that traders and merchants could make in dealing firearms to the Native tribes ensured that these efforts at gun control were rarely effective. In addition, the Indian Intercourse Act of 1834 formally granted Native Americans the legal right to possess rifles.[34]

Oddly enough, given the image of the Old West in American popular culture, several of America's frontier towns took gun regulation positions at odds with the century's general acceptance of an individual's unfettered right to bear arms. While newspaper reports and pulp fiction stories glorified the firearms skills and gunfighting exploits of "shootists" whose names became familiar even to people in the crowded cities of the East—names like Wyatt Earp, John Wesley Hardin, Jesse James, Wild Bill Hickok, Bat Masterson, and many others—these larger-than-life romanticized accounts offered an incomplete portrayal of life in the West's cattle towns. For permanent residents of these communities, the gunplay and violence that often accompanied the arrival of a group of transient cow-boys coming off a long cattle drive were unnerving and frightening. Their brawls and gunplay interfered with town growth and development by discouraging newcomers and new businesses. Thus, some of these towns set aside a section of town for the entertainment of visiting drovers, and they attempted to confine them to that area.[35] Other cow towns—such as Tombstone, Dodge City, Wichita, and Abilene—passed ordinances that prohibited the carrying of firearms within city limits. These ordinances[36] forced drovers and other visitors to check their weapons at some autho-rized location, such as the sheriff's or U.S. Marshals' office. Owners retrieved their firearms only when they departed town.

Although determined individuals could easy circumvent these early gun control efforts with derringers and the smaller and easily concealable pistols, evidence suggests that the towns took their regulations seriously and made genuine, albeit spotty, efforts to enforce them. For example, the ostensible cause of the infamous 1881 gunfight near the O.K. Corral in Tombstone, Arizona Territory, was Town Marshall (and U.S. Deputy Mar-shal) Virgil Earp's attempt to enforce the town's gun ordinance. Adam Winkler, a noted constitutional law professor specializing in gun issues, has asserted that, after drunk and disorderly conduct, carrying an illegal firearm was the most common cause of arrest in the Old West.[37]

More broadly on the judicial front, only a handful of court decisions focused on firearms during this period. For the most part, the courts' adjudications reflected the period's pro-gun attitudes. At the state level, in 1840, the Supreme Court of Tennessee addressed the appeal of William Aymette, who had been convicted of carrying a concealed Bowie knife. The court determined that the Second Amendment protected Aymette's right to *openly* carry firearms and other weapons (such as a Bowie knife), but it rejected his contention that the Second Amendment precluded *any* limitations on this right.[38] In 1846, in a similar case that involved the concealed carrying of a pistol, the Supreme Court of Georgia also ruled that the Second Amendment protected a citizen's right to openly carry firearms. As in the Aymette case, the court indicated that the legislature could prohibit the concealed carrying of weapons, but not open carry. Thus, the court overturned the state's ban on handguns as unconstitu-tional, and as the state had offered no proof that the pistol of appellant Hawkins Nunn was concealed, it quashed his conviction.[39]

At the federal level, in 1876, the U.S. Supreme Court adjudicated *United States v. Cruikshank et al.*, a case in which the federal government attempted to uphold the First and Second Amendment rights of Levi Nelson and Alexander Tillman, black Louisiana freedmen. William Cruikshank, along with several other white men, had been convicted of depriving Nelson and Tillman of their right to freely assemble and their right to keep and bear arms. Although the Court acknowledged that people, even independent of the Constitution, had the right to keep and bear arms, it noted that the Constitution limited only *federal* government infringements of that right. Thus, as First and Second Amendment protections applied only to the actions of the federal government (and not the actions of the state government or of private individuals), the Court, in a split decision, overturned the conviction of Cruikshank, indicating that citizens must rely on the protection of state and municipal governments when private parties infringe on civil rights.[40] It would take 124 years and another Supreme Court decision—*McDonald v. City of Chicago*—for the Court to fully incorporate the Second Amendment as applicable not just to the federal government but also to state and local governments.

Ten years after writing the majority opinion in *Cruikshank*, Chief Justice Morrison Waite presided over *Herman Presser v. State of Illinois*. Presser, a member of a private militia group, had been found guilty of unlawfully parading with an unauthorized body of armed men in the city of Chicago. Arguing that he was convicted under an unconstitutional law that violated the Second Amendment, Presser appealed to the U.S. Supreme Court. In a unanimous decision, the Court reiterated its earlier finding that Second Amendment protections of the right to keep and bear arms applied only to the federal government and that, unless prohibited by the state constitution, states were free to pass laws that regulated civilian associations engaged in military drills and parades. Thus, the Court rejected Presser's argument and upheld his conviction.[41]

From a cultural perspective, the significance of these state and national court proceedings is twofold. In line with the zeitgeist of the era, both the state and national judiciaries strongly endorsed a citizen's basic right to own and possess arms, with acknowledgment on both levels that this right even predates the Constitution. On the other hand, given the state's duty to provide for the common good, the courts also recognized that the state has the power to regulate this right in the interest of maintaining public safety—to the extent that such regulation "does not deprive the citizen of his natural right of self-defense, or of his constitutional right to keep and bear arms,"[42] with the determination of acceptable and unacceptable regulation left to court cases yet to come.

Nonetheless, despite the courts' tightrope balancing acts and the sporadic, localized attempts at weapons regulation in western cattle towns, positive attitudes toward guns and unquestioned gun acceptance characterized the 19th century. Even the towns that regulated firearms within the city recognized the usefulness and need for arms outside of town and returned them to their owners upon departure. The frontier persona of the cowboy/gunfighter/outlaw—real or mythical—inflamed the imagination of 19th-century Americans and turned the frontier gunfighter into a unique American icon. Complementing this icon were the stories of the shooting feats of army scouts such as Kit Carson, frontier provisioners such as Buffalo Bill Cody, and trick shooters such as Annie Oakley and Frank Butler, all later distilled down, elaborately embroidered, and broadcast worldwide through Cody's Wild West Shows. In many ways, the 19th century represented the age of firearms in America—"the tools of politicians, hunters, frontiersmen, trappers, Indian fighters, Indians, outlaws, army men, women, prostitutes, and, increasingly, law enforcement agents."[43]

Bedrock America's Iconic Embodiment: The Birth of the NRA

In 1871, William Church and George Wingate joined with several other former Civil War officers to establish the now widely respected and equally widely despised National Rifle Association—the NRA. In its early years, the organization was not particularly controversial. Concerned about the serious decline in American marksmanship that they had observed firsthand as military officers during the war, Church and Wingate wanted an association "to promote and encourage rifle shooting on a scientific basis."[44] Together with officers from the New York National Guard, and using the British National Rifle Association as a model, they incorporated the NRA in New York State—which is somewhat ironic given the state's current pro-regulatory orientation toward firearms. Setting about to acquire land for a shooting range suitable for both practice and competitions, they acquired Creed's Farm on Long Island in 1872, renaming it Creedmoor in an allusion to the moors of southern England. This first NRA range hosted its inaugural shooting match in 1873, and it hosted the country's first international match in 1874.[45]

The circumstances surrounding the establishment and rise of the NRA provide further evidence of the widespread cultural acceptance of firearms and shooting skills during this period in America. For example, General Ambrose Burnside, a nationally recognized Civil War leader, agreed to lend his prestige to the nascent NRA by serving as its first president. Similarly, Hermann Poppenhusen, the highly respected president of the Central and North Side Railroad of Long Island, favored the organization by selling Creed's Farm to the organization at a substantially discounted price. Even the State of New York supported the association, allocating most of the funds needed to purchase Creed's Farm from

Poppenhusen,[46] together with contributions from both Brooklyn (a distinct city at the time) and New York City.[47]

Moreover, the shooting competitions at Creedmoor proved extremely popular with spectators and were widely covered in the media. This popularity also contributed to the country's enthusiasm for firearms, which surged in 1874 when the NRA hosted a formidable Irish shooting team. Having decisively defeated the best English and Scottish rifle teams a year earlier, the Irish team was nevertheless outclassed in an extremely close match by the much less experienced American team, consisting entirely of NRA members and captained by Wingate. In a return match the following year in Ireland, the American team, again captained by an NRA official, proved that the first victory was no chance occurrence.[48] In the 90 years to follow, the NRA would grow into the country's premiere firearms organization, enjoying popular acceptance and wide respect for its substantial contributions to marksmanship, shooting expertise, and gun safety and training. The apolitical nature of the association would radically change in the last quarter of the 20th century, bringing with it a great deal of controversy and opprobrium. But in the 19th century, the newly formed NRA was both a producer and a product of the country's pro-gun culture.

The training and competitive successes of NRA-sponsored rifle teams centered attention on firearms and spurred the growth of local shooting clubs across the country. Target shooting grew into one of the most popular sports in the country, with riflemanship and the "cult of accuracy" becoming a national phenomenon. Songwriters penned popular songs glorifying rifle feats, which were "whistled, strummed, hummed, and danced to across the country."[49] Because abstinence from alcohol and smoking tended to improve a shooter's accuracy, ministers and preachers looked favorably upon congregants taking up the sport, and churches around the nation sponsored target matches in their basements. Further, popular magazines noted that target shooting was even fashionable among women, and they commented on the creation of all-women clubs in numerous American cities. *Chicago Field* magazine observed that shooting gave women skills to protect themselves and their families and was thus quite sensible and worthy.[50]

But even before the target shooting enthusiasm spurred by the NRA competitions, the celebration of popular gun-wielding military and political leaders had long served to promote America's gun culture. What could be more quintessentially American than having two nationally known, rugged individualists—both intimately familiar with the use of firearms and rifles—as partisan rivals, each vying to increase the political influence of his party? Andrew Jackson, hero of the Battle of New Orleans and leader of the Democrats, versus Davy Crockett, plain-spoken owner of "Old Betsy" (his celebrated flintlock rifle), king of the frontier, and standard-bearer for the Whigs. Although the Whigs' use of Crockett to trump Jackson's common-man appeal was ultimately unsuccessful, the party's effort to counter the allure of one iconic firearms professional with their own iconic rifleman is suggestive of the "common man's" high regard for politicians skilled in the use of guns and firearms.[51]

Similarly, Theodore Roosevelt, the 26th president of the United States, like Abraham Lincoln before him, took a keen interest in firearms,[52] and this passion, conveyed through his numerous books and speeches, was well-known among his contemporaries. His fondness for Winchester rifles—his first model acquired when he was 22 years old and blossomed into a collection of at least 20 others over his lifetime—manifested itself in gift presentations to favorite hunting companions and admired associates. So great was his enthusiasm for the various Winchester models— and so public his endorsements—that the Winchester Repeating Arms Company touted the president's frequent praise in its advertising campaigns.[53] Like the NRA, of which he was a life member and whose shooting goals he firmly endorsed, Theodore Roosevelt—the privileged Easterner, the western rancher, the Rough Rider, the big game hunter, and likely the most gun-oriented president ever to capture the White House—was both shaped by 19th-century America's gun culture and contributed to it.

Thus, by the end of the 1800s, the vast majority of Americans—both Easterners and Westerners—regarded rifles, pistols, and shotguns as quintessential American tools and an integral part of the American character. These tools helped tame the wilderness, win American independence, defeat Mexico, conquer the Plains Indians, and punish Spain. While doing this, they helped create iconic American heroes and a wonderful American mythology. The firearms industry's innovative designs, sophisticated manufacturing, high quality, and clever marketing led the world and spurred the growth of other American industries. For the individual, they offered personal protection and security, put meat on the table, and provided a chance to develop a challenging skill. Not least of all, they were fun to handle and shoot. In light of all this, it would be astonishing if 19th-century America had *failed* to develop a defining gun culture. But even more than this, the gun and the fundamental values of Bedrock America—self-sufficiency, rugged individualism, personal achievement, and independence—were so intimately entwined and complementary that they defined each other.

CHAPTER THREE

The Emerging Cultural Rift: 1910–1940

In May 1911, with little fanfare, New York State passed the Sullivan Act. Championed by State Senator Timothy ("Big Tim") Sullivan, of Tammany Hall fame, the act required residents to obtain a license to possess concealable firearms, knives, brass knuckles, razors, and other small weapons. The act made the possession of an unlicensed firearm a misdemeanor and the carrying of an unlicensed firearm a felony. Ostensibly enacted to address the rampant lawlessness and rising murder rate in New York City, the act became a gun control template for other states and municipalities and presaged the national enactment of further gun control laws several decades later.

What happened? Up to the early 20th century, Americans took ownership and possession of firearms for granted, despite the prior century's intricate judicial findings. Pragmatically, as gun control regulations had been virtually absent or not enforced,[1] the degree to which the government had the power to regulate arms and arms ownership had little practical significance for the average citizen. Additionally, the country already had a history of over 200 years of pro-gun culture. So why did the legislators of New York State suddenly feel compelled to challenge this culture? After all, violence and homicide had plagued New York City residents long before Tim Sullivan came along.

New York's Sullivan Act

Several elements factored into Sullivan's defiance of America's gun-friendly zeitgeist. On the most basic level and simply taking Big Tim at his word, one motivating force behind the Sullivan Act was a real desire to reduce violent crime. Sullivan's biographer[2] endorses this explanation, citing Sullivan's argument during debate over the legislation that "if this bill passes, it will do more to carry out the commandment thou shall not kill and save more souls than all the talk of all the ministers and priests in the state for the next ten years."[3] Sullivan had been experiencing a degree of political pressure because of the city's many gangs, which were notorious for robbing and beating well-to-do citizens unwary enough to wander into their territory, and even for occasionally uniting to fight pitched battles with the police on city streets. During his 1910 reelection campaign, Sullivan had promised to introduce legislation to control guns, and the January 1911 broad-daylight shooting murder of one of the era's well-known novelists, David Graham Phillips, by a well-off but deranged patrician, provided the perfect opportunity for Sullivan to move forward on this promise and push his act through the New York State Legislature.

State Senator Timothy Ferris opposed the bill, arguing that it "won't stop murders. You can't force a burglar to get a license to use a gun."[4] But a letter-writing campaign by George LeBrun, of the city coroner's office, enlisting the support of prominent New Yorkers for Sullivan's gun law, helped ensure that only five senators voted against it.[5] As the city's statistician responsible for providing the press with annual counts of accidental deaths in the city, LeBrun also tracked the increasing number of homicides in the city. He viewed the Sullivan Act as a law that would keep pistols and firearms—in his opinion too easily obtainable—out of the hands of rash and unsavory individuals.

Although the Sullivan Act certainly addressed a legitimate municipal issue, it also allowed Tammany Hall to maintain better control of the many thugs it paid to frighten the opposition and to assure favorable poll outcomes. Sullivan expected most gang members to ignore the law, ensuring that the police always had justification—legitimately or by planting a pistol—for arresting those thugs troublesome to Tammany's wishes.[6] Additionally, about the same time as the act's passage, a continuing influx of immigrants—particularly from Italy and Greece—was flooding into the city. Viewed suspiciously by New York's wealthier and better-established residents, they deemed the foreign arrivals as undesirable, hotheaded, and dangerous. Whether the new immigrants were problematic or not, the Sullivan Act provided a weapon to control even the *potentially* violent and unruly behavior of the newcomers, and it was so used. Thus, for example, one day after the act took effect, James Palermo, a recent Italian immigrant, found himself under arrest as he exited a hardware store with a newly purchased firearm.[7] Although Palermo was not convicted under the law, another Italian laborer, Marino Rossi, was less fortunate. Afraid of Italian extortionists, Rossi was on his way to work and carrying a concealed revolver for protection when he was arrested a week after Palermo. As the first person convicted under the act, Rossi received a year's prison sentence, with the magistrate commenting, "It is unfortunate that this [i.e., carrying guns] is the custom with you and your kind, and that fact, combined with your irascible nature, furnishes much of the criminal business in this country."[8] The *New York Times*, a staunch supporter of the Sullivan Act, also commented approvingly on the Rossi conviction, suggesting that "the judge's warning to the Italian community was timely and exemplary."[9]

Given Sullivan's extensive connections to New York City's criminal underworld and the heavy use of the act against newly arrived immigrant groups, some contemporaries of the period suggested that the act had nothing to do with reducing crime and violence and questioned its moral authority.[10] Others more pragmatically questioned its legal authority, believing the act in whole or in part an unconstitutional violation of the Second Amendment. Members of this camp included Charles Whitman, the New York district attorney; Francis Pendleton of the New York State Supreme Court; and Joseph Darlington, a New York City lawyer who deliberately violated the act to test its constitutionality in court. Despite both Whitman's and Pendleton's belief that the act exceeded the policing power of the state and infringed on a citizen's right to keep guns at home, the state appellate court ruled that the act could restrict handguns at home because it was simply regulatory and not prohibitive.[11] Thus, New York's Sullivan Act withstood judicial challenge and provided the first serious rejection of the country's pro-gun orientation. The act was without precedent in the nation in regulating not just the carrying of firearms but also their sale and possession.[12]

Nonetheless, one piece of legislation, even one as significant as the Sullivan Act, cannot in itself displace a culture rooted in several centuries' worth of traditions. Such legislation is as much a reflection of a larger shift in cultural values as it is a cause of such a shift. Putting aside the arcane particulars of big city politics and prejudices, the cultural origins of the Sullivan Act evolved from two major societal developments that were reshaping the entire nation: the end of the American frontier and the ramifications of the country's growing urbanization. These two forces created social dynamics that ultimately nurtured emerging anti-gun values in America.

Cosmopolitan America's Cultural Emergence

In 1890, the same year the U.S. Army completed its pacification of the Plains Indians at the Battle (or Massacre) of Wounded Knee and a year after the Oklahoma Land Rush, the U.S. Census Bureau determined that the United States no longer contained large areas of unsettled land (defined as having fewer than two persons per square mile) and proclaimed the frontier closed. Fredrick Jackson Turner, an eminent contemporary historian, perceived wide-ranging implications in this event. He argued that the transformative experience that had formed early Europeans into early Americans was the exploration and settlement of the frontier, and the further west the frontier advanced, the more Americans shed their European characteristics and acquired unique and distinctly "American" attributes.[13] As succeeding generations progressed westward, they became more individualistic, more egalitarian, more suspicious of authority, more self-reliant, more hardheaded, and even more violent.[14] But if the frontier had provided a defining source of American values and cultural uniqueness, its ending allowed the questioning of those values and the possibility of replacing them with other values perhaps more suited to the country's new circumstances. For Americans' traditional love of firearms, this seemed to be the case.

With the fading of the frontier, the customary justifications for owning and carrying firearms—survival, hunting, and self-defense—also began to fade. The rugged individualism that the American frontier had converted from a necessity into a virtue was neither as compelling nor as romantic in a developed nation now largely organized and settled. Although firearms still remained important tools on the ranches and farms of rural America, ongoing threats to personal safety were now exceptional.[15] And in major cities such as New York, Chicago, Houston, and San Francisco, professional municipal police departments had already been established for well over half a century. These developments helped diminish the previous attractiveness that firearms held for the typical American.

If the ending of the frontier dulled the luster of firearms, an intertwined contemporaneous development—urbanization—directly fostered attitudes and values antithetical to the country's dominant pro-gun culture. At the end of the 1700s, the country was rural and predominantly agricultural, with only about 5 percent of individuals residing in cities. With the extraordinary economic and social transformations that industrialization and manufacturing had wrought in the 19th century, by 1920, more than 50 percent of Americans lived in cities,[16] and a large portion of these city dwellers were newcomers to America. Although the country had always attracted immigrants looking for a better life, immigration surged from 3.5 million during the last decade of the 19th century, to 9 million in the first decade of the 20th century, to 15 million by 1915—a number approximately equal to the total number of newcomers arriving in the previous 40 years. And unlike earlier immigration waves, these foreigners came from the non-English-speaking countries of eastern and southern Europe,[17] bringing with them peculiar customs and languages that set them apart and made them objects of suspicion and fear. These free-floating fears and suspicions, in concert with the rampant crime already prevalent, spurred significant numbers of city dwellers—particularly the more established, well-to-do citizens—to question the ready availability of firearms in such high-density environments proffering so much ano-nymity and easy mobility.

Big city newspapers—the *New York Times, New York Herald Tribune, Chicago Tribune, Washington Post, Chicago Daily News*, and others—typically initiated campaigns decrying the prevalence of pistols and revolvers in their cities, and they often voiced forceful arguments for gun control in editorials and commentary.[18] For example, an editorial cartoon in the *New York Herald Tribune* entitled "Straining at a Gnat and Swallow-ing a Camel" contained drawings of a revolver and a pistol labeled "Man Killers: Designed and made openly and ostensibly with no other purpose in mind." Picking up on the man-killer theme, the *Chicago Tribune* noted, "As things are now, the man-killer is easy to get and inexpensive. A child may have one. The gun is around the house to be used in a fit of temper. Citizens are not defending their lives and property with them. They are bumping each other off when they get provoked."[19] The paper further stated that a pistol was not even essential for home defense, maintaining that law enforcement provided that defense. It concluded by arguing for national control of the manufacture and distribution of the "man-killer."

Comparable anti-gun sentiments also populated the editorial pages of some of the country's smaller newspapers. The *Grand Rapids Herald* declared that "any law which will make it more difficult for individuals to obtain one-hand guns . . . is bound to contribute to curtailment of the murder count." Similarly, after acknowledging that, in truth, laws could not prevent gun sales, the *Jersey Journal* nevertheless asserted that "the greater the number of obstacles placed in the way of the indiscriminate sale of guns, the fewer shootings there will be." Going even further, the *Ohio State Journal* argued for not only banning mail-order sales of guns and ammunition but also local sales.[20]

Alarmed at these growing anti-gun attitudes appearing in the country's newspapers and popular periodicals such as *Literary Digest, The Spectator*, and *World's Work*,[21] firearms proponents countered with arguments attacking the logic underlying many pro-gun control assertions. For example, the editors of *Field and Stream* magazine, addressing the claim that prohibiting the sale of pistols and revolvers would prevent crime, pointed out that the impact of such a law would likely be just the opposite, as criminals would still go armed while law-abiding citizens would obey the statute. Instead, the editors suggested "a law that every citizen of age must own a registered weapon, teach every public school boy how to use one, and impose a life sentence on armed robbery or assault. . . . We have had enough of prohibition; let's have a little common sense."[22] The *Wall Street Journal* expressed similar sentiments, noting that "so far as New York is concerned the Sullivan Law is a dangerous sham. . . . It sends to jail honest people ignorant of the law, and it makes the armed miscreant safe in carrying a gun, because it makes no distinction about robbery under arms."[23]

Reactions to the 1924 Sears, Roebuck and Company's announcement that the firm would discontinue the sale of firearms altogether (after having previously limited sales only to police officers) also illustrates the country's mixed attitudes toward small arms. While the *New York Daily News*—a leader in the campaign to limit "pistol-toting"—called the voluntary action "a shining example for other mail order houses to follow," the *El Paso Times* reacted less enthusiastically to the decision, noting that "like liquor, pistols will be obtained by those who want them as long as they are made. And the more prohibitory laws we pass regarding them, the more difficult we make it for law abiding citizens who intend to use them properly to get hold of them." Responding to the same announcement, the *Columbus Dispatch* observed that "the revolver still has its legitimate uses. . . . Otherwise, the murder of policemen would be an easy job, of every-day occurrence, to say nothing of the murder of ordinary citizens, and we would soon see crime waves in comparison with which those now complained of would be mere ripples." But rejecting this contention, the *Washington News* even doubted the value of firearms for home defense: "For every home that is saved from marauders by the presence of a gun, there is probably at least one into which tragedy came because some one 'didn't know it was loaded.'"[24]

Contradictory State Regulations

The legislative and judicial efforts of the period also mirrored mixed and contradictory attitudes toward firearms. Although World War I had dampened anti-gun discussions as large numbers of Americans prepared for and then engaged in combat, the 1920s unprecedented rise in crime and Prohibition-era mob violence, the country's growing xenophobia, and the intensifying fear of anonymous communist agents refocused the country's attention on the country's "gun problem" and the need for some type of gun control.[25] Thus, in 1924, a California court ruled that in the interests of public safety, the policing power of the state permitted the regulation of the right to bear arms and, in some cases, even its complete abolishment.[26] But when the legislature in neighboring Arizona passed a firearms bill that essentially only required a permit and a waiting period, the governor vetoed it as a serious infringement of individual liberties. Similarly, the legislatures of Arkansas and Michigan also evidenced inconsistent sentiment about handguns. Both states enacted handgun registration laws (in 1923 and 1925, respectively), but both states repealed these laws a short time later.

One law that received positive attention in a number of states during this period was the Uniform Firearms Act. Crafted by Karl Frederick, a former Olympic pistol champion and later an NRA president, this act shifted the focus of gun control from restricting certain types of firearms to restricting certain types of people from using firearms. Specifically, the act banned drug addicts, alcoholics, and persons under age 18 from possessing a handgun. Further, it mandated a waiting period of 48 hours between the purchase of a handgun and actual taking possession of it—a preventive measure assumed to reduce crimes of passion. The act also established gun dealer licensing and required individuals carrying a concealed weapon in a vehicle to obtain a permit. The National Conference of Commissioners on Uniform Laws endorsed the act in 1926, as did the American Bar Association in a reversal of its formerly anti-gun stance. Over the course of the next decade, at least eight states enacted this act or some variation of it. However, anti-gun New York was not among them. In that state, the Hanley-Fake Bill, a Uniform Firearms Act variant that would have replaced the Sullivan Act, actually passed both houses of the legislature but fell to the veto of New York State's governor at the time, Franklin Delano Roosevelt, who preferred the more severe restrictions of the earlier act.[27]

Attitudes toward firearms regulation in the cities were similarly rife with disagreement. For instance, after Chicago effectively refused to issue pistol carry permits, the courts mandated the city to honor outside permits because its pistol regulations diverged from state law. Chattanooga's carry ban was similarly voided by the courts. Officials in Philadelphia opted to arm their 1,600 firefighters rather than attempt measures to reduce the number of guns on the street. Meanwhile, the superintendent of the Pennsylvania State Police contended that outlawing pistols and revolvers was unlikely to decrease violent crime and might even increase such crime, "as thugs would no longer have any cause that their victims might be armed."[28] On the other hand, William McAdoo, the chief city magistrate of New York City and a fervent supporter of the Sullivan Act, argued that rather than arming themselves and resisting thieves and robbers, victims would be better off simply giving up their wallets. On this point, the *New York Times*—despite also championing gun regulation and the Sullivan Act—chose to disagree, noting that "the deterrent effect of resistance is, in the long run, considerable."[29] At least 17 states passed some type of gun control legislation over the course of the decade, but no consistent pattern characterized these regulatory attempts. The overall result from a regulatory perspective was unimpressive.[30]

National Regulation

In attempting to address the myriad social ills confronting the nation, reformers of the period started to look to the federal government as a force large enough and powerful enough to remedy these ills. After all, when nothing could be done on lesser levels to remedy the country's drinking problems, passage of a constitutional amendment banning the manufacture, sale, and transportation of intoxicating liquors within the United States seemingly offered a solution. When the patent unfairness of preventing half the country from voting simply became too great, another constitutional amendment addressed that problem. Not surprisingly then, gun control advocates saw the federal government as a potential ally in the ongoing fight against firearms. As one advocate put it,

> Let the W.C.T.U. and other reformers get busy in a reform that will mean something. . . . Let's fight the gun! . . . Let's put out of commission every manufacturer of arms for individual use. . . . Why not include the toy pistol as well and save our boys and little children from getting the habit. . . . Why not have another amendment to the Constitution. . . . Why not? If nobody had a gun, nobody would need a gun.[31]

Although federal efforts at gun regulation had been limited up to this point—it had taken multiple attempts to pass U.S. representative John F. Miller's bill outlawing the mail-order sale of pistols in the 1920s—gun control advocates had reason to believe the 1930s would be different. Violent crime in the cities had always been a problem, but the years of the Great Depression (1929–1939) saw an unprecedented escalation in violent criminal activity. Mobsters, bank robbers, and kidnappers, such as Al Capone, Pretty Boy Floyd, John Dillinger, Ma Barker, Clyde Barrow, and Bonnie Parker, periodically made national headlines with their lawless behavior and the devastating firearms they used. For example, Col. John

M. Thompson's .45-caliber submachine gun, designed for the trench warfare of World War I but arriving too late to be utilized in that conflict, was repurposed by New York and Chicago mobsters for gang warfare. The "tommy gun" proved stunningly effective in strewing city streets with the bodies of police and rivals alike. During these years, mobsters also discovered that, for unauthorized bank withdrawals and other close-up and personal encounters, the short-barreled shotgun—sometimes called a riot gun or "sawed-off" shotgun—was easily concealable, terrified tellers and other victims into instant submission, and required little skill to shoot effectively.[32]

Given this intensity of mobster violence and the casual indifference to life and law that it proclaimed, Franklin D. Roosevelt's New Deal unsurprisingly targeted crime aggressively. It did so by developing and championing national legislation to contain it. Homer Cummings, Roosevelt's attorney general, argued that pistol and firearms regulations needed significant tightening. He directed his staff to develop some draft proposals, one of which was the National Firearms Act (NFA). This act proposed to levy a federal tax not only on fully automatic weapons such as machine guns but also on most pistols and revolvers and on short-barreled rifles and shotguns. The act also imposed a tax on gun "silencers" (more accurately described as "sound suppressors" today) and on firearms disguised in some way (e.g., in belt buckles or walking sticks). The NFA required a federal license to manufacture, import, or sell such firearms; required the fingerprinting of buyers; and required a completed Internal Revenue Service form (with the appropriate tax stamp) each time a buyer sold or transferred the handgun, rifle, shotgun, or silencer to another person.[33]

The NFA immediately ran into powerful opposition from pro-gun advocates. Gun collectors, target shooters, and hunters fiercely objected to the proposed act, as did firearms manufacturers. The firearms manufacturers already had available a collective voice in firearms matters through the Sporting Arms and Ammunition Manufacturers' Institute (SAAMI), an association formed somewhat ironically at the behest of the federal government in 1926 to create industry standards for firearms safety, reliability, and quality. By 1934, this association consisted of 15 small arms manufacturers and about 70,000 dealers. The collective voice for hunters, shooters, and collectors was the National Rifle Association, now enlarged by the efforts of its executive director, C. B. Lister, who had broadened the organization's original focus on skilled marksmanship to include additional programs for youths and police officers as well as for hunters and sportsmen. At this time, the NRA had over 30,000 members and over 2,000 affiliated sportsmen's and shooters' clubs. It was the largest and best organized association of firearm users in the nation. The NRA considered the NFA a major infringement on the Second Amendment and opposed the act in its proposed form.[34]

In the congressional hearings that followed, the NRA leveled numerous criticisms of the act, noting practical limitations of several of the bill's presumed crime-fighting features and pointing out embarrassing inaccuracies in the bill's language in regard to common firearms definitions and terminology. The organization also fired up its membership, suggesting in its mail alerts that the NFA would eventually lead to mandated registration of all firearms, additional firearms taxes, and compulsory fingerprinting and photographing of all gun owners. In one of the firearms hearings, when a committee member suggested that gun registration could reduce murder, robbery, and other crimes, the executive vice president of the NRA, General M. A. Reckord, responded, "I do not think it would do a bit of good."[35]

Although the NRA accepted the NFA's restrictions on machine guns and sawed-off shotguns—gangster guns—the organization adamantly opposed handgun registration as an unnecessary infringement, despite the attorney general's last-minute assurance that members of organized groups (such as the NRA) could receive special consideration regarding registration. In the end, the revised act addressed many of the NRA's criticisms—most notably dropping the requirement for taxing and registering handguns—and the National Firearms Act became a federal law in 1934. Although the NFA became law, the attorney general's office nonetheless objected that the NRA had succeeded in gutting the act's most important provision—handgun registration. Indeed, in the wake of the battle over the NFA some in Congress began describing the NRA as the country's most influential organization opposed to firearms legislation.[36]

During the time of the NFA hearings, Congress also debated a second proposed bill focused on gun regulation. Sponsored by U.S. Senator Royal S. Copeland of New York, an ardent believer in strict gun control, this bill tapped into the federal government's authority to control interstate commerce. The proposed bill limited the shipping of concealable firearms across state lines to only federally licensed manufacturers, who could ship them only to federally licensed dealers in a state. It also banned the interstate shipment of machine guns; required manufacturers to maintain an inventory of at least one fired bullet from each weapon produced; and required an imprinted code on bullets indicating where they were sold. Aware of the NRA's impact on the final version of the National Firearms Act and anxious to ensure the enactment of at least some of his gun control restrictions, Senator Copeland involved the NRA and other pro-gun proponents in various drafts of the bill. Although the fired bullet inventory and the imprinted bullet code provisions did not make it into the bill's final version—experts pointedly derided the two provisions as virtually useless for practical crime solving[37]—the federal licensing requirements survived, including the need for license holders to follow detailed record-keeping procedures for sales and inventory. The bill also made it a felony to remove or obliterate a firearm's serial number or to possess a firearm whose serial number had been removed or altered in some way. Additionally, it created a class of "prohibited persons" (such as convicted felons and those under indictment) who were barred from transporting, receiving, or carrying firearms across interstate lines. Congress finally enacted Copeland's bill with little fanfare as the Federal Firearms Act (FFA) in 1938, and the FFA would remain the country's last national legislative effort on gun regulation for the next 30 years.[38]

Impact on American Gun Culture

The legal and statutory clashes of this period followed a distinct pattern: some immediate cultural spark igniting a call for gun regulation, extended arguments specifying the necessity of such legislation, countervailing arguments stating the unacceptability of the proposals, and, finally, the eventual passage of some usually negotiated regulation. The typical spark is often an event that was egregiously violent, even for a population jaded by violence. In the case of the Sullivan Act, the spark eventually leading to legislation was the attempted assassination of William Gaynor, the mayor of New York, in November 1910[39] and the broad-daylight murder of a popular writer in January 1911. Similarly, the spark for the National Firearms Act was the attempted assassination of president-elect Franklin Delano Roosevelt in February 1933, with the memory and images of the earlier St. Valentine's Day Massacre not yet faded from the public's mind. In the future, other singular acts of horrific violence will arrest the nation's attention, and these will revive new demands for further gun regulation.

The gun control arguments justifying the necessity of regulation—and the counterarguments disputing those contentions—will also follow a recurring pattern in the future. In the case of the Sullivan Act, the presumed reduction of violent crime provided the overriding justification for gun control. Based on the belief that regulation and enforcement can keep handguns out of the "wrong" hands—those hands typically belonging to thugs, mobsters, immigrants, and other suspected undesirables—the notion that gun control reduces violent crime will become a basic theme in all future discussions on the matter. The necessity of keeping guns out of the hands of suspected "undesirables" will also resurface, most notably in later confrontations with members of the Black Panthers in the 1960s and then again in the next century, with individuals listed on the federal government's "watch" and "no-fly" lists. The justifications for dismissal of these arguments will also resurface. Pro-gun advocates will point out time and again that criminals by definition ignore laws and will simply ignore gun regulations, whose only effect will be to disarm honest citizens no longer able to defend themselves. They will also note and decry the racial, ethnic, and regional assumptions seeming to underlie past gun control efforts to keep guns from supposed deviants.[40]

Although the NFA was also initially intended to reduce violent crime through handgun registration, its evolution through the legislative process resulted in creating a second cultural pattern that reemerged in later debates on firearms: the drive for legislation designed to protect the public from particularly dangerous or unnecessary weapons and instruments. In the case of the NFA, this category included automatic weapons such as machine guns, short-barreled rifles, silencers, and other such firearms. In the coming decades, gun control advocates attempted to expand the category to include semiautomatic "assault" rifles, "high-capacity" magazines, trigger accelerators, and related items.

Unlike 1934, when the NRA was open to gun control arguments focused on firearms deemed too dangerous or unnecessary, these later regulatory efforts encountered fierce opposition, as gun enthusiasts become increasingly wary of gun control agendas. As with the NFA, the FFA's passage through Congress transformed what was supposed to be a crime-fighting bill into something less: primarily an administrative and record-keeping regulation. Nonetheless, the justification for these regulatory procedures, which expanded the government's ability to track the flow of firearms from one federal licensee to another, rested on claims that they increased public safety. In coming decades, gun control proponents used the need for better public safety as the justification for more and more administrative regulations, and pro-gun supporters repeatedly rebuffed such efforts as ineffective and unnecessarily burdensome on law-abiding citizens attempting to exercise their constitutional rights.

Thus, by the end of the 1930s, a nascent rift in America's formerly unquestioned gun culture had clearly materialized. Further, the rift did not have the prosaic quality of benign neglect that characterized the English experience—where over time cultural ties to firearms seemed to fade of their own accord[41]—but rather the more fractious quality of a heated family disagreement. The developing rift seemed to signal not just that firearms no longer held a special place in American culture but that, according to some citizens, they had *no* place in American culture; as one contemporary put it, pistols and guns simply "do not fit into the pattern of a safe, healthy, and happy environment."[42] The virulent anti-gun attitudes that had surfaced during the debates surrounding the new federal laws suggested to many pro-gun advocates that the real but unstated objective of gun control was the eventual banning (at least for the average citizen) of *all* firearms for *any* purpose. Unlike earlier efforts at regulation, the effort this time appeared to regard even previously acceptable firearms such as target rifles and hunting shotguns as morally questionable and in need of strict regulation.[43]

Lee Kennett and James Anderson, noted historians of gun control, in their analysis of the period, have also attributed this changing attitude at least partially to the global zeitgeist and happenings in Europe. Simultaneously with events in America, England, Germany, and France were debating and legislating significant regulations limiting civilian possession of firearms in preparation for war. It is not hard to imagine a form of "cultural contagion" driving the development of a common transnational orientation inimical toward firearms in civilian hands. And, simply as a logical matter, rigidly regulating individual access to firearms might also make eminent sense to citizens committed to international disarmament.[44]

Taken together, the significant events that impacted American culture and shaped attitudes toward firearms during the first part of the 20th century—violent crime, urban growth, immigration, assassinations—cast a shadow on the continued viability of rugged individualism and on the values of Bedrock America that had long buttressed the country's gun culture. These same events, coupled with the growing belief in influential circles that America's gun policies were woefully out of step with the more progressive policies of the country's international peers in Europe, set the foundation for the rise of the anti-gun values of Cosmopolitan America.

Cultural Coexistence: 1940–1960

With war again on the horizon, the differing gun orientations of Bedrock America and Cosmopolitan America diminished in importance as the country geared up for the impending conflict. This is not to suggest that proponents deserted the cultural principles they advocated, merely that other significant events—the nation's preoccupations with war, its tremendous economic expansion, and its later postwar prosperity—took center stage and dominated the country's attention. Thus, for 20 years or so, an uneasy truce regarding firearms was forged between Bedrock and Cosmopolitan America, with the values of both groups warily coexisting.

In the evolving cultural environment, neither faction pressed its agenda aggressively, and the acrimony that would characterize encounters in later decades was absent. For example, in describing individuals opposed to gun rights, an editor of the *American Rifleman* (the NRA's flagship magazine) in 1955 proposed that they were simply people who were "sincere" and "conscientious" but "misguided"[1]—a description that opponents would likely reciprocate, disagreeing only on who was misguided. Despite this apparent detente, particular events and circumstances favored the cause of both Bedrock America and Cosmopolitan America at various times.

A Pro-Gun Resurgence

As the 1930s closed with the passage of the National Firearms Act and the Federal Firearms Act, the country's attitude toward handguns and rifles appeared to reflect a shift away from America's long-standing embrace of firearms toward a mounting distrust of them. World War II halted that shift. As patriotic Americans became reacquainted with military arms and weapons, their increased training and familiarity with rifles and pistols evolved into an enduring interest in small arms when they returned home and reentered civilian life. This interest reignited enthusiasm for target shooting and marksmanship, led to the formation of new shooting clubs, and spurred gun collecting as an engaging pastime. For example, between 1939 and 1958, the number of gun collectors in America grew over twelvefold, from about 50,000 individuals to about 650,000. During the same period, because of rising demand, prices for antique firearms also exploded, with prices for Kentucky rifles increasing over 400 percent and Colt pistols about 800 percent.[2]

Even more significantly, the war and its impact on Great Britain's civilian population vividly illustrated for Americans the value of guns in civilian hands. Because of severe gun control laws enacted years earlier, a substantial percentage of Englishmen were without firearms or weapons of any sort during this period. When it appeared likely that German forces would invade the United Kingdom, the country's home defense services were utterly ill prepared and unequipped—so much so that the only arms some members of the Home Guard could field were "Brown Bess" muskets. This firearm was the same musket British troops had carried during the American War of Independence almost 200 years earlier. In fact, the situation was so dire that a group of Americans—with the consent of the British government—formed a committee (the American Committee for the Defense of British Homes) to collect donations of privately owned pistols, rifles, revolvers, and shotguns from American citizens. These firearms were shipped overseas to aid in Great Britain's homeland defense.[3]

Further reinforcing Americans' reawakened belief in the value of firearms in civilian hands was the telling experience of citizens in countries occupied by the invading German forces. In virtually all cases, the German occupiers treated firearms in the hands of the civilian population as lethal threats. Time and again, they ordered civilians to surrender their rifles and guns and imposed severe penalties for noncompliance. In some cases, such as Czechoslovakia, Denmark, and Poland, prior gun registration lists expedited the German confiscation of weapons; in other cases, the occupying forces simply relied on the threatened penalties (e.g., immediate execution for possession) listed in the posted notices and proclamations to ensure the surrender of privately owned arms. Thus, in 1941, when U.S. Attorney General Robert Jackson urged Congress to pass legislation establishing a national registry of firearms, Congress instead responded by passing legislation with provisions that specifically blocked firearms registration and any manner of infringement on the right of an individual to keep or bear arms.[4] In later years, the idea of a national firearms registry will periodically resurface in the clash between Bedrock and Cosmopolitan America. As it did then, and for the same reasons, the National Rifle Association will fiercely oppose such efforts, pointing to events in Europe before and during World War II as a cautionary warning against gun control in general and gun registration in particular.

Although wartime European experiences underscored what the NRA framed as the unintended consequences and hidden dangers of gun control, it was not the only factor that made Americans wary of anti-gun attitudes and enabled firearms to regain some of their former luster. Influences that had prompted cries for gun regulation in past decades— violent crime, foreign immigration, civil disorder, and political assassinations—were much less in evidence during this period. For instance, crimes of violence, such as homicide, aggravated assault, and robbery, had markedly decreased to low levels during the war years and remained at these unusually low levels throughout the 1950s.[5]

Similarly, by opening up jobs formerly held by millions of men now in uniform, the American war effort provided new economic opportunities for migrating blacks and poor Southerners seeking work in northern factories and for wartime immigrants urgently needed to fill in for workers vacuumed up by the military. Thus, with good-paying jobs alleviating unemployment (the usual cause of civil unrest) and with the pragmatic need for workers overcoming Americans' usual suspicion of immigrant newcomers, the power of these past gun control triggers was missing.[6] Even the attempted assassination of President Harry Truman by Puerto Rican nationalists in November 1950 and the shooting of five U.S. congressmen on the floor of the House of Representatives four years later failed to create a clamor for gun legislation.

The resurgence in pro-gun attitudes during these decades also stemmed from a sea change in American popular culture, which had rediscovered and begun to celebrate the country's Western and frontier roots during these decades. Both motion picture producers and television writers entertained their audiences with scripts centered on cowboys, gunslingers, frontiersmen, and gamblers. Throughout the 1940s and 1950s, Hollywood created a proliferation of action-driven, B Westerns that simultaneously propagated America's Western myths and incorporated the American characteristics of self-reliance and fair play into their themes and plots.[7] Gene Autry and Roy Rogers were the first of the "singing cowboys"—a new twist on the cowboy genre—and their popularity was such that each eventually produced and starred in weekly television Westerns entitled eponymously. William Boyd popularized the Hopalong Cassidy character in a Saturday morning series, and Clayton Moore did the same for the Lone Ranger on Thursday evenings. Guns were prominent features in all these television Westerns, but producers actually kept violent gunplay to a minimum. Both John Wayne and Gary Cooper not only starred in iconic Western films—*Red River* and *High Noon* immediately come to mind—but they also went on to achieve later acclaim in other film genres. Hollywood Westerns also prominently featured guns and firearms, but violent gunplay was more common than in television programming of that era.

For a generation of viewers, these shows and films showcased soft-spoken, white-hatted heroes whose actions illustrated the meaning of personal integrity, self-reliance, and fair play, and the villains invariably suffered the consequences of their shameful and despicable behavior. Many of the leading actors in these films would enter the pantheon of American Western film iconography—with their character portrayals almost invariably wearing a holstered six-shooter or carrying a Winchester rifle. The image was not lost on filmgoers of the era: good men carried firearms and as a last resort used them to right the wrongs perpetrated by evil men.

The wide popularity of cowboy-oriented entertainment did not escape the notice of advertising and marketing executives either, and they enlisted the most recognizable actors to tout an impressive range of products—breads, cereals, candies, books, watches, guitars, and bicycles—including many Western-themed items specifically geared to the highly receptive children's market. For instance, at the height of his appeal, Autry endorsed not only children's clothing, such as cowboy outfits, boots, hats, and neckerchiefs, but also toy firearms, such as six-shooters and rifles. Following the same path, Roy Rogers and his wife, Dale Evans, eventually surpassed Autry both in popularity and in endorsements, with over 450 products bearing their names, including a selection of Roy Rogers's and Dale Evans's holsters, cap guns, and rifles for both boys and girls.[8]

Western-themed entertainment and its associated marketing had enormous effects on Americans' acceptance of guns during this period. By the end of the 1950s, cap pistols and rifles were poised to become the largest category of toys for boys, with sales approaching $100 million annually—a far cry from the 1930s when U.S. Senator Arthur Capper described children playing with toy guns as a "real American tragedy" and the

United Parents Association of New York City considered even toy guns harmful because they symbolized gangsters and violence.[9] Nor was this acceptance limited to children's toys. The Hollywood films and television Westerns also renewed adults' interest in firearms. Lee Kennett and James Anderson suggest that it was during this period that gun collecting as a serious hobby first emerged, with Colt's Model 1873 Single Action Army (SAA) revolver becoming a particular collector favorite. They note that Colt had produced more than a quarter million SAAs by 1947, when the firm ended the gun's run. However, collector demand for the revolver was so great that Colt determined it was worthwhile to resume production in 1955.[10] Even today, the SAA revolver continues to hold a special mystique among gun enthusiasts, with one expert asserting, "From the most cosmopolitan urban centers to the most remote outposts of civilization, the Colt Single Action Army revolver is the most recognizable handgun ever made. . . . The Colt Single Action Army was and is the gun of the cowboy."[11]

In addition to the impetus the entertainment industry provided, the country's revived interest in firearms also reflected a reaction to the relative unavailability of handguns and rifles during the war years, when military requirements absorbed virtually all weapons-manufacturing capacity. When the war ended, Remington, Smith & Wesson, Colt, and other manufacturers turned much of their production capacity back to civilian firearms to satisfy the pent-up demand for guns that the war had generated. From an economic viewpoint, courting the suppressed civilian market was a pragmatic imperative for the arms manufacturers, given their enormous expansion during the war years. For instance, Remington had expanded 2,000 percent in filling its military orders. Smith & Wesson, which had produced more arms during the war years than it had in its preceding 90 years of existence, had so increased its scope that its manufacturing capacity now exceeded that of all other revolver manufacturers combined.[12] The firms' strategic shift in focus from military to civilian also appropriately converged with a budding new segment of the gun market that had formed from many of the millions of returned veterans whose military experiences had sparked an abiding interest in firearms. These newcomers to civilian shooting would gravitate across the traditional demarcations separating firearms enthusiasts and blur distinctions between hunters, target shooters, and collectors.

Accompanying the country's renewed acceptance of firearms was the emergence of an array of commercial products and services catering to gun enthusiasts. Notable among these ancillary ventures was the development of a thriving gun-oriented press that examined specialized firearm topics and significant issues relevant to the shooting community. Where previously anyone looking to read about pistols and rifles had only *Gun Digest* (an annual publication) and *American Rifleman* (a monthly published by the NRA) to peruse, by the 1950s, the gun enthusiast had a slew of additional periodicals to examine: *Guns* and *Gun Reports* (1955); *Guns and Ammo* and *Guns and Hunting* (1958); and *Gun World* and *Shooting Times* (1960). Additionally, firearms-related books, a limited market before the war, became more profitable to publish, and sales of such titles flourished during this period.[13]

Target shooting and marksmanship reemerged as worthwhile leisure pursuits, and shooting clubs regained whatever stature they might have lost in the 1930s. One activity some clubs sponsored—no doubt inspired by the cowboy-oriented films and television shows that dominated the era—was dubbed "fast draw."[14] Typically using working replicas of Single Action Army revolvers and suitably attired as 1870s cowpokes, individuals competed to determine who was the fastest in drawing the revolver from the holster and accurately firing it. Variations on this theme proliferated, with club members practicing such lost (Hollywood) gun-handling skills as the "road agent's spin," the "border shift," and "up-twist fanning."[15]

While serious shooters dismissed these activities as childish, the challenges (and amusement) they offered attracted newcomers to the shooting fraternity and lured new members into the clubs. By one estimate, half a million Americans took up the hobby during the 1950s and early 1960s, with participants purchasing 150,000 Western-style six-guns annually. More than 800 clubs specifically focused on fast draw, with some holding weekly "shootdowns" that allowed members to exhibit their quickness and accuracy. When enthusiasts held broader regional gatherings to show off their skills to fellow aficionados, such meeting attracted as many as 12,000 spectators.[16] Fascination with the activity was enough that even a non-shooting-oriented periodical such as *Popular Science* took note and examined the mechanics of the fast draw.[17]

The country's resumed love affair with firearms not only benefited local shooting clubs and associations—growing the membership of established clubs and encouraging the founding of new ones—but it also stimulated the growth of the National Rifle Association. Prior to the war, the NRA could boast of about 3,500 affiliated clubs. By 1948, that number had almost doubled to about 6,500 clubs. Similarly, its individual membership numbers reflected the period's endorsement of firearms: 50,000 members before the war and about 500,000 by the end of the 1950s.[18]

Although government policies certainly account for part of this growth—the government authorized the NRA to sell surplus rifles and pistols to its members at discounted prices—part of this growth is also likely due to the high esteem the NRA now commanded among citizens. Whatever controversy the NRA may have engendered during the legislative fights of the 1930s disappeared under the weight of the organization's wartime contributions. For instance, the NRA had furnished firearms manuals and training films to the government, which the military then adopted for official use. Similarly, the NRA had provided the plans for forming Home Guard units, which many states used, and had recruited trainers and dogs for Coast Guard Beach Patrols through its network of sportsmen. Further, NRA-affiliated clubs had opened their rifle and pistol ranges to the government, and NRA members had trained about 10 percent of all service members in marksmanship. President Truman applauded the NRA's contributions to the war effort in a 1945 letter to the NRA, and in doing so, he implicitly endorsed the value of civilian gun training and ownership.[19]

Anti-Gun Sentiment: Muted but Present

While World War II and the offerings of the country's entertainment industries subdued calls for gun control and rehabilitated the image of the gun in the minds of most Americans, other developments during this period nonetheless kept the need for potential firearms restrictions in the national consciousness. Ironically enough, some of these developments originated in the firearms fraternity itself. For example, many participants in the early fast draw competitions actually used live ammunition in their revolvers. Not surprisingly, given the numbers involved in the sport, a significant percentage had trigger fingers that were faster than their hands, and these relatively untrained individuals often ended up with gunshot wounds to the leg, foot, or groin.[20] Eventually, clubs banned the use of live ammunition in these competitions, insisting that participants use wax bullets instead, but such shooting accidents remained frequent enough that a medical journal described them as a national malady, publishing an account entitled "Gunshot Wounds of Lower Extremity: Fast Draw Syndrome."[21]

Similarly, many neophyte shooters took up hunting as a pursuit during these decades, with a predictable spike in hunting accidents and tragedies. Reported dramatically in the press and discussed somberly in national periodicals, these hunting mishaps brought significant unwanted attention to the activity and so alarmed the shooting fraternity that the NRA introduced a hunter safety course in 1950 and started to collect statistics on hunting accidents. Further exacerbating fears that issues with the sport might result in new restrictions on hunting and firearms, popular magazines published a number of articles examining the ethical implications of hunting and killing animals. Even when an article defended hunting as appropriate game management and necessary to keep the animal population and wider ecosystem healthy, the lingering impression for many readers was frequently negative: hunters simply liked to kill.[22]

Aside from these safety and ethical issues, a development having even greater bearing for firearms restrictions and gun control originated with the firearms manufacturers themselves. These firms, already unhappy with the NRA's government-sponsored program offering the sale of surplus U.S. military rifles and pistols to civilians at steeply discounted rates, were alarmed over the huge numbers of surplus *foreign* firearms that American entrepreneurs began to import in the 1950s. Because of low customs valuations, even with added tariff costs, importers could price these arms much below the prices American manufacturers charged for their wares. Many gun enthusiasts took advantage of the price differential, purchasing the foreign rifles and then easily "sporterizing" (modifying) the firearms to improve their suitability for hunting and target practice.

The arms manufacturers' strategy for dealing with this economic threat involved regular attempts (one large importer estimated at least 11) to use restrictive federal legislation to eliminate the unwanted source of competition. At the time, both Connecticut and Massachusetts were home to several of the country's major firearms manufacturers, so their congressional members took the industry's complaints particularly seriously. The Massachusetts Senate petitioned Congress to restrict imports, Congressman Albert Morano of Connecticut introduced legislation to ban the importation of surplus foreign arms, and Senator John Kennedy of Massachusetts offered a similar bill in the Senate.

These restrictive legislative attempts put the NRA—the acknowledged representative of the gun community—in a bit of a bind. On the one hand, the NRA did not want to offend the manufacturers by opposing the legislation and perhaps lose advertising revenues in the *American Rifleman*, but on the other hand, the group worried that closing the spigot of inexpensive arms might harm the shooting sports' burgeoning expansion. Like the shooting press in general, the association chose simply to report legislative activity rather than take a definite stand.[23]

Ultimately, the zeitgeist of the era trumped these legislative efforts, and none of the federal firearms bills introduced in the 1950s made it out of committee.[24] Similarly, on the state level, few of the various firearms-related bills proposed each year posed any significant new threats to gun rights. Throughout these years the NRA could declare in its annual evaluation of legislative activity that "no unduly restrictive legislation was passed."[25]

Nonetheless, despite these legislative victories and the country's seemingly positive orientation toward firearms, other gauges indicated that the anti-gun attitudes of Cosmopolitan America were far from banished. An August 1959 Gallup poll indicated that 75 percent of all those surveyed—and 65 percent of actual gun owners—believed that anyone wanting a handgun should first obtain a police permit. Even more startling, a second poll in September revealed that, except for police, 59 percent of those polled favored banning handguns altogether—and this in a time when half the homes in the nation contained firearms.[26]

Although the press inexplicably showed little interest in these findings, the shooting fraternity became so worried that the results might spark new calls for gun regulation that it decided to undertake preemptive actions. In addition to broadcasting its misgivings in editorials, the NRA created a new feature in its flagship magazine highlighting numerous instances where peaceable citizens had used guns to foil criminal activity and to protect themselves and their communities. Not long afterward, *Field and Stream* magazine facilitated the creation of the National Shooting Sports Foundation (NSSF), a collection of firms involved with firearms and related accessories. The NSSF then supervised a publicity campaign touting the numerous benefits and positive facets of sport shooting and firearms.[27] Thus, regardless of the absence of restrictive legislation during these decades, the polls—and the worried response of the firearms community—signaled that much anti-gun sentiment existed below the country's exterior acceptance of civilian-owned handguns and rifles.

Assessing Cultural Coexistence

In evaluating this odd period in the history of gun control, Kennett and Anderson conclude that extraordinary circumstances simply overwhelmed Cosmopolitan America in its struggles with Bedrock America. World War II had introduced a new generation to military armaments and reinvigorated the country's traditional fascination with firearms. It had also flooded the country with an ocean of easily available rifles and pistols: war souvenirs brought back by returning veterans, foreign imports from overseas, excess inventory from the U.S. government, and brand-new offerings from American high-capacity firearms factories. Further, the era's economic prosperity provided individuals with enough leisure time to explore new shooting interests sparked by the gun-oriented films and shows of the day. Then, too, the political tensions of the decade— troubles with North Korea and the emergence of the Cold War with the Soviet bloc—ensured that the country still continued to regard firearms as essential instruments for preparedness, and this also endowed them with a certain prudent respectability.[28]

Additionally, the social dynamics usually fostering Cosmopolitan America's anti-gun orientation—crime, civil unrest, and urban turbulence— were hardly in play during this period. Crime rates were at historic lows, and while one national publication attributed the anti-gun attitudes uncovered by Gallup to civil rights violence erupting in the South,[29] civil rights issues and urban mayhem did not really roil the country until the next decade. And, despite the sobering number of self-inflicted wounds and shooting accidents fast draw enthusiasts generated, calls for gun safety did not become a major rallying cry for Cosmopolitan America until decades later. Thus, advocates of gun control had few reasons and little opportunity to thrust their values into the national spotlight. They could only watch on the sidelines as the country's traditional orientation toward firearms—and Bedrock America's pro-gun values—reasserted themselves. All this would radically change, however, when gun control conflicts and legislative restrictions returned to dominate the next decades.

CHAPTER FIVE

Cultural Upheaval:
1960–1970

For proponents of Cosmopolitan America, the cultural zeitgeist of the 1960s—the "Decade of Assassinations"—simply started as an extension of the previous year. To the extent the country saw a problem with firearms, that problem centered on the continuing availability of firearms through the mails. Although the Federal Firearms Act of 1938 had indirectly addressed this issue by allowing interstate gun dealers to send firearms only to individuals who had a firearms permit, this restriction only applied in those states that required individuals to possess a permit to own a gun. Just seven states had such a requirement.[1] Consequently, mail-order sales to minors, criminals, and other prohibited individuals represented an ongoing concern of Cosmopolitan America, and its proponents pushed for new legislation to remedy the problem. Their champion in this matter was Senator Thomas Dodd of Connecticut.

As chairman of the Senate Judiciary Subcommittee to Investigate Juvenile Delinquency, Dodd had become interested in mail-order gun sales to minors as early as 1961. Working with the NRA and other firearms representatives, the committee began public hearings on mail-order firearms in January 1963. That August, Dodd introduced S. 1975, "A Bill to Regulate the Shipment of Interstate Firearms," a proposal primarily aimed at limiting mail-order sales. In addition to banning the importation of "Saturday Night Specials" (inexpensive and typically shoddily made foreign pistols favored by street thugs and poor working men), the bill in its original form required that mail-order handgun buyers include a notarized statement with their order, attesting to their legal eligibility to make such a purchase. Although the shooting fraternity initially looked upon the proposed legislation favorably, Dodd's bill received little attention in the Senate and languished in Senator Warren Magnuson's Committee on Commerce, where it had been referred. Gun legislation was simply not a high priority at this time, for the Senate or the country.[2] But less than four months later, Lee Harvey Oswald used a mail-ordered Mannlicher-Carcano bolt-action rifle to assassinate President John F. Kennedy in Dallas. In the aftermath of this horrifying event, gun control came to dominate the attention of the nation.

Kennedy's assassination was the first of four prominent gun murders—five if we include the murder of Oswald himself by the revolver-wielding Jack Ruby—that defined and forever marked the 1960s: John Kennedy in 1963, Malcolm X in 1965, and Martin Luther King Jr. and Robert Kennedy in 1968. For Cosmopolitan America, these murders gruesomely illustrated that the casual cultural acceptance of widely available and easily obtainable firearms truly had appallingly blood-stained consequences. Members of Cosmopolitan America demanded that this cultural acceptance of firearms be fully repudiated. For Bedrock America, the assassinations evoked fears that civil instability and racial unrest existed just under the surface and were increasingly dividing the country. These beliefs simply confirmed the necessity of firearms and underscored their essential value for self-protection and family security. In addition to the assassinations during this period, two other societal developments also contributed to the escalating tensions separating Bedrock and Cosmopolitan America: a resurgence in violent criminal activity and fears and uncertainties associated with the nascent civil rights movement.

JFK's Assassination and Gun Legislation

The president's assassination resulted in a deluge of mail flooding Congress, most of it pressing for more severe gun control measures. Congress responded. Less than a week after the assassination, legislators had put forth a dozen firearms bills.[3] Senator Dodd, who described Kennedy's assassination as a "tragic opportunity" to enact long-needed gun controls, expanded his bill to cover *all* mail-order firearms (not just pistols and other handguns). He also added the requirement that the chief law enforcement official of the purchaser's locality certify the notarized statement of eligibility. In this form, the bill would have made mail-order firearm purchases more difficult than in-person, local gun store purchases virtually everywhere in the country. However, because the certification requirement seemed tantamount to licensing, the NRA requested that Dodd change this aspect of the bill so that the buyer only had to provide the seller with the name and address of the official, with the requirement that the seller then provide the official with the buyer's particulars and the type of firearm purchased.[4]

Dodd agreed to the change, and in return, the NRA, noting the country's unprecedented wave of anti-gun animosity, cautiously supported the amended bill.[5] Nonetheless, other members of the shooting fraternity were not convinced that S. 1975 was as harmless to their values and interests as the NRA assumed. Opposition may have arisen due to confusion over the bill's provisions, with many gun advocates thinking the bill required gun registration. Others may have opposed the bill because they believed its emotional origins would ensure that more restrictive measures would follow should this measure pass.[6] This fear was not entirely unfounded. Gun control was understandably receiving a great deal of attention in the news media at the time, and the dominant theme of these articles was the need for more robust restrictions on the availability of firearms. One *Newsweek* article[7] was typical. Not only did the article question the necessity for mail-order firearms, suggesting that purchasers more often than not had criminal intentions, it also expressed doubts about the relevance of the Second Amendment, arguing that numerous gun owners retained an odd frontier mentality and "miss the fact that the frontier is secure and the armed forces, National Guard, and local police protect the nation."[8]

Although debates about the practical relevance of the Second Amendment had periodically occurred in the popular press at least since the passage of the Sullivan Act in 1911, the cultural significance of the amendment to both Bedrock and Cosmopolitan America was such that these arguments became increasingly acrimonious over the next several years. Indeed, one's position on the Second Amendment served (and continues to serve) as a reliable indicator of whether one belonged to Bedrock America or Cosmopolitan America. For Cosmopolitan America, the amendment's prefatory clause—"a well-regulated militia being necessary to a free state"—determined the intent and scope of the amendment. The right to bear arms was clearly a *collective* right, exercised in defense of the country in militia service. The *Newsweek* article plainly exemplified and fostered this orientation. For Bedrock America, the prefatory clause was exactly that: prefatory. The substantive clause was what followed: "the right of the people to keep and bear arms shall not be infringed." It was here that the intent and meaning of the amendment resided. While the country's need for a militia might at some point fade, the need of the people to continually protect themselves from tyrannical overreach would not.[9] A Creator-ordained right to bear arms offered such a safeguard, an individual right constitutionally upheld by this amendment.

Using these different lenses, the two sides naturally assessed Dodd's bill (and the associated media calls for even more severe restrictions) quite differently. Kennett and Anderson, in summarizing voluminous committee testimony, noted that "there were few in the debate who did not quote the Second Amendment. . . . Statistics on crime, gun ownership, and the correlation between them were variously interpreted,"[10] but the testimony broke no new ground, with many of the arguments reminiscent of those occurring 50 years earlier, during clashes over New York's Sullivan Act. However, the tone of the new exchanges were sometimes more hostile and perhaps more dramatic. When John Lindsay, a pro–gun control New York congressman who later became mayor of New York City, appeared before the committee wielding a Mannlicher-Carcano rifle, Senator Ralph Yarborough of Texas sharply told him to follow all NRA gun-handling safety rules. Lindsay shot back, "I can't help but do that, because they run the show."[11] His statement to the committee effectively captured Cosmopolitan America's position on gun control (then and now): "Today the nation no longer depends on the citizen's weapon, nor does the citizen himself. And, most significant, the population is now densely packed into urban areas. . . . In our changed and complicated society, guns have become more dangerous. . . . The Constitution must be interpreted in the light of the times."[12]

Bedrock America's position was that more effective solutions to the gun problem were available and that these deserved more consideration than they were receiving. For example, instead of focusing on the gun, Congressman Robert Casey of Texas suggested focusing on the gun user. He proposed a federal law that would subject individuals committing certain crimes with a firearm to a possible 25-year prison sentence. This idea received little support from gun control proponents, and this seeming unwillingness to consider any alternatives other than gun restrictions further polarized the debate and hardened each group's stance.[13]

Returning to the constitutional question, we might ask whether the constraints proposed in S. 1975 violated the Second Amendment, exceeding the limits earlier judicial rulings had placed on the right to keep and bear arms. Certainly, Cosmopolitan America did not think so, considering the bill's restrictions had garnered the support of the NRA, the arms industry, and more than three-quarters of those polled by Gallup. But Bedrock America could also point to judicial rulings upholding a citizen's right to arms and severely limiting the legitimate constraints the government could place on the exercise of that right. It is unclear what role such considerations played in committee's deliberations, but in any event, Bedrock America's opposition was sufficient to stall Dodd's bill; in 1964, it died at the end of the 88th Congress, having never proceeded beyond committee hearings.[14]

Urban Riots

While the Kennedy assassination harshly limned the appalling consequences of firearms used criminally, the birthing shudders of the civil rights movement—and the violent response to its rise, especially across the South—also offered vivid national images of a country embroiled in chaos and violence. It prompted many Americans to weigh the appropriate role of guns in such disordered social conditions. Concerns that the nation was speeding toward anarchy intensified in July and August of 1964, when major clashes between police and black Americans erupted in New York, Rochester, Jersey City, Paterson, Elizabeth, and Philadelphia.

The New York riot occurred after an off-duty white police lieutenant, Thomas Gilligan, shot and killed James Powell, a 15-year-old black teenager who with some friends had been confronting a building superintendent that had water-hosed and disparaged them. In his account of the incident, Gilligan claimed that when he arrived on the scene, the teenager lunged at him while wielding a knife. He first fired a warning shot but then shot Powell in self-defense. Others at the scene disputed Gilligan's account, asserting that Powell held no knife and merely raised his arm protectively when Gilligan fired his first shot. Ultimately, it mattered little which account was objectively correct. Because of accumulated racial tensions and past perceptions of police harassment and brutality, the shooting sparked six days of confrontations and clashes in Harlem and Bedford-Stuyvesant that involved about 8,000 rioters. As the rioting dragged on, people on rooftops pelted the police with bottles, bricks, and debris, as mobs on the ground threw Molotov cocktails at police cruisers and beat "Whiteys" as they encountered them. Responding to Police Commissioner Michael Murphy's statement that he would treat the riot as "a crime problem and not a social problem,"[15] the Black Nationalist leader Malcolm X replied, "There are probably more armed Negroes in Harlem than in any other spot on earth. If the people who are armed get involved in this, you can bet they'll really have something on their hands."[16] In the end, the New York riot took one life, injured more than 100, resulted in 465 arrests, and caused property damage of almost $1 million.[17]

Less than three days later, a second riot occurred, this time in Rochester, New York. After the arrest of an apparently intoxicated black 19-year-old at a street block party, Rochester police arrived at the scene with a K-9 dog, fueling rumors among the black crowd of excessive police force and brutality. As the rumors spread and the crowd grew, people turned hostile, and the riot began. Nelson Rockefeller, the governor at the time, activated the New York National Guard, quelling the disturbance after three days of chaos. The riot resulted in four deaths, about 350 injuries, almost 1,000 arrests, and over 200 shops and stores looted or damaged.[18]

A week later, in Jersey City, New Jersey, a third riot ensued, triggered by the arrest of a 26-year-old black woman, Dolores Shannon, on a disorderly conduct charge. As with the earlier riots, rumors of police brutality and simmering prior tensions with the police inflamed the neighborhood, and a crowd of almost 1,000 black protestors morphed into a mob throwing rocks and stones at passing automobiles; pulling drivers and passengers out of stopped cars; hurling bricks, bottles, and garbage can covers at police; and ransacking businesses over a wide area. The riot lasted three days and nights, with at least 46 people injured, 52 arrested, and 71 shops damaged.[19]

Rioting would again erupt in New Jersey seven days later, but on a smaller scale in, Paterson and, in a separate but simultaneous incident, in nearby Elizabeth. In Paterson, the initial incident began with black teenagers throwing rocks at passing police cars. As hostilities escalated, Paterson's mayor, Frank Graves, decided to "meet force with force" and ordered the police (equipped with tear gas, sawed-off shotguns, armored personnel carriers, and riot gear) to crack down on the rioters. As in the Jersey City riot, the mob attacked the police and passing automobiles with rocks, bricks, and even Molotov cocktails, but the aftermath was more subdued. Estimates suggest that somewhere between 100 and 500 people were involved, with only 46 arrests, less than 10 injured, and no one killed.[20] The Elizabeth riot began on the same day as the Paterson riot, ignited by several carloads of black youths using Molotov cocktails to set stores and businesses along the Hudson River waterfront ablaze. As the disturbance progressed, around 700 blacks took to the streets, often confronting the police with a mix of bricks, stones, and Molotov cocktails. By the third day, the riot had run its course, with 18 people arrested.[21]

Two weeks later, at the end of August, the nation would confront the sixth race riot of that summer—ironically the same summer Congress passed the Civil Rights Act of 1964—in Philadelphia, Pennsylvania. A domestic dispute between a black couple, Rush and Odessa Bradford, was the immediate cause of the uprising, although, as in all the other riots, relations between the police and the black community had long been antagonistic. On this day, Odessa had stopped her car in the middle of a busy intersection to continue arguing with Rush. When approached by two police officers and instructed to move the vehicle out of the intersection, she refused. A growing crowd of observers watched as the officers attempted to pull Odessa from the car and arrest her. Bystanders who felt the officers were using excessive force against a woman intervened, and the crowd began to pelt the two officers with bottles and other projectiles. At some point, a rumor spread through North Philadelphia that a pregnant black woman had been beaten to death by white police officers.

That evening and over the next two days, rioters burned and looted mostly white-owned businesses in the area. Because the police were heavily outnumbered, Mayor Howard Tate and Police Commissioner Howard Leary initially ordered the police to withdraw, to refrain from firing on the mob, and to not interfere with looters. After receiving information that armed rioters were positioned on rooftops, Commissioner Leary rescinded this order and allowed police to engage rioters and employ firearms when necessary. The authorities then imposed a citywide curfew, prohibited liquor sales, and initiated heavy police patrols in the rioting areas. To help with these efforts, community leaders also escorted Odessa Bradford throughout the neighborhood to show that she was alive and unharmed. By the time the rioting finally ended, two were dead, 350 were wounded, over 1,000 were arrested, and the damage to 225 stores was estimated at $4 million.[22]

On a national macrolevel, the riots of the summer of 1964 underscored the deeply rooted racial divisions and social problems of the era: poverty, unemployment, job and housing discrimination, and police brutality. But on the microlevel of the average white law-abiding citizen, the riots also underscored the threats and dangers of living in a culturally complex, multiracial society. The riots prompted countless individuals to consider (or reconsider) means and methods for safeguarding their own lives and property. For the rugged individualists of Bedrock America, the riots confirmed what they already knew: personal protection is ultimately a personal responsibility, because in times of urgent need, police protection is often problematic—as Philadelphia chillingly demonstrated. For these Americans, the riots simply validated the need for personal ownership of firearms.

Oddly enough, considering that the riots all occurred in urban centers—the heart of Cosmopolitan America—the beliefs of gun control proponents were not unduly shaken by the violence and chaos of the disturbances. To the contrary, they remained steadfast in their position that guns were the problem, not the solution. Cosmopolitan America continued to call for additional restrictions on firearms, and in March 1965, at the behest of the Johnson administration (which was at that point gearing up for what would become known as the "War on Crime"), Senator Dodd introduced S. 1592, "A Bill to Amend the Federal Firearms Act of 1938." This legislation was a revised and expanded version of his bill that had previously died in committee.[23] In his efforts to get the bill passed, Dodd made it a point to assure hunters and shooting enthusiasts that the provisions of S. 1592 would only impact crime and criminals and that legitimate gun owners and sportsmen would suffer just "minimal inconvenience."

As is typical with most congressional legislation, potential difficulties reside in the details, and such was the case with S. 1592. In examining the bill, gun advocates recognized the license fee increase on firearms dealers, and most of the firearms prohibitions (on mail-order sales, underage sales, and out-of-state sales; on military surplus imports; on mortars and other "destructive devices") from Dodd's prior bills. However, S. 1592 also contained some new provisions that appeared to give the secretary of the treasury substantial leeway to create additional "necessary" rules, regulations, fees, and forms regulating the sale and shipment of firearms. In all, seven sections of the bill shifted regulatory power from Congress to the treasury secretary, and the type and nature of these "necessary" future regulations were obviously unknowable—casting doubt on Dodd's reassurance that the bill would not inconvenience legitimate gun users.[24]

Although the NRA had worked with Dodd and provided support for Dodd's earlier bill, the organization did not endorse S. 1592. Dodd felt betrayed, and he accused the NRA of merely giving lip service to his proposals at the same time that it attacked them in the pages of the *American Rifleman*, its membership magazine.[25] In defending the bill's crime-fighting orientation, Dodd rhetorically asked—as gun control opponents often did—whether it was even reasonable to expect gun regulation to have any impact on murder and crime, as criminals "who want guns manage to get them, whatever the law says." In answer to this common objection, Dodd argued that "the facts are on the side of those who believe that we can solve this problem." He presented murder and robbery statistics purporting to show that cities with lax gun laws had homicide rates by firearms that were substantially higher than cities with more stringent gun laws.[26]

Of course, his analysis did not go unchallenged. Gun advocates were quick to point out that Dodd's figures did not reference the *overall* murder rate but the murder rate *by firearms*. They argued that an examination of the overall murder rate painted a different picture and revealed that overall homicide rates were not necessarily lower in those cities with strict gun regulations. Further, they asserted that robbery rates in cities with strict gun control—where the criminal knows that the shopkeeper is likely to be unarmed—were often much greater than in areas with little regulation.[27]

Kennett and Anderson have described such exchanges as "a tedious and repetitive dialogue of the deaf,"[28] with pro- and anti-gun proponents no longer even listening to the other's arguments. In this case, that characterization is probably too harsh. As noted in an earlier chapter, because of the complex nature and inherent limitations associated with crime statistics, it is impossible to establish unquestioned equivalency between "before-and-after" evaluations or "region A to region B" comparisons. Consequently, partisans can always legitimately dispute empirical attempts claiming to "prove" the effectiveness or ineffectiveness of gun restrictions, and they can continue to believe whatever they wish to believe. In any case, despite Dodd's statistical arguments and the persistent clamoring of the national media for action on firearms regulation, S. 1592, like its predecessor, eventually stalled in committee.

The Assassination of Malcolm X

Even as hearings on S. 1592 progressed, the racial tensions and violence that confronted the nation in 1964 continued to rend the country and capture headlines in 1965. Early in the year, the assassination of Malcolm Little—better known as Malcolm X—seized the attention of the nation and again propelled gun-perpetrated violence and race relations onto the national stage. A charismatic but controversial figure, Malcolm X was, for much of his adult life, a notable leader in the Nation of Islam, a black separatist movement that taught that white people were devils, that blacks were superior to whites, that the races should remain apart, and that black people should have their own separate country in America. He rejected Martin Luther King's nonviolent approach to civil rights, arguing that blacks must defend themselves "by any means necessary."[29] Commenting on the Kennedy assassination, he shocked the nation by suggesting that it was simply a case of the "chickens coming home to roost;" and that did not sadden him at all.[30] Not surprisingly, mainstream America saw the Nation of Islam—and Malcolm X—as a group of hate-mongering, racist, violence-seeking extremists, but many of his black followers felt he captured their concerns and frustrations better than Martin Luther King Jr.[31]

In March 1964, less than a year before his assassination, Malcolm X broke with the Nation of Islam, having become disillusioned with its policies and approach to Islam and with the personal failings of its leader and his former mentor, Elijah Muhammed. As the rupture between these past friends grew—Malcolm X having founded a competing organization and Elijah Muhammad perhaps feeling challenged and overshadowed by the popularity of his erstwhile disciple—members of the Nation of Islam took to threatening their earlier colleague. Muhammad, for example, speaking to Louis Farrakhan (then known as Louis X), suggested that "hypocrites like Malcolm should have their heads cut off,"[32] and FBI surveillance tapes captured a call to Malcolm's wife in which the caller warned that "he was a good as dead."[33] A photograph in *Ebony Magazine* depicted Malcolm's response to these threats: it shows him glancing out a curtained window with a rifle in hand, prepared to fight.[34]

In February 1965, in spite of his bravado, Malcolm X was gunned down as he prepared to speak to a large gathering in a Manhattan auditorium. A disturbance occurred in the crowd, and in the confusion, a Nation of Islam assailant with a sawed-off shotgun blasted him in the chest, backed up by other Nation of Islam members firing handguns.[35] Elijah Muhammad, while denying any connection to the assassination, noted that "Malcolm X got just what he preached. . . . We knew such ignorant, foolish teachings would bring him to his own end."[36]

For both pro- and anti-gun advocates, the life and death of Malcolm X posed significant strategic challenges. For Cosmopolitan America, a firearms-driven assassination of a prominent public figure—tragic though it may be—provided a superlative opportunity to underscore once again the tragic consequences associated with the unfettered availability of guns in American society and to reiterate the absolute need for better and more stringent gun regulation. Further, the weapons used in the assassination—a sawed-off shotgun and semiautomatic pistols—were precisely the type of firearms that past gun control efforts focused on, thus vindicating these past efforts. Nonetheless, perhaps because Malcolm X was an unsympathetic figure to much of the country, Cosmopolitan America's reaction to this assassination was uncharacteristically muted.

For Bedrock America, Malcolm X's personal philosophy and his beliefs regarding the place of firearms in American society—minus the racial animus—certainly would have firmly ensconced him as a Bedrock American. In one of his notable speeches, he argued that "the Constitution of the United States of America clearly affirms the right of every American citizen to bear arms. And as Americans, we will not give up a single right under the Constitution."[37] In another, commenting on the controversy over rifles and shotguns, he noted that "Article number two of the constitutional amendments provides you and me the right to own a rifle or a shotgun. It is constitutionally legal to own a shotgun or a rifle."[38] But because of his initial extremism and endorsements of violence—he apparently reconsidered some of his more radical positions when he broke with the Nation of Islam—Bedrock America, unsurprisingly, never claimed him as one of their own. In many minds, he perhaps illustrated precisely why "good people" needed guns. Nevertheless, Malcolm X's beliefs about race, firearms, and society would still significantly impact America's gun culture. This was especially evident later in the decade, when the Black Panthers, a black militant organization, adopted his perspective on guns as their own.

Resurgence of Crime and Violence

As the 1960s began, the historically low crime rates of the previous decade started to rise, and they would continue to climb over the next 20 years.[39] In particular, organized criminal activity—focused on gambling, prostitution, extortion, bribery, and drugs—erupted in many of America's big cities. The typical newspaper reader of this era acquired an uncomfortable familiarity with the names of America's most notorious mobsters and the crime families to which they belonged. Figures such as Joseph Bonanno, Joe Colombo, Carlo Gambino, Joey Gallo, and Tommy Lucchese dominated the New York crime scene, with Philadelphia, Chicago, New Orleans, and other regions each having their own set of feared and prominent gangsters. By this time, crime bosses had learned the lessons of the St. Valentine's Day Massacre and clearly realized that public violence and its attendant publicity created enormous operational problems. While they tried to control such disasters, personal rivalries and territorial disputes periodically sparked internecine warfare as families (and ambitious but frustrated underbosses) jockeyed for greater power. The mobster Al Capone, from an earlier crime era, reputedly claimed, "You can go a lot further with a smile and a gun than you can with just a smile," and that maxim often appeared to guide interactions among the families and the rival gangs under their control. Further, this internal violence was in addition to the vicious and sometimes deadly crimes perpetrated against the victims ensnared in the families' criminal enterprises.

Frightened by these illegal developments and their societal reach, many individuals wanted reassurance that the violence and crime they read about in their daily paper would not touch them or their families. For some, that reassurance would come in the form of a firearm. Over the course of the decade, the number of guns in America increased by 37 percent, from about 78 million in 1960 to about 107 million in 1969.[40]

For others, reassurance came from the federal government in the form of President Lyndon Johnson's "War on Crime." Aside from crime itself, a major impetus for this initiative was the presidential campaign of the previous year. In that campaign, both Senator Barry Goldwater of Arizona (the Republican nominee) and Governor George Wallace of Alabama (running as an Independent) treated "crime in the streets" as an issue of national concern and made a return to "law and order" a major theme in their speeches. They promised to rid the nation of the crime problem by rigorous policing and strict enforcement of criminal statutes while simultaneously painting Johnson as "soft on crime."[41]

Johnson prevailed in the election, however, and although his own preference was to concentrate on what he considered the root cause of crime—poverty—he also directly responded to the nation's anxieties over rampant lawlessness by establishing the President's Commission on Law Enforcement and Administration of Justice in July 1965. The creation of this commission signaled to all Americans—but particularly to Cosmopolitan America—that the national government recognized crime and violence as a national problem that urgently needed resolution and that they could count on the government to resolve it. The findings of the commission would in fact guide efforts to control crime in the coming years,[42] but success in actually quelling crime would remain elusive.[43]

Less than a month after President Johnson signed the executive order establishing the commission, the city of Los Angeles exploded in the worst civil disturbance and race riot in its history (up to that point). Ignited by the arrest of Marquette Frye, a 21-year-old black resident, for drunk and reckless driving, the Watts riots roiled the city over a period of six days. According to some estimates, the riot involved more than 30,000 active participants and more than twice that number of inactive but sympathetic supporters.[44] Quelling the riot required over 900 Los Angeles police officers, over 700 Los Angeles County sheriff's officers, and about 2,300 California National Guardsmen.[45] At the height of the riot, one estimate suggested that some 16,000 law enforcement personnel patrolled the city, setting up blockades and threatening the use of deadly force.[46] Rioters ripped up concrete and bricks to launch at police and guardsmen, assaulted white motorists, blocked fire department vehicles, and looted white-owned businesses. Governor Pat Brown asserted that the authorities were encountering "guerillas fighting with gangsters,"[47] and the Los Angeles police chief, William Parker, saw the riot as an "insurgency" that had changed a 46-square-mile area of Los Angeles into an all-out war zone. He responded by initiating a paramilitary response that included curfews and mass arrests.

By the time order was restored, about 3,400 rioters were in custody, more than 1,000 individuals had been injured, and 34 people were dead. The rioters had destroyed 268 buildings, damaged or burned another 272, and looted 192 more, and they had damaged, burned, *and* looted another 288. Altogether, the riot caused about $40 million in damages[48]— about $400 million in 2017 dollars. Although the authorities initially attributed the underlying cause of the riot to criminal elements in the community, other observers suggested that deeply rooted racial tensions and long-standing resentment of discriminatory police treatment were more likely explanations. Regardless of its underlying causes, the collapse of social order in Watts concerned all law-abiding Americans, but given their antithetical orientations, Bedrock America and Cosmopolitan America drew vastly different lessons from the collapse and about the role of firearms policies in alleviating those concerns.

Throughout this period, committee hearings on Dodd's gun control bill, S. 1592, had continued with little noticeable progress as both sides recycled variations of arguments heard earlier in 1911 and again in 1934. Then, in August 1966, a University of Texas student named Charles Whitman ascended to the 28th floor of the UT tower carrying a deer rifle. For an hour and a half, he proceeded to snipe at random students, workers, and visitors crossing the campus below. Whitman killed a total of 17 people and wounded 31 others before finally being shot and killed by two Austin police officers.[49] On the following day, President Johnson called for stricter gun laws and gun registration, a call that was echoed in the nation's major news media. In response, several gun-oriented magazines opposed this emotional appeal, as did conservative journalist and commentator William Buckley Jr. Buckley argued in the *National Review* that neither Dodd's proposed legislation nor any other reasonable bill would have prevented Whitman from acquiring a firearm. Although the country's horror at the Whitman shooting and the president's plea for increased gun regulation appeared to give S. 1592 a boost, the bill nevertheless remained in committee, and it died again in 1966.[50]

The Black Panthers

If the nation's political elite thought that climbing crime rates, race riots, and mass shootings showed that too many people had access to guns and that violence in America was too great,[51] these worries gained further urgency in May 1967, when Bobby Seale and 29 other Black Panthers—a militant black organization founded by Seale and Huey Newton six months earlier in Oakland—took to the steps of the

California State Capitol building, armed with powerful revolvers, 12-gauge shotguns, and .45-caliber pistols.[52] Adopting the radical principles of the assassinated Malcolm X, Seale announced to America in general, and California in particular, that racist legislatures would no longer keep black people disarmed and powerless; the time had come for blacks to arm themselves. When he finished reading his statement, he led his group—loaded weapons and all—right into the California statehouse. One commentator, Adam Winkler, a professor of law at UCLA, has suggested that Seale launched the modern gun rights movement that day.[53]

Guns had always formed a core element in Panther identity, and the Black Panther Party had accumulated an arsenal of machine guns, rifles, handguns, explosives, and even grenade launchers. Further, Panther instructors—often black Vietnam veterans—had ensured that recruits acquired basic competency in gun-handling and shooting skills.[54] Because California law at that time permitted "open carry" (carrying or wearing firearms in public, provided the firearm is both visible and not pointed at anyone), Panthers had taken to parading their guns in public. Further, as California law also allowed civilians to observe police officers making an arrest, armed Panthers had for some time been following police cars, and whenever the officers stopped and questioned a black person, the Panthers stood off to the side and offered legal guidance to the individual.[55] Although the Panthers may have believed their actions merely enacted the core purpose of the Second Amendment—armed citizens checking governmental tyranny—these behaviors incensed both the police and much of the public.

Seale's dramatic statehouse demonstration was a defiant reaction to proposed gun control legislation specifically aimed at curtailing the armed Panther patrols. State assemblyman Donald Mulford had proposed a bill forbidding individuals from openly carrying loaded firearms in any California municipality, and the statehouse theatrics were Seale's way of objecting to Mulford's gun control efforts. Instead of their intended discouraging effect, the Panthers' actions triggered a legislative backlash. The bill was quickly passed in the aftermath of the Panthers' defiant statehouse visit, with an additional clause that specifically prohibited bringing loaded weapons into the State Capitol building. Governor Ronald Reagan, who later as president was a staunch gun-rights supporter but at this time was still a gun control proponent, strongly endorsed the Mulford Act, claiming that law-abiding citizens walking American streets did not need to carry around loaded weapons and that the act would have little impact on the honest citizen.[56] He signed Mulford's bill into law in July, and a citizen in California could no longer legally carry loaded guns in public.

Urban Upheavals II

About two months later, during the "long hot summer of 1967,"[57] major race riots in Detroit, Michigan, and Newark, New Jersey, pushed the maneuverings of the Black Panthers to the back of the nation's consciousness. Once again, headlines and newscasts mesmerized the country with scenes of police, National Guardsmen, and U.S. Army Regulars—sometimes with tanks and machine guns—battling rioters, snipers, looters, and arsonists. The Detroit disturbance, covering a period of five days, started with a police raid on an unlicensed after-hours drinking club. After arresting an unexpectedly large group of partygoers, the police faced a sizable mob of angry, harassing observers who began looting adjacent stores and businesses when the police departed. Crowds formed throughout the area, and as the chaos grew, a major fire enveloped a grocery store, which was soon followed by others. Rioters shot at firefighters to prevent them from extinguishing the flames, and sometimes succeeded. Looting, fighting, and wanton destruction ensued. Over the course of the riot, the initially undermanned Detroit police force received reinforcements from county and state police as well as from Michigan National Guardsmen, but the rampage was not contained until President Johnson, acting under the Insurrection Act of 1807, sent in veteran troops from the U.S. Army's 82nd and 101st Airborne Divisions.[58]

The riot was one of the most violent in American history. An estimated 10,000 people actively engaged in the rioting, with many others adopting a more passive stance. The disturbance resulted in over $40 million in damage (about $400 million in 2017 dollars), destroyed more than 2,500 buildings, resulted in over 7,200 arrests (including 26 for sniping), injured almost 1,200 people, and left 43 dead. During the riot, looters stole an estimated 2,500 rifles and about three dozen handguns from local businesses.[59] Public opinion surveys conducted after the riot indicated that the area's black radicals thought it was justifiable to break into gun shops to seize weapons and that it was not immoral to kill whites.[60]

Two Newark police officers sparked the Newark riot when they arrested a black taxi driver, John Smith, for a traffic infraction and then proceeded to punch and beat him for resisting and making disparaging comments. A rumor that he had been battered to death while in police custody sped through the neighborhood, and when a large crowd gathered outside the precinct house, the police confronted the group. Several officers sustained injuries from hurled stones and bottles. That night, agitators set off false fire alarms, looters smashed store windows to pilfer merchandise, and other rioters targeted liquor stores to steal alcohol. Looting continued the next day, with Molotov cocktails setting entire buildings on fire. As the riot grew and spread, authorities brought in the state police and called out the National Guard. By the time the police and guardsmen had regained control several days later, the riot had left 26 people dead, over 350 injured, and about 1,500 arrested. Damage estimates exceeded $10 million.[61]

After the Newark and Detroit riots, the country experienced an explosion of racial disturbances across the nation, with riots erupting in several other cities in Michigan as well as in Ohio, Maryland, Texas, and Arizona.[62] For Bedrock and Cosmopolitan America, the riots and the earlier antics of the Panthers acted like a national Rorschach test, with both sides projecting their own value orientations onto the events. Cosmopolitan America, noting the abundance of firearms on display during the disturbances and pointing out how rioting snipers easily used them to stymie the efforts of police and firefighters, continued to see gun control as an essential element in resolving urban violence. Such beliefs received confirmation from the conclusions of a federal analysis of the riots in 1968. That report endorsed effective gun regulations as a fundamental requirement for "domestic peace and tranquility."[63]

Citizens of Bedrock America drew different lessons from the riots. For Bedrock America, noting the inability of the authorities to speedily contain and control these disturbances or to protect hapless civilians inadvertently caught in the turmoil, the urban riots confirmed the necessity of accepting personal responsibility for one's own safety, and for having available the means to ensure that safety. They pointed to the experiences of people like Joe Von Battle, the owner of an influential record shop and recording studio, as stark object lessons. Founded in 1945, and located in the heart of Detroit's rioting area, the record and recording shop owned by Von Battle sported a "Soul Brother" sign in its window and an armed Von Battle standing outside, on guard with gun in hand. Rioters bypassed his business. But after the first day of rioting, the authorities prohibited Von Battle and other business owners from guarding their shops. When he returned to his store days later, he discovered that the police had been unable to protect his place, and the shop had been transformed into a mass of "wet, fetid debris." Von Battle never reopened the store.[64]

MLK and RFK Assassinations

Although S. 1592 had died in committee in 1966, Senator Dodd—not one to give up easily—introduced an identical bill, S. 1, in 1967. Despite the riots and President Johnson's advocacy, this bill made little progress, and it suffered the same fate as his earlier bills, never reaching the congressional floor.[65] For Senator Dodd and other gun control proponents, national gun control legislation was fairing no better in the new year when, in April, James Earl Ray (a convicted criminal searching for notoriety) assassinated Martin Luther King Jr. as he stood on a motel balcony in Memphis, Tennessee. Unlike the Kennedy assassination of 1963, in which the murder weapon was a foreign-made mail-order rifle, Ray used an American-made Remington Model 760 purchased in Alabama to extinguish the life of the noted civil rights leader and Nobel Peace Prize recipient.

In addition to igniting another round of violent race riots across the nation,[66] the King assassination renewed strident cries for gun control in the media and refocused the public's attention on congressional efforts in this arena. On the same day as the assassination, the Senate Judiciary Committee approved President Johnson's Omnibus Crime Control and Safe Streets Act, a series of extensive laws his administration had proposed in response to the era's rampant crime and violence. Two months later, the full Senate was still debating the details of the bill and voting on proposed amendments and counter-amendments, when Sirhan Sirhan, a young Palestinian immigrant upset with Senator Robert F. Kennedy's support of Israel, shot and killed Kennedy with an Iver-Johnson .22-caliber pistol at the Ambassador Hotel in Los Angeles.

Coming so closely on the heels of the King assassination, the Kennedy assassination opened floodgates of anti-gun sentiment around the country. The murder set in motion "a series of reactions and occurrences which were without parallel,"[67] starting with the passage of the Omnibus Crime Control and Safe Streets Act by an overwhelming House vote after previous approval by the Senate. With the bill's passage, President Johnson himself addressed the nation, noting that the act was just a start; the country still needed a comprehensive gun control law: "Surely this must be clear beyond question. The hour has come for the Congress to enact a strong and effective gun-control law, governing the full range of lethal weapons."[68] His characterization of the Omnibus Crime Control and Safe Streets Act as a comparatively weak firearms regulation was probably accurate, in that the section of the bill dealing with firearms merely banned interstate trade in handguns and raised the minimum age for purchasing pistols and revolvers to 21. But his clarion call for comprehensive gun control did not go unheeded.

A huge anti-gun campaign exploded in the media. *Advertising Age*, the flagship publication of the advertising industry, ran an editorial headlined "Guns Must Go." The *New York Times*, the *Washington Post*, and the *Los*

Angeles Times all ran a full-page letter urging readers to contact their congressional and state legislators and to plead with them to support strong gun regulation. The letter carried the signatures of numerous prominent members of the entertainment industry as well as church and business leaders and important medical, legal, and government figures.[69] *Time* and *Newsweek* ran major feature articles in support of gun control. The *Time* article[70] disputed the claim that Americans had a constitutional right to bear arms, attacked the use of firearms for home defense, and dismissed NRA concerns that gun registration was the first step on the path to gun confiscation. The *Newsweek* article[71] echoed the same refrains, arguing that the Second Amendment was not an individual right. It also asserted that, in any case, outright gun confiscation was not an objective of gun control legislation or gun control proponents. The *New Republic* also weighed in on gun control, with recommendations that went far beyond those of *Time* and *Newsweek*, and even disputed *Newsweek*'s assertion regarding confiscation:

> Put simply, private citizens should be disarmed. A modest effort in this direction would include the following first steps: No person should be permitted to buy or possess a hand gun or ammunition for any hand gun. Possession of all automatic and semi-automatic firearms should be banned. So should all rifles. However, licenses for the purchase of shotguns for sporting purposes could be obtained from the local police chief.[72]

Nor was the *New Republic*'s position an isolated stance. The *Detroit Daily Press* editorialized, "No private citizen has any reason or need at any time to possess a gun."[73]

Cosmopolitan America did not limit its assault on guns to just a media campaign. Holding the NRA at least partly responsible for the assassinations, individuals picketed the NRA headquarters building in Washington, D.C., carrying signs saying, "Lobby for Murder," "Blood Is the Color of the NRA," "Ban Weapons," and "Stop Violence, Stop the NRA." Callers twice phoned the headquarters claiming that they had placed a bomb in the building, and others suggested to the telephone operators that everyone in the NRA should be shot and killed. Additionally, police authorities took an anti-gun stance. In Chicago, the police superintendent urged private citizens to turn in their personal firearms to avoid the "bloodshed and tragedy that can result from misuse or accident." Even the American Civil Liberties Union questioned the civil liberty of owning or possessing a gun, arguing that "the freedom to bear arms must be sacrificed to the more important freedom of 'free and fearless debate.'"[74]

In responding to this almost universal attack on firearms—the American Bar Association, the International Association of Chiefs of Police, the American Civil Liberties Union, most of the nation's newspapers, the majority of the periodical press, and 75 percent of citizens polled were all anti-gun[75]—Bedrock America ironically benefited legislatively from the plethora of gun control voices demanding attention. Responding to their constituents' demands, legislators put forth such a wide array of proposals and measures that their very numbers tended to dissipate focused effort.[76] Eventually, however, post-assassination gun control battles swirled around three main issues: gun registration, mail-order sales, and certain foreign imports.[77] The City of Chicago enacted gun registration in 1968, as did New York City, adding rifle and shotgun registration to the handgun registration requirements of the Sullivan Act. In New Jersey, a legislator put forth a bill proposing the confiscation of all privately owned handguns and requiring the registration of all long guns, but it was defeated. Nationally, a trio of Democratic senators, Joseph Tydings of Maryland, Henry Jackson of Washington, and Edward Brooke of Massachusetts, all sponsored bills that involved some type of gun registration, but fierce opposition from Western and Southern states—Bedrock America strongholds—ensured the defeat of all three bills.[78] But on the other two issues, Bedrock America could not deflect the country's anti-gun sentiments.

In October, President Johnson signed into law the Gun Control Act of 1968 (GCA), the first major federal legislation regulating firearms since the 1930s. This new act repealed the earlier Federal Firearms Act (but comprehensively revised and included many of the FFA's provisions) and incorporated the National Firearms Act of 1934 as Title II of the new act. In addition to defining categories of individuals prohibited from owning or possessing firearms and establishing federal licensing requirements for those engaged in the business of selling firearms, the act banned the direct mail-order sales of all firearms and prohibited the importation of surplus military firearms and specified foreign handguns. Although pro-gun advocates in Congress had heatedly fought the act during debate, they ultimately supported its passage to avoid possibly more stringent regulation.[79] Bedrock America may have staved off gun registration, but Cosmopolitan America had succeeded in barring both direct mail-order sales and certain foreign imports.

CHAPTER SIX

The Rift Widens: 1970–1990

Although the unofficial representative of Bedrock America, the NRA, decried the Gun Control Act (GCA) of 1968 as "the most sweeping Federal legislation ever imposed on U.S. firearms owners,"[1] the more cynical supporters of Cosmopolitan America looked upon the act in frustration. In their view, a mountain had labored to deliver a mouse, with the act's title its most significant accomplishment. In any case, both proponents and opponents of the act recognized that the conflict over gun rights versus gun regulation was far from settled as they entered the new decade. Bedrock America began by chipping away at the GCA. An early controversial provision of the act required dealers to maintain records of all ammunition sales, a measure that not only inconvenienced shooters but was in effect a backdoor form of registration. Pro-gun advocates argued that the requirement was worthless as a crime prevention technique, and despite opposition from Senators Dodd, Kennedy, and Brooke, they succeeded in getting the provision repealed.[2]

The zeitgeist provided Cosmopolitan America with multiple opportunities to respond. The conclusions of President Johnson's National Commission on the Causes and Prevention of Violence set the stage. Published in December 1969, the commission's final report was virulently anti-gun. The report argued that individuals had no constitutional right to bear arms, that guns were not especially useful for self-defense, and that stringent gun regulation could reduce gun violence. It went on to recommend a handgun licensing scheme that required an individual to provide "good reason"—a special need—for pistol ownership and the confiscation of all handguns currently possessed if the owners could not show such special need. Additionally, it recommended the registration and licensing of rifles and other long guns.[3] Although the newly elected Nixon administration chose to ignore the commission's proposals, the recommendations nonetheless reassured Cosmopolitan America that gun control remained a significant political issue and that their efforts to rein in gun proliferation were finally gathering meaningful momentum.

Additionally, as in other eras, the 1970s had its complement of angry and deranged individuals, some of whom outraged the nation by targeting prominent members of society for assassination. Such attempts gave anti-gun politicians the impetus for introducing new firearms legislation that was especially focused on the registration and regulation of handguns. Other developments also impacted the shooting world. The Bureau of Alcohol, Tobacco, and Taxes was transformed into a firearms regulatory agency, and hard-line gun activists transformed (or at least finished the evolution of) the National Rifle Association (NRA) into the country's most politically powerful pro-gun advocacy organization.

Taking Aim at Handguns

Although Cosmopolitan America considered the Gun Control Act a step in the right direction, it was merely a step. The act failed to address many aspects of firearms regulation that gun control advocates believed were critically important. Topping the list of their concerns was the continuing proliferation of handguns. Thus, early in the decade, sympathetic senators and congressmen introduced a number of bills specifically focused on this issue. Emmanuel Celler, a representative from New York whose earlier bill, H.R. 17735, had helped shaped the Gun Control Act, sponsored new legislation outlawing all handguns and requiring the registration of all rifles and shotguns. Similarly, Senator Philip Hart of Michigan, echoing the recommendations of the National Commission on the Causes and Prevention of Violence, sponsored legislation banning handgun ownership by anyone other than police officers and security guards, with the government reimbursing gun owners at fair market value for their confiscated handguns. Senator Ted Kennedy of Massachusetts introduced a less extreme measure that nonetheless mandated the registration of all firearms, while Senator Adlai Stevenson III of Illinois proposed a bill requiring both the licensing and registration of all handguns. Congressman Abner Mikva, also from Illinois, went further and introduced legislation simply prohibiting handgun ownership. All these measures encountered fierce opposition from pro-gun rights organizations and garnered little support from the Nixon administration. None became law.[4]

Taking a different tack, Senator Birch Bayh of Indiana crafted a more focused bill directly centered on "Saturday Night Specials"—a term coined by law enforcement officers to describe the small, cheaply made, inaccurate, and often unreliable revolvers favored by street thugs and other individuals who could not afford a higher quality but more expensive firearm. As serious gun owners typically had no use for such firearms—their unreliability making them a poor choice for self-defense and their lack of accuracy unsuitable for target shooting—the thinking was that Bedrock America would at least accept legislation banning these firearms. Further, the bill was still wending its way through the legislative process when Arthur Bremer used a short-barreled .38-caliber Charter Arms revolver to shoot Governor George Wallace of Alabama, a candidate in the 1968 presidential campaign. Eager for fame, Bremer had first set his sights on Nixon before switching his attention to Wallace, an easier target. Although the Charter Arms firearm was not actually a Saturday Night Special—it cost two or three times the going rate for the typical SNS—the horror of the assassination attempt (Wallace was left permanently paralyzed) and the ensuing outcry against gun violence boosted the bill's chances of passage.

Yet despite the anti-gun emotions sparked by the shooting and the bill's narrower focus, this measure also stalled in Congress and never became law. In part, this came about because the bill defined a "Saturday Night Special" quite broadly, and its definition would have actually outlawed a much larger segment of the handgun market than its title implied—about 30 percent of all handguns manufactured in the country. The bill would have made two of the most popular pistols in America illegal, the .22-caliber Colt Woodsman and the .22-caliber Ruger Standard. These were quality firearms used by serious gun owners, not Saturday Night Specials, and Bedrock America and the NRA strongly opposed any measure banning them.[5]

Further, the nation's print and broadcast media and well-known gun control advocates had used the Wallace shooting to call for additional stringent gun regulation. The *New York Times* argued that clamping down on snub-nosed revolvers "must become the jumping off point for a much broader and conclusive effort,"[6] and Richard Daley, the mayor of Chicago, expressed the hope that "this would be the opportunity to do some soul-searching by the Congress to outlaw handguns."[7] Further, *ABC Nightly News*, on the evening of the attack, featured an editorial by Howard K. Smith claiming that new gun laws would merely register guns, not take them away[8]—although several of the bills in Congress actually proposed to do just that. Such anti-gun rhetoric and confusion alarmed Bedrock America and contributed to its opposition to Bayh's bill. In addition, some opposition likely reflected a simple pragmatic recognition: banning snub-nosed revolvers has little efficacy if a common hacksaw can turn a revolver's eight-inch barrel into a two-inch barrel.[9]

While Bedrock America may have prevailed in stymieing handgun regulation on the federal level, Cosmopolitan America continued to make headway on the state and local levels. Following up on victories obtained in the latter half of the 1960s, when gun control advocates successfully campaigned for favorable new state legislation in Connecticut, Illinois, New Jersey, and New York, as well as new stringent municipal ordinances in Chicago, Philadelphia, and New York City,[10] Cosmopolitan America succeeded in shepherding a Firearms Identification Act through the Massachusetts state legislature in 1974 (the State of Illinois had passed similar legislation in 1968). The act required residents wishing to purchase or possess a firearm (or even ammunition) to first obtain a Firearm Owners Identification (FOID) card—essentially a firearms license—from the local police department. The act imposed mandatory prison sentences for possession of any type of gun without a FOID.[11] Thus, despite setbacks on the national stage, Cosmopolitan America's battle for gun regulation, far from being over, simply continued in different arenas.

Enter Federal Agencies and Other Organizations

Less than a year after the Wallace shooting, Senator John Stennis of Mississippi encountered two teenaged muggers, Tyrone Marshall and his brother John, outside his residence in Washington, D.C. The muggers threatened to shoot Stennis if he did not hand over his valuables. Stennis gave them his wallet, credit cards, a gold pocket watch, and his Phi Beta Kappa key. After taking his valuables, one of the brothers simply said, "Now we're going to shoot you anyway," and did so. The bullet pierced Stennis's stomach and pancreas and nicked a major vein in his left thigh, but Senator Stennis survived the attack.[12]

As with the Wallace shooting, the Stennis assault touched off a flurry of articles and press reports demanding that Congress act on some form of gun control. Several lawmakers offered proposals, and Senator Kennedy sponsored a bill that outlawed all pistols with barrels under 10 inches—virtually a ban on almost all handguns as very few models have barrels that long. None of the proposed legislation made it into law, at least in part because both Wallace and Stennis, despite having been shot, continued to oppose gun control.[13]

Between the two shootings, a less dramatic but a substantively more significant event occurred, one that would seriously impact the country's gun culture in coming years: the creation of the Bureau of Alcohol, Tobacco and Firearms. Tracing its heritage back to the Alcohol Tax Unit (ATU) of the 1930s, the unit morphed into the Alcohol and Tobacco Tax Division (ATTD) in the 1950s and then into the Alcohol, Tobacco, and Firearms Division (ATFD) when the agency became responsible for enforcing the Gun Control Act of 1968. In 1972, ATFD officially became an independent bureau (BATF) within the Department of the Treasury.[14] Given its enforcement role, BATF would become the bane of many federally licensed gun sellers, who would bitterly complain that its regulatory approach too often accentuated technical paperwork violations and that it was harshly punitive over trivial or honest record-keeping mistakes. Congressional committees eventually investigated these complaints and found that a large percentage of BATF gun prosecutions were, in fact, brought against ordinary citizens having no criminal intent rather than against individuals adding to the proliferation of illegal street guns.[15]

However, the adversarial relationship between Bedrock America and BATF actually preceded the creation of BATF. At least a year before the agency's founding, agents of the ATFD engaged in a joint operation with two Maryland police departments and conducted a disastrous raid on the residence of Kenyon Ballew, a former U.S. Air Force security policeman who had become a Boy Scout troop leader and printing pressman employed at a local newspaper. Acting on a teenaged housebreaker's tip that Ballew had live hand grenades in his apartment, the ATFD agents and county police battered down Ballew's back door after failing to get a response to their knock. Alerted by the screams of his girlfriend (later his wife) in the bedroom, a nude Ballew rushed from the bathroom to confront the intruders. Holding a working replica of an early Colt cap-and-ball revolver—Ballew was a gun collector and an NRA member—Ballew encountered armed men streaming into his apartment. Although the agents and police wore identifying armbands, they were all nonetheless in plainclothes. Seeing the naked Ballew holding a revolver, several of them fired their own weapons, and a bullet struck Ballew in the head. A search of the apartment uncovered no live grenades, but it did turn up unloaded inert grenades, which were often sold at army navy stores and gun shops as curios. ATF regulations classified such dummy grenades as nonweapon curiosities, without any need for federal registry, and possession did not violate the Gun Control Act.[16]

The raid left Ballew permanently paralyzed, and his case became a cause célèbre within the gun-owning fraternity. The NRA made sure that the incident received widespread publicity and devoted a six-page feature article to the case in the *American Rifleman*.[17] The organization also often brought the crippled and wheel-chair bound Ballew to NRA gun shows and other events, placing him on stage—head hanging and face slack—with a sign proclaiming, "Victim of the Gun Control Act."[18] The Ballew raid began Bedrock America's sharply critical and highly adversarial relationship with the bureau. Neal Knox, an NRA board member, later suggested that the shooting was "the first of a long chain of Gestapo-like raids, sieges, and questionable arrests"[19] by BATF. Virulent animosity still characterized Bedrock America's relationship with the agency a quarter of a century later, with the NRA's executive vice president, Wayne LaPierre, in a 1995 fund-raising letter, describing BATF agents as "jack-booted government thugs"[20] in the wake of fatal confrontations at Ruby Ridge, Idaho, and Waco, Texas.

The same year the Treasury Department established BATF, Cosmopolitan America acquired a second would-be ally in another governmental agency: the U.S. Consumer Protection Safety Commission (CPSC). Created by the Consumer Product Safety Act to regulate the manufacture and sale of myriad consumer products, its authority did not extend to firearms and ammunition—these items were under the purview of BATF. Even so, the CPSC's first chairman, working with congressmen from Illinois and Michigan in 1975, proposed an amendment that would have extended the CPSC's regulatory authority to include guns and ammunition, and he indicated that the CPSC would ban handgun bullets as a "hazardous substance."[21] Seeing the proposed amendment as a backdoor attempt at gun prohibition, and in effect a usurpation of congressional legislative power by a federal bureaucracy, numerous members of Congress reacted negatively and instead passed legislation that explicitly excluded firearms and ammunition from CPSC oversight.[22] However, this legislation did not necessarily dampen the CPSC's commitment to restrictions on ammunition. Forty years later, both a former commissioner[23] and a current commissioner[24] of the CPSC passionately advocated for the enactment of some type of bullet control.

Although the CPSC failed to gain regulatory control over firearms and ammunition, Cosmopolitan America saw in the attempt a new strategy for achieving gun control, and the idea of controlling ammunition to control firearms would periodically resurface in the future. In 2003, Senator Jon Corzine of New Jersey and Representative Patrick Kennedy of Rhode Island proposed the Firearms Safety and Consumer Protection Act, a bill allowing the Treasury Department (instead of the CPSC) to *administratively* ban not just ammunition but also guns, laser sights, and other firearms accessories. Treasury officials could recall guns in private hands and would have emergency authority to confiscate guns without following normal administrative procedures.[25] Although this bill died in committee, proponents of gun control would continue to seek administrative ways to outflank Bedrock America.

In 1974, the country witnessed another political assassination attempt, this time on the life of President Richard Nixon. Convinced that Nixon was oppressing the poor, Samuel Byck, a depressed and delusional ne'er-do-well, stole a .22-caliber revolver from a friend and made his way to Baltimore/Washington International airport. After killing an aviation administration police officer, Byck—in a chilling foreshadowing of terroristic events a quarter century later—planned to hijack a Delta Airlines DC-9 scheduled for an Atlanta run and crash it into the White House. Anne Arundel County police foiled the hijacking attempt, and in a standoff with the police, Byck shot and killed himself.[26]

High-profile assassination attempts involving firearms typically provide Cosmopolitan America with an emotional opportunity to rekindle demands for more stringent gun regulation and to shape the attitudes of uncommitted individuals. Oddly enough, perhaps because Byck's weapon was stolen, or because his attempt was ultimately unsuccessful, or because Nixon was an unsympathetic public figure at the time, gun control advocates failed to exploit this opportunity. Yet, 1974 was nonetheless a significant year for Cosmopolitan America: it marked the founding of the modern gun control movement with Dr. Mark Borinsky's establishment of the National Council to Control Handguns (NCCH). NCCH later evolved into Handgun Control Inc. (HCI), and, in turn, HCI became the Brady Campaign to Prevent Gun Violence—arguably the leading gun control advocacy organization in the country.[27]

Dr. Borinsky was a graduate student in psychology when, in 1973, three young thugs accosted him and a friend as they walked to the University of Chicago, demanding his valuables. Although he complied, one of the thugs kept urging the others to shoot him and his friend. For whatever reasons, the robbers chose not to do so. Nonetheless, the incident deeply impressed Borinsky, and after finishing his doctoral studies and moving to Washington, D.C., he rented a small office, hired a secretary, and, using his own funds, started the National Council to Control Handguns. As his work schedule prevented Borinsky from handling the daily operations of NCCH, he brought on Edward O. Welles, a retired CIA officer. In 1975, Borinsky and Welles added N. T. "Pete" Shields, a former marketing manager, to the group. Shields (whose son had been murdered with a handgun) and Welles significantly shaped NCCH into a highly effective lobbying group, working with the Bureau of Justice Statistics, the Centers for Disease Control, and numerous congressional representatives, focused solely on gun control.[28]

NCCH changed its name to Handgun Control Inc. in 1980. HCI had a short-lived partnership with the National Coalition to Ban Handguns (now known as the Coalition to Stop Gun Violence), an umbrella organization created by the United Methodist Church that consisted of various religious, educational, labor, and nonprofit groups interested in minimizing gun violence in America. Policy differences between the two organizations—CSGV advocating for even more stringent gun regulation than HCI[29]—soon doomed this partnership, but over the next 20 years, HCI grew into Cosmopolitan America's standard-bearer in its fight against guns. In 2001, HCI renamed itself the Brady Campaign to Prevent Gun Violence.[30]

Radicalization of the NRA

Since at least the 1960s, when the debates between the two Americas became markedly more vitriolic and bitter, proponents of Cosmopolitan America periodically painted the National Rifle Association as a radical extremist organization that is unreasonably opposed to even innocuous gun regulations that virtually all Americans—even NRA members—endorse. The implication was that NRA leadership, in service to the gun manufacturers, had usurped the organization and that it no longer truly represented the wishes of its rank and file. The irony here is that, in reality, the impetus for radicalization was just the reverse: NRA leadership did not drag its members into opposing gun regulation; its members dragged the NRA into opposing regulation. As Lee Kennett and James Anderson have suggested, even up until the late 1970s, NRA leadership would have preferred a moderate and conciliatory approach to firearms control. After all, the NRA had a distinguished history and a reputation for service to the nation in times of war, a mutually beneficial relationship with the federal government as an unofficial adviser on firearms (even helping to shape most of the federal laws regarding firearms), close ties with both the U.S. Army and the Pentagon, and a successful governmental arrangement distributing surplus military rifles and pistols through its civilian marksmanship program. It also knew that continuous, unrelenting intransigence on gun control legislation would endanger all this. Nonetheless, because the rank-and-file membership—made up of tens of thousands of highly committed gun enthusiasts—insisted that every legislative trench be defended, NRA leadership had no options if the commanders were to direct the infantry.[31]

The issue of the association's nature—whether it would revert to its former incarnation as a marksmanship and shooting sports organization or continue on its path as a gun rights and Second Amendment advocacy organization—resolved itself quite dramatically in 1977. During the previous year, the executive vice president of the NRA, Maxwell Rich, had revealed that the association would henceforth put more effort into growing its outdoor and environmental endeavors and less into its political and lobbying activities. In anticipation of this strategic change, the NRA planned to relocate its headquarters from Washington, D.C., to Colorado Springs. This shift in focus alarmed the uncompromising hard-liners among the NRA, in particular Harlon Carter, the head of the organization's recently created lobbying arm, the Institute for Legislative Action (NRA-ILA). A former chief of the U.S. Border Patrol, Carter was a libertarian who firmly believed that the NRA's critical mission was in championing gun rights and advocating against firearms legislation. Seeing all gun control regulation as unacceptable, Carter argued for a simple platform: "No compromise. No gun legislation."[32]

In November 1976, the NRA's board of directors fired Carter and about 80 other employees sympathetic to Carter's views. Outraged with these developments, Carter and other NRA activists met secretly, and at the association's 1977 annual meeting in Cincinnati, they engineered a takeover of the organization. By using the NRA's parliamentary procedures, they commandeered the meeting agenda from the floor, changed the selection procedures for board of director seats, and proceeded to replace the old-guard leadership with their own candidate choices. Carter became executive vice president, supplanting Maxwell Rich. They also voted to restore the ILA, and Carter's chief deputy, Neal Knox, a hard-liner with positions even more unyielding than Carter's—he wanted the repeal of all existing gun laws, including the ban on machine guns—took over the ILA. As executive vice president, Carter canceled the move to Colorado Springs and changed the organization's motto on its headquarters' building to reflect its renewed focus: "The Right of the People to Keep and Bear Arms Shall Not Be Infringed."[33] During Carter's tenure at the helm, NRA membership tripled to over 3 million.[34]

In 1981, Carter was reelected as NRA executive vice president. In covering that event, the *New York Times* revealed that, as a 17-year-old teenager 50 years earlier, Carter had been convicted of murder. Carter, carrying a shotgun, had confronted Ramon Casiano, a 15-year-old boy whom Carter thought knew something about the family's stolen car. Casiano rejected Carter's demands to come with him, and the two traded curses and taunts. When Casiano brandished a knife, Carter fatally shot him. Although the Texas Court of Appeals overturned the conviction because of incorrect jury instructions regarding the laws of self-defense, the *New York Times*[35] went into some detail regarding the incident, the ensuing trial, and its aftermath. If the purpose of including the shooting narrative in a reelection report was an attempt to discredit Carter or to question his moral character, the attempt backfired. In fact, as one scholar noted, "the hard-liners in the NRA loved it. Who better to lead them than a man who really understood the value of a gun for self-protection?"[36]

A New Wave of Assassination Headlines

Between the founding of HCI in 1974 and the radicalization of the NRA in 1977, two assassination attempts on the life of President Gerald Ford roiled the country and helped ensure that the issue of gun violence remained one of national prominence. Lynette "Squeaky" Fromme carried out the first attempt. A devoted follower of mass murderer Charles Manson and a member of his "family," Fromme was an environmental extremist—she resolutely advocated ATWA (Air, Trees, Water, Animals), a Manson-endorsed notion referring to the environment's interconnected life support systems. Fromme had determined to kill Ford as a protest against environmental pollution. She got her chance during Ford's September 1975 visit to Sacramento, California, where he had a scheduled breakfast speaking engagement. Dressing in red "for the animals" and borrowing a .45-caliber Colt pistol from a friend, Fromme waited with a group of spectators as Ford, walking to the State Capitol after the breakfast, shook hands and worked the crowd. When he was just feet away, Fromme drew the semiautomatic pistol from a leg holster, pointed it at the president, and pressed the trigger. The gun failed to fire. Although the pistol contained a magazine with live rounds, Fromme either forgot to rack the pistol's slide to chamber a round or, as she later claimed, she was actually ambivalent about killing Ford.[37]

The second attempt on Ford's life occurred later that same month and was also in California and carried out by a woman. Sara Jayne Moore, a five-times divorced mother of four known in radical political circles for her mood swings and fiery temper, had become mildly obsessed with publishing heiress Patty Hearst's 1974 abduction by the Symbionese Liberation Army (SLA) and her subsequent involvement in the terrorist activities of the SLA. Moore became the press person and bookkeeper for People in Need (PIN), the food distribution organization that Randolph Hearst had set up at the behest of the SLA in an effort to win the return of his daughter. Although the leader of the SLA and several members of the terrorist group had died 18 months earlier in a pitched battle with the Los Angeles Police Department—perhaps the most formidable police shootout in U.S. history, with more than 4,000 rounds fired by SLA members and more than 5,000 by law enforcement officers[38]—the Hearst girl was not among them, and police would not apprehend her until four days prior to Moore's attempt on Ford's life. How these events might have influenced Moore is uncertain.

Moore's activities with leftist activists linked to PIN had resulted in her recruitment as an FBI informant,[39] but she was also funneling information about the FBI's interests to the activists—even becoming known as the "FBI Lady." The assassination attempt may have signaled her decision to finally commit to the extremists by demonstrating her allegiance to the "cause."[40] Whatever her motives, Moore was in San Francisco awaiting President Ford in the crowd outside the St. Francis Hotel on September 22. Ford had just finished addressing a World Affairs Council meeting, and before entering his limousine, he had paused to wave to the spectators. Armed with a newly purchased .38-caliber Smith & Wesson revolver— the police had confiscated her .44 caliber handgun the day before, after she had advised them she might "test" Ford's security detail—Moore got off two shots. Unfamiliar with the new revolver's sights, she narrowly missed the president with her first shot, and Oliver Sipple, a former marine standing near her, grabbed her arm and deflected her second shot.[41]

Predictably, the assassination attempts galvanized Cosmopolitan America. Two days after the second attempt on Ford's life, California governor Jerry Brown signed into law a pair of gun control bills, one imposing a mandatory prison sentence for anyone using a gun in the commission of a serious crime and the other imposing a 15-day waiting period on purchases of firearms.[42] Senator Edward Kennedy of Massachusetts admonished the nation that "if America cares about the safety of its leaders, it can no longer ignore the shocking absence of gun control."[43] Chicago mayor Richard Daley opined that "you don't see someone shooting rabbits with handguns. The only thing you hunt is human beings."[44] Of course, handgun hunters, who do shoot rabbits and other small game, sharply disagreed.

Other gun control proponents revived old bills and introduced new ones. John Conyers of Michigan proposed to ban all handguns, Senators Jacob Javits and Charles Percy introduced a bill mandating handgun registration, and Congressman Peter Rodino called for the registration of handguns and the licensing of gun owners. Public opinion polls at the time suggested that the assassination attempts had increased support for handgun registration, but they had decreased support for handgun bans—presumably on the grounds that a ban would simply disarm the law-abiding, making them more vulnerable to lawbreakers.[45] In any case, the discussions were academic. As with similar past legislative efforts, Cosmopolitan America watched in frustration as all of these proposals died in committee.

About five years later, and barely a year into the new decade, handguns once again featured in assassination-screaming global headlines, but this time the assassinations had more tragic human consequences. The first involved the murder of John Lennon, the world-renowned musician and songwriter, outside his residence in the Dakota Apartment Building in New York City. Formerly an avid fan and admirer of the ex-Beatle, Mark David Chapman, a religiously oriented delusional psychotic, had at some point determined that Lennon was a blasphemous hypocrite. Chapman raged at Lennon's claim that the Beatles were "more popular than Jesus" and that Lennon "told us to imagine no possessions [while he had] millions of dollars and yachts and farms and country estates, laughing at people like me who had believed the lies . . . and built their lives around his music."[46]

On December 8, 1980, Chapman waited for Lennon at the entrance to the Dakota. Earlier in the day, as was his habit, Lennon had given autographs and signed albums for fans waiting outside the building, and he had even signed an album cover for Chapman. On his return several hours later, Chapman fired a .38-caliber revolver five times as the musician strolled by. He struck Lennon in the back and shoulder with four of his shots. As Lennon lay dying, Chapman waited for the police to arrive, reading J. D. Salinger's novel *The Catcher in the Rye*, perhaps reliving Holden Caulfield's fury at perceived "phoniness."[47] As with the political assassinations in the 1960s, Lennon's murder shocked and saddened the country and reignited emotional pleas for gun regulation. Up to this point, Handgun Control Inc. had been struggling with limited resources, but Lennon's shooting again pushed the gun debate to the center of public consciousness and swelled HCI membership rolls past the 100,000 mark. Two years later, HCI had sufficient means to establish an educational outreach organization, the Center to Prevent Handgun Violence (CPHV).[48]

Four months after the Lennon murder, at the end of March 1981, the second assassination incident occurred. A mentally disturbed John Hinckley Jr., obsessed with actress and Yale student Jodie Foster and despairing over the recent slaying of the former Beatle, decided to show Miss Foster the depth of his longing for her by assassinating President Ronald Reagan.[49] Armed with a Rohm RG-14 .22-caliber revolver—considered a Saturday Night Special in shooting circles—Hinckley waited outside the Washington Hilton Hotel on March 30 as Reagan addressed members of the AFL-CIO labor organization. Ironically, the Secret Service had regarded the hotel as one of the safest venues in Washington, D.C., as it had an enclosed, secure passageway (the "President's Walk"), which was built after John Kennedy's assassination. Although Reagan entered and exited the hotel through the President's Walk, he still had to walk about 30 feet from the hotel to his limousine, and the Secret Service had unaccountably allowed unscreened spectators to get within five yards of the car.[50]

As Reagan passed right in front of him, Hinckley pulled his revolver—loaded with Devastator cartridges designed to explode on impact—and fired six times in less than two seconds. The first shot hit James Brady, Reagan's press secretary, in the head. That bullet detonated (the only round that did so) and crippled him. Other shots hit D.C. police officer Thomas Delahanty in the neck and Secret Service agent Tim McCarthy—who used his body to shield the president—in the abdomen. Two shots missed individuals completely, doing no damage, but the last bullet struck the armored door of the limousine and ricocheted into Reagan's side, grazing a rib and puncturing a lung. As Secret Service agents quickly wrestled Hinckley to the ground and arrested him, others sped the president to George Washington University Hospital, where he underwent emergency surgery. In 1982, a jury found Hinckley not guilty by reason of insanity. Hinckley spent the next 34 years in a psychiatric hospital before gaining his release (with severe restrictions on his movements) in 2016.[51]

These shootings did not result in any new federal gun regulations—at least not immediately (the Brady Handgun Violence Prevention Act was still well over a decade away)—but they nonetheless had significant ramifications for Cosmopolitan America. Reagan's shooting reignited discussions about Saturday Night Specials and suggested to gun control advocates a novel *judicial*—as opposed to *legislative*—strategy for limiting handguns. After recovering from the surgical extraction of the Devastator round from his neck—physician volunteers had donned bulletproof vests for the operation—Officer Thomas Delahanty brought suit against Rohm Gesellschaft (RG), the gun manufacturer. Delahanty argued that as the RG-14 was a Saturday Night Special (small, cheap, and unreliable) and had no purpose except to facilitate criminal undertakings, the court should hold RG responsible for his injuries.[52] Although the D.C. Court of Appeals rejected this argument, Cosmopolitan America will in the future periodically return to this legal strategy, exploring ways to get courts to hold gun manufacturers liable for a customer's illegal misuse of their firearms.

The second ramification of the Reagan shooting was more long-term in nature and perhaps more important. With the crippling and paralysis of James Brady and the eventual involvement of his wife, Sarah Brady, in the gun control crusade, Cosmopolitan America gained two powerful figures in its fight. James Brady, a poignant symbol of the toll that firearm violence takes, captured the very heart of the crusade, and Sarah Brady emerged as a prominent and savvy advocate for the cause. For much of their adult lives, Jim and Sarah Brady were at the forefront of the crusade for firearms regulation, and for 15 years before her death in 2015, Sarah Brady would serve as the chairperson of the Brady Campaign to Prevent Gun Violence, Cosmopolitan America's answer to Bedrock America's NRA.

Legislative Developments

The rest of the 1980s were relatively uneventful years for the two Americas. On the federal level, Congress passed three gun-related bills of limited scope. In 1984, the Reagan administration included the Armed Career Criminal Act (ACCA) as part of its Comprehensive Crime Control bill, a major revision of the U.S. criminal code. For individuals convicted of three or more violent crimes, the ACCA enhanced the penalties for the possession or use of firearms from the 10-year *maximum* imprisonment under the Gun Control Act of 1968 to a *minimum* of 15 years, up to an implied maximum of life.[53] Then, in 1986, Congress enacted a similarly narrow bill, the Law Enforcement Officers Protection Act (LEOPA), regulating the manufacture, importation, and sale of armor-piercing ammunition. The bill essentially banned "cop-killer" bullets, those capable of penetrating bulletproof vests and garments.

The third federal bill, the 1986 Firearm Owners Protection Act (FOPA), also tweaked specific provisions of the GCA, but it held broader implications for Bedrock America than either ACCA or LEOPA. In response to complaints about the Bureau of Alcohol, Tobacco and Firearms (BATF) harassing gun shop owners with repeated unwarranted compliance inspections and time-consuming conferences, FOPA limited BATF—in the absence of any evidence of record-keeping violations—to one inspection per year. The act also eased restrictions on the sale and interstate transportation of firearms and ammunition and removed record-keeping requirements on the sale of non-armor-piercing ammunition. Additionally, while FOPA banned the sale of newly manufactured, fully automatic firearms (i.e., machine guns) to civilians, the act allowed civilian possession and transference of machine guns manufactured prior to the act's passage. As another concession to gun advocates, who were perpetually suspicious that any form of firearms registration would inevitably morph into firearms confiscation, FOPA explicitly forbade any government agency from creating a permanent registry linking guns not controlled by the National Firearms Act to their owners.[54]

Although not on the federal level, a significant legislative event occurred in California in the final year of the decade, when the state passed the Roberti-Roos Assault Weapons Control Act of 1989 (AWCA). The act stemmed from an appalling mass shooting that left 5 schoolchildren dead and about 30 others wounded in Stockton, California. Patrick Edward Purdy, a 26-year-old unemployed drifter with alcohol, drug, and mental problems, walked from behind a school building and used a Chinese variant of an AK-47 semiautomatic rifle to spew over 100 rounds into the playground, which was mostly filled with children of Southeast Asian immigrants playing at recess. Investigators later learned that the children were targeted because Purdy fiercely resented Asian immigrants for "taking jobs" from native-born citizens. After three or four minutes, Purdy stopped firing, drew a Taurus PT92 9mm pistol from his jacket, leveled the gun at his head, and killed himself.[55]

The shooting received national press coverage, and *Time* magazine captured the nature of much of this coverage: "Why could Purdy, an alcoholic who had been arrested for . . . selling weapons and attempted robbery, walk into a gun shop . . . and leave with an AK-47 under his arm? The easy availability of weapons like this, which have no purpose other than killing human beings, can all too readily turn the delusions of sick gunmen into tragic nightmares."[56] California subsequently enacted AWCA, a law that banned as "assault weapons" the sale and possession of over 50 specifically named brands and models of semiautomatic rifles, pistols, and shotguns and identified certain firearm characteristics that, if present, would categorize even unnamed guns as assault weapons and also subject to the ban.[57] This legislation in California would foreshadow similar "assault weapon" bans on the federal level in the 1990s.

Taking a larger perspective, two decades after passage of the Gun Control Act of 1968, "gun violence" remained as divisive an issue in America as ever. If anything, the gulf between Bedrock and Cosmopolitan America had grown, with positions hardening in both camps. With Bedrock America's NRA embracing a no-compromise stance to halt further legislative erosion of gun rights, and with Cosmopolitan America's HCI and its organizational allies espousing novel administrative and legal strategies intended to ban bullets and bankrupt gun manufacturers, the contest between the two Americas became even more hostile. At heart, the reactions of the two Americas to the events of the 1970s and 1980s—the shootings, murders, and assassinations—account for this hostility and underscore a recurrent difference separating the two camps. Cosmopolitan America studies the horrific murders and the devastated shooting victims and sees carnage wrought by guns. Whether the firearm is Mayor Daley's handgun or *Time* magazine's AK-47, the conclusion is relentless and identical: guns have no significant role in society other than to kill or maim human beings. If this is the problem—if guns victimize even the most well-protected among us and endanger even the most innocent among us—the solution is glaringly evident: ban the possession and sale of firearms or, at the very least, impose and enforce rigorous and stringent controls.

In contrast, Bedrock America studies the same shootings and killings and sees carnage wrought by mentally unbalanced, deranged individuals or by sociopathic, criminal assailants. Such damaged and defective people may do harm using guns, if firearms are handy, but those bent on violence will find a method to harm the innocent, no matter how. If such individuals are the problem, if society wants a shield against the violently deranged and the criminal sociopath, the solution is indeed evident, but that solution is to ensure that peaceable citizens have at hand a powerful means of protection and defense—firearms. Far from being the obvious answer declared by Cosmopolitan America, gun control merely endangers the law-abiding and exacerbates the problem of gun violence.

CHAPTER SEVEN

Further Rifting: 1990–2000

For the next 15 years or so, as the ideological positions of the two Americas progressively hardened, their political skirmishes became both more acrimonious and more sophisticated. On the national stage, gun politics began to play an increasingly critical role in presidential politics, with a candidate's stand on guns—distilled to its most basic assessment: pro or con?—scrutinized minutely and judged accordingly. Legislatively, Cosmopolitan America mounted an ongoing campaign against "assault" weapons—a campaign that Bedrock America derisively mocked and vehemently opposed. On a second front, Cosmopolitan America again focused its attention and resources on restricting handgun sales and adamantly demanded background checks and waiting periods for such purchases. Bedrock America again decried these demands as constitutional infringements and rigorously contested these efforts as well.

During this period, gun control proponents adopted two relatively new tactical procedures in their fight against firearms. The first was reminiscent of Officer Thomas Delahanty's legal action against the gun manufacturer Rohm Gesellschaft (RG). The tactic centered on the premise that firearms producers and firearms dealers are liable for the economic and psychological costs that municipalities and victims sustain when individuals who have been sold a firearm misuse that pistol or rifle. The second tactic, foreshadowing Cosmopolitan America's nascent realization that many ideologically uncommitted Americans are simply mistrustful of government-sponsored "gun control,"[1] began to reframe firearm regulation as gun "safety" rather than gun "control." Opening yet another front in the battle, they called for legislation requiring firearms manufacturers and dealers to provide child-protective trigger locks with each handgun sold. This tactical shift forced Bedrock America into the awkward position of either accepting a mild form of firearms regulation or appearing coldly indifferent to the safety of innocent children. The timing of this child-safety skirmish would take on a certain morbid irony in that the Columbine High School massacre—youths killing youths—occurred before the Senate had reached a resolution on the efficacy of even trigger-lock safety.

The Fight to Ban Assault Weapons

Prior to the late 1980s, few individuals within the shooting fraternity (and even fewer outside the fraternity) would have described any of the semiautomatic rifles and pistols then commonly available as "assault weapons." While the term had occasionally been used by some gun manufacturers[2] as marketing hyperbole, such usage merely played on the cosmetic surface similarities between a civilian semiautomatic version of a military rifle (such as the AR-15) and the actual automatic military rifle (such as the M-16). The primary feature that truly distinguishes a military rifle from a civilian rifle—the ability to have continuous fire with one press of the trigger—converts the rifle into a machine gun, and the National Firearms Act had effectively banned civilian ownership of machine guns since the 1930s. Nonetheless, the surface similarities of the two types of firearms and the vaguely menacing associations of the "assault" term gave Cosmopolitan America a significant opportunity in its war with Bedrock America.

Josh Sugarmann, the individual usually credited with initiating and popularizing Cosmopolitan America's "assault weapons"[3] strategy, is an ardent gun control proponent and the founder and current director of the Violence Policy Center (VPC), a Joyce Foundation–funded nonprofit advocacy organization focused on gun control legislation and policy.[4] After working as the communications director for the National Coalition to Ban Handguns, Sugarmann founded VPC in 1988. That same year, he authored a VPC study called *Assault Weapons and Accessories in America*. Although this examination acknowledged that "assault" rifles were simply semiautomatic firearms, it nonetheless contended that because of their rate of fire and large-capacity magazines, these military look-alikes were more lethal than standard semiautomatic hunting rifles. The book asserted that such "assault" rifles had no role in modern society except as human killing machines and that they posed a mounting health and safety threat to the lives of peaceable Americans. In urging a policy of severe governmental restrictions on such firearms, the book additionally argued that gun control proponents could use the "assault weapon threat" to further the cause of gun control generally. Suggesting that efforts to restrict assault weapons were more likely to succeed than efforts to restrict handguns, Sugermann maintained that "the weapons' menacing looks, coupled with the public's confusion over fully automatic machine guns versus semiautomatic assault weapons—anything that looks like a machine gun is assumed to be a machine gun—can only increase the chance of public support for restrictions on these weapons."[5]

In January 1989, less than a year after the publication of *Assault Weapons and Accessories in America*, Patrick Purdy went on his appalling shooting rampage in Stockton, California, using a semiautomatic AK-47 rifle—an assault rifle in VPC terms—to kill or maim dozens of Southeast Asian schoolchildren as they played during recess. Subsequently, despite VPC's stated advocacy of gun regulation, the partisan nature of the analysis, and the obvious gun control agenda driving its conclusions, the book had a significant impact in shaping the public's perception of specific types of semiautomatic rifles, and it succeeded in getting them labeled as "assault weapons." For instance, in the two years before Purdy's mass murder attack, the media used "assault weapon" as a descriptor 140 times. Two years after the shooting, as congressional debates on a potential ban gained steam, the term occurred in the media almost 2,600 times.[6] Further, even before 1989 ended, California enacted the Assault Weapons Control Act (AWCA), which used many of the cosmetic features identified in the PVC report to classify and ban as "assault weapons" over 50 different brands and models of semiautomatic rifles and pistols.[7] These developments alarmed and astonished members of Bedrock America, who asserted that semiautomatic firearms were being classified as assault weapons simply because of surface similarities.

The developing battle between Cosmopolitan and Bedrock America soon ensnared the administration of Republican president George H. W. Bush. A life member of the NRA and a hunter, Bush had taken positions opposing gun bans during his presidential campaign. Nonetheless, a few months after the Stockton shooting, William Bennett (the administration's "drug czar") and First Lady Barbara Bush convinced the president to temporarily suspend the importation of certain types of foreign-made semiautomatic rifles. During the suspension, BATF was instructed to determine whether they were "assault rifles" with no sporting purpose. Under the Gun Control Act of 1968, BATF had the authority to ban foreign imports judged not suitable for sporting purposes. During the suspension, importers could provide BATF with evidence and information demonstrating that buyers used the rifles for hunting and target shooting—sporting purposes—but BATF acknowledged that any determination was still a fairly subjective process.[8]

Although BATF's ultimate determination regarding semiautomatic *imported* rifles would have no impact on the manufacture or sale of *domestic* semiautomatic firearms—that type of restriction was beyond BATF's authority and required congressional legislation—the political stakes for Bush and Bedrock America were still high. If BATF determined that the imports had no sporting purpose, the indefinite suspension would become a permanent ban and raise obvious questions about the domestic versions of the same rifles and their suitability for civilian ownership and possession. Noting the temporary suspension, Democratic senator Howard Metzenbaum of Ohio was quick to congratulate Bush, who had asserted less than a month earlier that he was "not about to" ban semiautomatic firearms, despite repeated calls for such restrictions. Metzenbaum went on to pointedly observe that legislation banning the domestic sale and manufacture of such guns was also required.[9] Bedrock America took a wait-and-see position on the suspension. The NRA noted that 20–30 million Americans owned and hunted with semiautomatic firearms and that they used such rifles and pistols extensively in target shooting and competitions. The association also pointed out the difficulties in creating a meaningful legal distinction between "assault" and "sporting" firearms, but it nevertheless welcomed the BATF review as an opportunity to get a "cool-headed look at the facts" regarding semiautomatic guns and get beyond "media hysteria."[10]

Less than four months later, in July 1989, BATF completed its review of the firearms in question and determined that 43 of the 50 reviewed models did not meet the "sporting purposes" standard, subjecting them to a permanent ban. Stephen Higgins, the director of BATF at the time (he retired shortly after the government's disastrous raid on David Koresh's Waco, Texas, compound in April 1993), announced that viable differences distinguished semiautomatic "assault-style" rifles from semiautomatic rifles traditionally used in hunting and in shooting sports. These distinguishing features included the use of large-capacity detachable magazines, often holding five times the number of cartridges a hunting rifle might hold, and the use of centerfire cartridges less than 2.25 inches long.[11] Asked about the ban, the president's spokesperson indicated that Bush fully supported the decision.

President Bush's support of the BATF decision pleased neither Cosmopolitan nor Bedrock America. Senator Metzenbaum and Democratic representative Pete Stark of California still criticized Bush for not going far enough—for not also advocating for severe restrictions on home-grown assault firearms. Stark suggested that with the import ban, Bush had effectively acknowledged that assault-style weapons had no role in civilian hands. It followed, then, that Bush must sign an assault weapons ban should any of the bills currently wending their way through Congress make it to his desk.[12] On the other hand, the NRA indicated that it would fight the import ban "in the courts, on Capitol Hill and at the ballot box."[13] Similarly, Larry Pratt, the executive director of Gun Owners of America, characterized Bush's action as "a slap in the face to millions of Americans who voted for George Bush because of his well-publicized opposition to new gun control." He went on to assert that the import ban would do nothing to alleviate the country's crime and drug problems, but it would "simply be another infringement on the Second Amendment rights of law-abiding American citizens."[14]

In the end, the ban for which Metzenbaum and Stark and other members of Cosmopolitan American had lobbied did not happen during George Bush's Republican administration. It would eventually come about but under a new president, William "Bill" Clinton, and during a Democratic administration. Accounting for the delay—in addition to the usual political machinations surrounding any legislation focused on firearms—were two events that occurred in the months surrounding the transition between the Bush and Clinton administrations. One was the standoff and siege of the Weaver homestead at Ruby Ridge, Idaho, in August 1992, and the other was the siege and destruction of the Branch Davidian compound at Waco, Texas, in February 1993. Both incidents galvanized the country, ignited fiery debates about federal law enforcement procedures and tactics, and pushed the assault weapons controversy to the back burner. Each vividly displayed the incredible violence that the federal government could bring to bear on citizens deemed troublesome and unlawful. For many individuals, and particularly for members of Bedrock America, Ruby Ridge and Waco provided a sobering reminder that sometimes it is not just from "bad guys" that an individual may require protection.

Ruby Ridge, Waco, and Governmental Gun Violence

The Ruby Ridge standoff, which centered on Randy Weaver, an unconventional religious fundamentalist with white separatist leanings who anticipated the Apocalypse, lasted 11 days and initially involved about a dozen members of the U.S. Marshals Service and the FBI's Hostage Rescue Team. Before it ended, the event had engaged several hundred agents and officers from the Marshals Service, the FBI, BATF, the

Idaho State Police, the County Sheriff's office, the local police, and the Idaho National Guard.

After a BATF informant claimed that Weaver had supplied him with illegal sawed-off shotguns and Weaver had missed a court date to respond to the weapons charge (the letter notifying him of the required court appearance contained an incorrect court date), U.S. Marshals staked out the family's remote cabin in the Idaho woods hoping to arrest Weaver. In a reconnaissance mission gone bad, a team of three U.S. Marshals first chanced upon Weaver on a logging trail in the woods. When they identified themselves as U.S. Marshals and ordered him to stop, he hurriedly disappeared back to his cabin. About a minute later, traveling along a different logging trail, the agents spotted Weaver's 14-year-old son, Samuel; Kevin Harris (a family friend); and Samuel's dog, Striker. Perceiving Striker as a threat, one agent shot and killed the dog, and Samuel, upset and enraged, returned fire. A gun battle then ensued between the federal agents and Weaver and Harris. In the brief firefight, one marshal wounded Samuel in the right elbow. As the wounded boy retreated, another marshal shot him in the back, killing him. In turn, Kevin Harris fired at the agents and one of his rounds hit and killed a marshal. He then retreated back to the Weaver cabin.[15]

With the shooting death of an agent, the Marshals Service activated its Special Operations Group, alerted the FBI about the marshal's death, and requested immediate support from Idaho law enforcement. The Boundary County Sheriff's Office and the Idaho State Police quickly responded. Additionally, the governor declared a state of emergency, thus allowing the use of Idaho National Guard resources, including armored personnel carriers. In all, several hundred federal agents eventually surrounded the Weaver cabin. On the following day, the FBI's Hostage Rescue Team (HRT) deployed sniper/observer teams with rules-of-engagement later described in a Senate investigative report as "virtual shoot on sight orders."[16] Thus, when Randy Weaver, his daughter, and Harris eventually ran from the cabin to the shed where they had placed the body of Samuel the day before, FBI HRT sniper Lon Horiuchi saw his opportunity and, from a distance of about 200 yards, shot Weaver as he raised the door latch on the shed.

The bullet struck Weaver in the back, wounding but not killing him. As the group raced back to the cabin, Horiuchi fired a second shot as Harris reached the cabin's open doorway. Inside the cabin, standing slightly back from the doorway, was Weaver's wife, Vicki, holding their 10-month-old daughter. As Harris entered the cabin, Horiuchi's second bullet tore through his chest, wounding him, and then hit Vicki in the head, killing her instantly. Although the siege would last for another nine days, no further bloodshed occurred. Civilian negotiators ultimately convinced the Weavers and Harris to surrender. In the subsequent criminal trials, the jury found Weaver innocent of all charges except missing his court date. Harris, indicted for murder, was also acquitted. Later, both he and Weaver brought civil suits against the federal government. Weaver and his daughters settled their wrongful death claim out of court for $3.1 million, and Harris eventually received a $380,000 settlement from the government. FBI sniper Lon Horiuchi was indicted in 1997 on manslaughter charges in the death of Vicki Weaver, but the charges were later dropped after a change of leadership in the prosecutor's office.[17]

About six months later, federal and state agents confronted a second sect of religious nonconformists in Waco, Texas, and after an extended standoff, the government's siege of the Branch Davidian compound would also end lethally, again with the use of terrifying force and violence. The incident revolved around David Koresh, the charismatic leader of a fringe religious sect awaiting Armageddon and the Second Coming of Christ. While awaiting the Apocalypse, Koresh had convinced his followers that God wanted him to separate married couples, allowing only Koresh to have sexual relations with the wives, while the husbands and other men practiced celibacy. God's plan, he insisted, was to have Koresh procreate with all the women of the group to create a "House of David" and build an "Army for God" in preparation for the "end of days."[18]

A local paper picked up on the unusual sexual arrangements and religious beliefs of the Branch Davidians and published a series of articles profiling the sect in February 1993. The paper detailed allegations that Koresh advocated polygamy (at least for himself), took multiple underage girls as brides, fathered at least a dozen children, had "rights" to any female in the group, and physically abused children living in the compound. But even before the articles, rumors had been circulating in the area intimating that Koresh and the Branch Davidians had begun stockpiling firearms in anticipation of Armageddon. Other reports had individuals hearing "automatic" gunfire coming from the compound. Firearms capable of automatic firing—machine guns—are generally illegal for civilians to own or possess, and the rumors and reports prompted BATF to open an investigation in June 1992. After following paper trails to confirm some unusual firearm parts purchased by the sect, the agent spearheading the probe, David Aguilera, interviewed the local gun dealer used by the Branch Davidians, Henry McMahon, in July. McMahon phoned Koresh, who offered to let the agent come out and inspect the compound's firearms and associated paperwork. Although McMahon suggested that the agent talk with Koresh directly, for some reason Aguilera refused.[19]

Instead, BATF began to monitor the compound from a nearby residence and sent in an undercover agent to gather additional information. Based on a former sect member's claim that the Branch Davidians did, in fact, have M-16 parts that could convert semiautomatic AR-15 rifles (which the Branch Davidians also had) into illegal automatic rifles, BATF obtained search and arrest warrants for David Koresh and several other Branch Davidians. On the day of the raid, 76 agents drove from Fort Hood in a multivehicle convoy that stretched for about a mile along the highway. Although the agents had hoped to surprise the Davidians and execute the search and arrest warrants before the group had a chance to prepare and arm themselves, Koresh had received a tip from his brother-in-law that agents were coming and that a raid was imminent. Koresh directed the women and children to take shelter in their rooms, and he and other male members armed themselves and dispersed around the compound. Shortly afterward, gunfire erupted. BATF agents later claimed that the first shots came from within the compound, but Branch Davidian survivors insisted they came from agents outside.[20]

Within minutes of the first shots, Wayne Martin, a member of the sect and a Waco lawyer, called the sheriff's office and pleaded for a cease-fire, exclaiming, "Here they come again! That's them shooting! That's not us!"[21] However, it was not until about 45 minutes later, with agents running low on ammunition (the Branch Davidians themselves had stockpiled tens of thousands of rounds), that shooting even slowed down. Another hour passed before a negotiated cease-fire occurred, and the Davidians allowed the agents to withdraw with their dead and wounded. During the gun battle, the Davidians had killed four BATF agents and wounded 16 others, and they had themselves sustained five deaths. Early on, Koresh himself had been shot in the wrist. Later reports analyzing these events noted that violent cults that create an enclave to minimize contact with the world while they await the end-time usually engage in defensive violence; they do not act on their beliefs that the end-time has arrived unless provoked. The Davidians appeared to fall into this category. They expected to achieve destined salvation by defending their sacred retreat and thus had no need—and did not try—to maximize the killing of ATF agents.[22]

After this initial siege, BATF called in the FBI (a common procedure after the killing of federal agents) and a standoff of over 50 days ensued. Teams of FBI negotiators communicated with Koresh and the Branch Davidians during this time, attempting to find a resolution to avoid further bloodshed. The negotiations produced progress—the Davidians eventually let 19 children and 11 adults leave—but a faction within the FBI contingent that saw the situation as a *hostage* crisis pressed for a more aggressive tactical solution. The commander of the FBI Hostage Rescue Team, Richard Rogers—the same individual who commanded the HRT at Ruby Ridge—also worried that the continuing stalemate severely tied down HRT resources; he wanted a speedy resolution to the standoff. Additionally, FBI and Texas Ranger interviews with the released children suggested that some of the children had been subjected to ongoing physical and sexual abuse prior to the standoff. Given these factors, Janet Reno, President Clinton's new attorney general, signed off on the HRT's recommendation to mount an assault on the compound and force out the Davidians.[23]

The Hostage Response Team's assault objective was to clear the compound using an infusion of tear gas and to avoid harming the Davidians, if at all possible. To this end, the agents planned on using Combat Engineer Vehicles (CEVs) to punch holes in the compound's various buildings and then pump in increasing amounts of tear gas over a two-day period. Loudspeakers would assure the Davidians that the agents planned no armed assault and that they would not fire unless fired upon. The hope was that, at some point, the Davidians would find the tear gas so unbearable that they would abandon the buildings and surrender. Instead, even after about six hours in which two CEVs battered different walls of the compound and agents fired multiple rounds of tear gas grenades (so many that the FBI had to ask the Texas Rangers for a resupply), no members of the sect left the buildings. Meanwhile, quick-moving, raging fires had broken out in three separate locations within the compound. In the end, only 9 Davidians escaped the destruction of the compound, and 76 others perished. Evidence indicated that Steve Schneider, Koresh's top aide, shot Koresh and then shot himself.[24]

Of the surviving Branch Davidians, the government brought charges against 12. Authorities won convictions for voluntary manslaughter, illegal firearms use, or both against 8 of the defendants. In a legal sense, the convictions substantially vindicated the BATF and FBI actions in the flawed operation. For many individuals in Cosmopolitan America, the Waco siege—tragic though the outcome was—simply confirmed the belief that firearms and high-powered weapons in the hands of often unstable civilians was a lethally dangerous idea. But for many other Americans, the federal actions and firefights at Ruby Ridge and Waco cast an uneasy shadow on the national government. For Bedrock America, with its inherent wariness of federal intentions, the unbridled violence unleashed against admittedly strange but relatively innocuous citizens was particularly alarming. These two incidents would ripple through the fabric of American society, giving impetus to the sudden growth of the militia/patriot movement in the United States and culminating in 1995 (on the April 19 anniversary of the final Waco assault) with the horrific truck bombing of the Alfred P. Murrah Federal Building in Oklahoma City by Timothy McVeigh and Terry Nichols, domestic terrorists.[25]

Waiting Periods, Background Checks, and an Assault Weapons Ban

With the defeat of Republican George H. W. Bush in the 1992 presidential election and the inauguration of Democrat Bill Clinton as the 42nd president of the United States, Cosmopolitan America had finally found a champion in the White House. During the campaign, Clinton had promised he would fight for stricter gun laws, and as president, he kept his word. He lobbied for passage of both the Brady Handgun Violence Protection Act (the Brady Bill) and the Public Safety and Recreational Firearms Use Protection Act (the Assault Weapons Ban (AWB)), both of which Congress enacted.

The Brady Bill was named after James Brady, the press secretary who had been shot and severely disabled in John Hinckley Jr.'s assassination attempt on President Reagan in 1981. This legislation mandated that federally licensed gun dealers conduct background checks on individuals attempting to purchase handguns, and it also imposed a five-day waiting period before buyers could receive their firearms. The background check was to determine that the buyer was eligible to own a firearm and not a "prohibited person" as defined in earlier federal legislation. Noting that a background check likely would have prevented Hinckley from purchasing the revolver used in the assassination attempt—Hinckley had been arrested on gun charges earlier and was also undergoing psychiatric treatment—Sarah Brady and Handgun Control Inc. had made passage of the Brady Bill a legislative priority as early as 1987. Until Clinton assumed the Oval Office, however, opposition from the NRA and other gun rights advocates had stymied these legislative efforts.[26]

In 1991, Representative (later Senator) Chuck Schumer of New York again introduced Brady legislation. The bill passed both the House and the Senate, but it was later attached to a comprehensive crime bill that never came to a vote; thus, the Brady legislation also died in the Bush administration.[27] President Clinton, however, was more favorably disposed to gun control, and he lobbied Congress to reintroduce the Brady Bill. Schumer did so, and in 1993, Clinton signed the Brady Act into law.

Influenced by NRA concerns, the final version of the bill also mandated the creation of a National Instant Criminal Background Check System (NICS) by 1998, at which time NICS would replace the five-day waiting period with instant computer checks.[28]

Perceiving another federal infringement on the Second Amendment, gun rights proponents in nine states quickly challenged the Brady Bill as unconstitutional. In 1997, these challenges reached the U.S. Supreme Court in the case of *Prinz v. United States*. The Court determined in *Prinz* that one of the Brady Act's provisions—compelling state and local law enforcement officials to conduct background checks—violated the Tenth Amendment's principle of federalism and was consequently unconstitutional. The Court otherwise upheld the act and also noted that state and local authorities could still conduct background checks if they freely chose to do so. A year later, the NICS came on line under the administration of the FBI. With NICS operational, the need for state or local involvement in background checks disappeared and the required five-day waiting period was also eliminated.[29]

Nonetheless, background checks continued as a contentious issue for both Bedrock and Cosmopolitan America. Before long, they soon renewed combat in a clash over firearm sales by private individuals—or what gun control proponents termed the "gun show loophole." Because the Brady Bill's background check requirement applied only to Federal Firearms License (FFL) holders—typically gun store owners—private individuals not dealing in firearms as a business could legally sell guns from their personal collection at gun shows or any other venues without conducting background checks on their buyers or completing any paperwork.

This "loophole" dated back to 1986, when Congress passed the Firearm Owners Protection Act (FOPA), a law designed to ensure that private law-abiding citizens were not unduly burdened by the firearms licensing requirements of the earlier Gun Control Act. FOPA restricted the administrative and operational burdens associated with federal licensing to only those individuals dealing in firearms as an ongoing regular business—that is, those individuals trying to make a living from the repetitive purchase and resale of firearms. FOPA specifically excluded from the obligations imposed on FFL dealers those individuals who simply bought and sold firearms as a hobby or to enhance or reduce their personal firearms collection. Because of this "private seller" exemption (which was also open to FFL dealers, provided they were selling from their own private gun collection), prohibited individuals had a way to skirt background checks, and acquire firearms illegally by buying in this secondary market.[30]

In essence, the gun show loophole was, and continues to be, a private seller loophole, and aside from an honor system where private sellers might voluntarily bring buyers to an FFL dealer for background checks, the only truly effective way of closing the loophole would require universal firearms registration. Because the NICS database is limited to person-centric information, NICS cannot serve in this capacity. The background search merely determines whether a potential buyer falls into one of the "prohibited person" categories, for example, the name or Social Security number belongs to a convicted felon. If so, the FFL dealer receives an electronic notification to reject the sale. If the check raises no flags, the sale goes through. In either case, neither the FBI nor BATF obtain or store information identifying *specific firearms* involved in the transactions.[31] Universal firearms registration—linking particular firearms to specific owners—is deliberately not possible because, in the eyes of much of Bedrock America, registration lists are at risk of becoming confiscation lists. Thus, firearms registration, even as a solution to the private seller problem, is anathema to many gun rights activists. Nonetheless, Cosmopolitan America will continue to press for legislation to close the gun show loophole throughout the decade and into the new century.[32]

Less than a year after Cosmopolitan America's Brady Bill victory, President Clinton championed another gun control bill authored by Democratic senator Dianne Feinstein of California and provided the gun control movement with a second major legislative triumph: the Public Safety and Recreational Firearms Use Protection Act, better known as the Federal Assault Weapons Ban (AWB). Gun control advocates had been pushing for an assault weapons ban since the late 1980s, but the effort met with little success in the Bush administration. Under President Clinton, who was supportive of the bill's goals, and spurred by Gian Luigi Ferri's 1993 mass shooting inside a San Francisco law firm, the legislation gained additional momentum. The Democrat-controlled Congress ultimately included the AWB in the Violent Crime Control and Law Enforcement Act of 1994. Like earlier bills, the AWB defined "assault weapons" as those having certain external physical characteristics (such as bayonet mounts and folding stocks) as well as AR-15s, various versions of the AK-47, the MAC-10, the TEC-9, and the Uzi. The law specified a 10-year ban on the manufacture of these firearms and imposed a 10-round maximum capacity on ammunition magazines. Significantly, the law did not apply to firearms or magazines that individuals already possessed, and it had a sunset provision that allowed the law to lapse in 10 years if not renewed by Congress.[33]

After enactment of the AWB, gun rights proponents challenged the ban on several constitutional points, but none of the challenges were successful. Regarding the effectiveness of the ban for reducing crime and violence in the years after passage, various analyses produced differing results. Some suggested that insufficient evidence existed to determine whether the AWB prevented violence, and others insisted that the impact of the ban was too small to measure reliably. Research by John Lott, a prominent gun rights advocate, indicated that the ban had no effect on violent crime rates.[34] In contrast, the Brady Center to Prevent Gun Violence—a gun control organization—reported that the ban had noticeably reduced the number of assault weapons appearing in BATF crime-gun traces.[35] As noted earlier, convincing determinations of gun law effectiveness in reducing crime or violence are extremely difficult to generate. Analyses are invariably open to criticisms of methodology, time periods, geographic locations, criteria appropriateness, and other limitations. This makes it easy for advocates on both sides to dismiss any findings inconsistent with their preferred view. Consequently, when the AWB was set to expire 10 years after passage, Cosmopolitan America touted the success of the ban and pressed for its renewal, while Bedrock America reaffirmed the ban's utter lack of utility and lobbied for its expiration. In September 2004, after much debate along largely partisan lines, Congress let the ban expire.

Lawsuits, Liabilities, and the Firearms Business

Politically, the Brady Bill and the AWB were pyrrhic victories for President Clinton and Cosmopolitan America, in that some Democrats supporting the bills lost their 1994 reelection bids—losses in part attributed to their votes on the two bills—allowing Republicans to gain control of the House of Representatives. This loss effectively blocked additional enactments of the president's firearms agenda and also discouraged future forays into gun control's political minefield during Clinton's second term.[36] Thus, with the loss of the House frustrating Cosmopolitan America's legislative advance, gun control advocates mounted a second campaign four years later. This one, however, was fought in the judicial system. Using novel theories of product liability, coalitions of gun control activists, litigation attorneys, and municipal politicians saw an avenue in the country's tort system for reining in and regulating America's firearms industry. By broadening traditional notions of product liability, and suing gun manufacturers and distributors into compliance with proposed regulations or into bankruptcy, they hoped to achieve judicially outcomes that had proved impossible to achieve legislatively.[37]

New Orleans filed the first of the major product liability and negligence lawsuits against the gun industry in October 1998. Designed to establish that firearms manufacturers bore responsibility for the epidemic of gun violence in the country's urban areas, the suit claimed that gun makers neglected to incorporate safety mechanisms into their firearms that could have prevented accidental shootings, thus making the guns "unreasonably dangerous." The suit also claimed that the manufacturers and distributors saturated the gun market with more firearms than legal purchasers could possibly buy, thus ensuring that criminals and juveniles would eventually acquire many of the guns.[38] An assembly of anti-tobacco trial lawyers, working with the Brady Center to Prevent Handgun Violence and the mayor of New Orleans, brought the suit against 10 firearms manufacturers using the same novel legal strategies that had brought down the tobacco industry.

As with the tobacco litigation, the New Orleans suit was only the first of a projected series of filings that the coalition of lawyers, mayors, and the Brady Center planned to bring. Thus, less than two weeks later, in November 1998, the City of Chicago and Cook County filed a $433 million suit against 38 gun manufacturers, distributors, and dealers, alleging that the industry deliberately oversupplied the gun market in outlying areas, knowing that thousands of firearms would illegally flow into Chicago, purchased by gang members and other criminals. The novel legal premise was not that the firearms were defective—the basis of traditional product liability cases—but that the distribution and marketing of the guns was tantamount to a public nuisance, similar to a factory polluting a town's water supply or poisoning the air.[39]

Chicago mayor Richard Daley, in commenting on the lawsuit, claimed that "gun manufacturers and retailers know exactly what they're doing. They knowingly market and distribute their deadly weapons to criminals in Chicago and refuse to impose even the most basic controls. If money is the only language they understand, then money is the language we will use to make them understand that they have no business in Chicago."[40] The lawsuit noted that the $433 million in estimated costs to the city in responding to gun violence since 1994 was a conservative figure when considering the staggering aggregate of police, hospital, and custodial resources involved. Additionally, the suit also asked for an injunction requiring manufacturers to train and monitor the sales practices of gun retailers.[41] Responding to the lawsuit, the general counsel for one of the defendants in the suit, Sturm, Ruger & Co., noted, "You don't sue the manufacturers of lawful, non-defective products for criminal acts beyond their control. . . . We don't want to see the bad guys armed, but how can we prevent that?"[42]

In January 1999, the new year opened with two additional suits brought against the firearms industry. Using the legal strategies of the two earlier cases, officials from Bridgeport, Connecticut, and Miami-Dade County, Florida, argued that the gun manufacturers' failure to equip firearms with safety features such as load indicators, trigger locks, and personalization technology constituted negligent and defective design. They also charged that the industry engaged in negligent marketing, first by oversupplying too many guns and then by overpromoting to the general public certain firearms more appropriate to the military and law enforcement markets.[43] Philadelphia mayor Edward Rendell, who headed the U.S. Conference of Mayors' Gun Violence Task Force, noted that the municipalities were not looking for monetary damages in an attempt to put the gun manufacturers out of business, but for improved safety features on firearms and for changes in the way firearms were sold.[44] The plaintiffs may not have specifically been seeking "monetary damages"; however, the Dade County suit sought reimbursement for "hundreds of millions of dollars" in law enforcement, paramedic, and hospital expenses related to gun violence, and Bridgeport sought $100 million from the gun makers.[45] Further, other municipalities—Atlanta, Cincinnati, Los Angeles, Newark, Philadelphia, and San Francisco—were also preparing lawsuits against the firearms industry, using the same novel liability strategies.

Recognizing the lawsuits' potentially devastating consequences for the industry, gun manufacturers and their supporters fiercely rejected shifting responsibility for controlling gun crime from the municipalities to the gun manufacturers. They also questioned whether the litigation had an ulterior purpose that went beyond gun safety. Georgia Nichols, the president of the American Shooting Sports Council, argued that "as an industry, [we] really feel there is no basis for a suit against the legitimate sale of a product. We don't want our guns used for criminal purposes." She called on federal and municipal authorities to strictly enforce existing firearms laws and to arrest and prosecute rogue dealers selling guns illegally as better approaches for solving urban gun violence.[46] Her colleague at the council, Jack Adkins, the director of operations, contended, "That this industry should somehow have established its own private police force to shadow every gun buyer is ludicrous. By filing these suits, the mayors are admitting their own failure to protect their citizens."[47] Taking a different tack, the vice president and general counsel for Glock, Paul Jannuzzo, characterized the lawsuits as a "naked attempt at gun control.

It is not hidden whatsoever."[48] At the retail level, gun dealers also claimed that the litigation was unjust and unreasonable, with one gun shop owner noting, "What could any retailer know about what someone is going to do with a gun when they walk out of the door? If they have a current gun card and I try to refuse them, I would be violating their civil rights."[49] The firearms industry, almost universally reflecting these sentiments, strenuously fought each suit in court.

In the end, the municipalities' unusual interpretation of tort law, clever though it was, proved unsuccessful. The courts refused to apply (or were legislatively blocked from applying) the liability approaches laid out in the gun cases and dismissed the lawsuits. In December 1999, a Connecticut state judge, ruling that the city did not suffer any direct injuries from guns and had no statutory or common-law basis to recoup their claimed expenditures, rejected Bridgeport's suit. Three days later, a state judge in Florida, noting that the county, unlike an individual filing a product liability or negligence suit, had not suffered a specific injury resulting from a defective product, rejected the Miami-Dade suit. The judge further commented that "public nuisance" cannot apply to the design, manufacture, and distribution of a lawful product.[50] In April 2001, the Louisiana Supreme Court, upholding a retroactively passed state law blocking the New Orleans lawsuit, rejected that city's case, ruling that the city lacked a right of action to pursue the suit.[51] Several years later, in 2004, the Illinois Supreme Court concluded that Chicago had no legal basis for holding gun manufacturers responsible for the acts of third parties and dismissed that city's litigation.[52]

Gun rights advocates hailed these court decisions as landmark rulings in line with the country's traditions of firearms ownership and individual responsibility. Commenting on the New Orleans dismissal, James Baker of the NRA suggested that the outcome was "a major victory for gun owners, taxpayers, and all who believe that we must hold criminals accountable for their crimes. These reckless lawsuits against the firearms industry have no place in our judicial system."[53] Similarly, Chris Cox, another NRA representative, applauded "the Illinois Supreme Court for upholding common sense in the face of politically motivated lawsuits. These lawsuits seek to undermine our country's long-standing heritage of firearms ownership. Now perhaps Mayor Daley and other big-city politicians can concentrate on . . . getting criminals off the streets."[54]

Gun control advocates had a substantially different reaction to the decisions. Remarking on the dismissals of the Miami-Dade and Bridgeport suits, John Lowy, the senior lawyer for the Center to Prevent Handgun Violence, suggested that both judges misapplied the law and "simply got it wrong. This is a tough battle. We knew that and we know we're in it for the long haul. Tobacco won cases for decades, then they started losing."[55] Lowy's comment held ominous implications for the firearms industry. It suggested that gun control activists believed that even if one or two judges in one or two courts dismissed the litigation, other judges in other courts—over two dozen lawsuits were pending—might see merit in the municipalities' arguments. Further, as a representative of the gun industry noted early on, even if the manufacturers prevailed on the merits of the cases, fighting litigation in 30 or 40 jurisdictions might still destroy the industry financially.[56] Thus, despite the court defeats, Cosmopolitan America's judicial assault on the country's firearms industry did not truly end until October 2005, when gun manufacturers obtained a federal legislative shield from these novel kinds of product liability lawsuits—the Protection of Lawful Commerce in Arms Act (also known as the Child Safety Lock Act of 2005).

Trigger Locks and Gun Safety

During the same years that the two Americas warred over the liability of gun makers for firearms violence, they also fought a second battle over trigger locks. These are external devices that prevent handguns from firing while they are in place, such as a padlock around the gun's trigger guard, blocking access to the trigger, or a cable lock threaded through the gun's open ejection port, which prevents loading and operating the firearm. The fight over trigger locks dated back to 1997, when President Clinton kept faith with Cosmopolitan America in his State of the Union Address and urged that all handguns sold in the United States be equipped with child safety locks. Such locks were an important element in Cosmopolitan America's attempt to frame strict gun regulation not only as a means for reducing street crime and violence but also as a way to increase gun safety by minimizing shooting accidents and impulse suicides.

While not inherently opposed to these aims, Bedrock America harbored intense suspicion about the actual goals of such gun safety regulation. Members questioned the overall need for trigger locks, noting that fatal firearms accidents had been declining since the 1930s and lagged far behind deaths due to car accidents—and considerably behind deaths due to falling, poisoning, drowning, fire, and even suffocation due to ingested objects.[57] Thus, anticipating an extended legislative fight in Congress over mandatory locks, the Clinton administration instead quietly negotiated with a majority of firearms manufacturers to voluntarily provide child safety locks with any handgun sold. The agreement ensured that about 80 percent of handguns sold in the country would come with locks.[58]

Although the Clinton administration and some child advocacy groups hailed the agreement as a "breakthrough" gun safety initiative—"it will save many young lives"[59]—not everyone was as enthusiastic, with detractors occupying both Bedrock and Cosmopolitan America. Representatives of the NRA, while noting that the organization certainly favored voluntary actions over mandates, nonetheless commented, "If President Clinton really cared about reducing firearms access among children, he would stand up and use the bully pulpit of the White House to urge everyone to take an N.R.A. firearms safety course."[60] On the other side, a representative of the Violence Policy Center scathingly remarked, "By endorsing this voluntary effort by the industry . . . President Clinton has guaranteed that no mandatory federal standards will be developed. . . . The big winners today are America's gun manufacturers—not America's children."[61]

Already displeased that three major California handgun producers refused to accept the voluntary agreement[62]—resulting in a less than 100 percent coverage rate—Senator Barbara Boxer of California introduced an amendment in July 1998 that directed all dealers to include a trigger lock with every handgun sold. Although the Senate killed that amendment, it did approve an amendment mandating that dealers have locks available for sale; and funded gun safety and educational programs.[63] These votes normally would have moved the trigger lock matter to the legislative back burner, but 10 months later, in April 1999, the senseless and heartrending student massacre at Columbine High School occurred, ensuring that gun regulation remained front and center in the nation's consciousness.

Carried out by 18-year-old Eric Harris and 17-year-old Dylan Klebold, the Columbine shooting attack left 12 students and 1 teacher dead and 24 individuals hurt or wounded. It was the most lethal assault ever committed at an American high school until the massacre at Stoneman Douglas High School in February 2018.[64] Investigators have attributed various motives to the teen-aged assailants, including a desire to rival the destruction and deadly outcomes of the Waco, Texas, siege and the Oklahoma City bombing.[65] The psychopathic killers had used illegally obtained firearms—two shotguns, a semiautomatic TEC-9 pistol, and a semiautomatic Hi-Point carbine—during their murderous spree, and the massacre almost immediately produced public outcries for some type of legislative action. Congress responded, and a month later, after 10 days of often acerbic debate, the Senate passed a crime package bill aimed at stemming juvenile violence. The bill not only mandated handgun trigger locks, but it also mandated background checks for all gun sales at gun shows and pawnshops—partially addressing the gun show loophole that so vexed many ardent gun control advocates. As president of the Senate, Vice President Al Gore cast the tie-breaking vote, ensuring the bill's passage.[66] A month later, in June 1999, when the bill came before the House, Democrats and Republicans could not agree on a number of amendments to the proposed legislation, and the juvenile crime bill, with the first major additions to the country's gun regulations in five years, went down in defeat, rejected by a House vote of 280 to 147.[67]

At first glance, Bedrock America's intransigence on a gun safety feature as innocuous as trigger locks may appear inexplicable and self-defeating. From a public relations perspective, the practical arguments marshaled against such locks—increasing gun owners' costs, delaying emergency gun use, unlikely owner compliance, low existing firearm accident rates, and so on[68]—surely cannot offset the advocacy advantage given Cosmopolitan America in portraying gun rights proponents as coldhearted, unfeeling extremists more concerned about their guns than about their children. So why fight a battle where winning is so potentially costly?

Understanding the animus here is to grasp how gun rights advocates regard virtually all the regulatory demands of Cosmopolitan America. Regardless of how reasonable and acceptable a gun control proposal may first appear, it will invariably have consequences that are neither reasonable nor acceptable. As a case relevant to gun safety regulations, Bedrock America points to the Gun Free School Zones Act (GFSZA), passed as part of President George H. W. Bush's Crime Control Act of 1990. The act prohibits unlicensed individuals from carrying firearms on school property and on public property within 1,000 feet of a grade school or high school.[69] Despite its original benign intent, in developed areas of the country with numerous grade and high schools, the GFSZA has made it almost impossible for an unlicensed but legal firearms owner to travel any distance with a gun without entering a gun-free zone, breaking the law. Similarly, the GFSZA has prevented hunters from using locally approved hunting areas because the hunting forest was within 1,000 feet of a local school. In another application of the act, a prosecutor secured a conviction against a woman who kept a firearm in her public housing apartment because the publicly owned apartment fell under the jurisdiction of the act, being within 1,000 feet of a school. Even off-duty law enforcement officers cannot carry firearms in a school zone without violating GFSZA.[70] More astonishingly, BATF has noted that, while a licensed gun owner can

CHAPTER EIGHT

Cultural Ascendancy: 2001–2016

With President George W. Bush, a Republican and former Texas governor, taking up residency in the White House in January 2001, the political winds blowing across the country shifted in favor of Bedrock America. Gun rights proponents saw Bush as one of their own, even though he often endorsed "commonsense" gun controls[1] and tended to vacillate on important gun issues. Like his father, former president George H. W. Bush, his firearms stands sometimes angered both sides. During his first presidential campaign, Bush had stated that he favored the assault weapons ban, and as the ban's expiration deadline approached, he even implied a readiness to make it permanent. This stance significantly provoked the gun rights community, with one Internet firearms publisher noting, "There are a lot of gun owners who worked hard to put President Bush into office, and there are a lot of gun owners who feel betrayed by him."[2] But when the extension never happened, Cosmopolitan America excoriated Bush for not putting enough pressure on Congress to extend the ban: "In a secret deal, [Bush] chose his powerful friends in the gun lobby over the police officers and families he promised to protect."[3]

Nonetheless, despite his seemingly ambivalent attitudes toward gun control—Bush supported calls for trigger locks, *if* they were voluntary programs; he supported background checks, *if* they did not entail a waiting period; and he supported handgun possession, *if* the individual was 21 or older[4]—Bedrock America achieved major victories in both legislative and judicial arenas during Bush's eight-year presidency, and that momentum continued well beyond his administration. In the years that followed his two terms, despite the Democrats reclaiming the White House with an anti-gun president, Cosmopolitan America struggled to deter gun rights advocates determined to not just impede new gun control regulations but to expand gun rights by repealing (or at least relaxing) prohibitions already in place. This lack of success was all the more notable since Cosmopolitan America had an ally in the Oval Office in the person of President Barack Obama. During this ongoing struggle between the two Americas, severely disturbed mass murderers on several occasions used semiautomatic firearms to spree kill, with each new shooting focusing attention on the weapons involved and reviving clamors for regulatory solutions. But even these horrifying incidents failed to slow Bedrock America's growing ascendency in the gun culture war.

The PLCAA: Saving the Firearms Business

From a gun rights perspective, the Protection of Lawful Commerce in Arms Act (PLCAA) of 2005 was the outstanding legislative accomplishment of the Bush administration. Hailed by the NRA's Wayne LaPierre as the "most significant piece of pro-gun legislation in twenty years,"[5] the PLCAA shielded gun manufacturers and distributors from the kinds of tort lawsuits brought by New Orleans and Chicago years earlier. Based on novel extensions of traditional product liability law, these municipal lawsuits aimed to establish gun regulation through litigation, with gun manufacturers either agreeing to implement the municipalities' firearms limitations and measures or face eventual bankruptcy defending themselves in court. Although the gun industry fought and won the first of these liability cases brought to court, the threat of ongoing municipal litigation remained real, as was the possibility of eventual bankruptcy.

To avoid the cost of litigation, one major American firearms manufacturer, Smith & Wesson (S&W), had even negotiated a compact with the Clinton administration in 2000 in which it promised to implement a menu of "gun safety" measures. The S&W compact went well beyond just adding additional safety mechanisms to the guns themselves. S&W agreed to supply firearms only to those dealers and distributors willing to enforce waiting periods and who would carry substantial liability insurance. Additionally, these dealers and distributors could not carry certain legal semiautomatic rifles and magazines and had to agree to not sell firearms at gun shows that allowed legal private sales. S&W itself promised to avoid marketing firearms to young shooters and to earmark 1 percent of its revenues to advertising campaigns highlighting dangers associated with gun ownership. The company further agreed to support efforts to develop "smart" gun technology, to carry out "ballistic fingerprinting" of every handgun manufactured, and to several other demands favored by gun control advocates.[6]

While the S&W compact may have precluded the litigation worrying the industry, it did so by voluntarily accepting many restrictions that the shooting fraternity had vigorously fought. Not surprisingly, gun rights proponents reacted extremely negatively to the S&W compact, with the NRA labeling the pact a "sellout" and suggesting that "the true intent of this agreement is to force down the throats of an entire lawful industry anti-gun policies rejected by Congress, rejected by legislatures across America, and rejected by the judges who have dismissed their lawsuits in whole or in part nearly without exception."[7] The CEO of the National Shooting Sports Foundation, Robert Delfay, noted that S&W had "violated a trust with their customers and with the entire firearms industry."[8] Gun groups and retailers organized boycotts of the company, and individual gun buyers inundated the company with angry calls and faxes. Distributors either abandoned the S&W handgun line or threatened to do so.[9]

Ironically, gun control advocates were also unhappy with the pact. Kristen Rand, of the Violence Policy Center, criticized the agreement for loopholes that would likely allow S&W to skirt the more innovative elements of the pact, such as smart gun technology, while getting credit for actions that the firm had already instituted (e.g., the inclusion of trigger locks with their handguns). She argued, "To settle these lawsuits that have put a lot of pressure on the industry and that have the potential of leading to real regulations, it was a tremendous step backwards." She also noted that, short of having a watchman in every gun shop in America, S&W could not really police the restrictions imposed on their dealers.[10]

Other gun control advocates were equally unenthusiastic. Garen Wintemute, the director of UC Davis' Violence Prevention Center, felt that the agreement, while "a good first step," fell short of adequately regulating the industry. Similarly, the director of the Johns Hopkins Center for Gun Policy and Research, Stephen Teret, saw benefit in the pact but feared few other manufacturers would accept it. Kristen Rand echoed this concern: "There will be a firestorm in the industry in which other gun manufacturers will treat Smith & Wesson as a pariah. In the gun culture, Clinton equals Satan, and they will see that Smith has just made a deal with Satan."[11]

Realizing that the agreement with S&W was of little value unless the rest of the industry joined the pact, the Clinton administration proposed that police forces purchase firearms only from manufacturers endorsing the accord. The administration also threatened to file a federal lawsuit against recalcitrant manufacturers, joining the suing municipalities in court. Regardless, no other firearms manufacturers joined S&W, and the backlash that S&W suffered was substantial. Before the year was out, the company had to suspend most of its manufacturing and layoff 15 percent of its workforce. Ed Shultz, the CEO, had to step down, and in 2001—a bit more than a year after S&W had made its "deal with Satan"—the British conglomerate that owned the company sold the firm for a small fraction of its purchase price 20 years earlier.[12]

Although the firearms industry prevailed over S&W's potentially disastrous defection, the original problem confronting the manufacturers—ruinous litigation—remained. But by this time, the generally gun-friendly Bush administration controlled the White House, and President Bush adamantly opposed the municipal lawsuits targeting the firearms industry.[13] The industry lobbied the Bush administration and the GOP-controlled Congress for a legislative solution to their litigation difficulties, and in October 2005, Bush signed the PLCAA into law. The act gave firearms manufacturers and dealers broad immunity from suits stemming from the criminal or unlawful misuse of firearms or ammunition—the kind of suits brought by the municipalities—but it did not shield them from legal actions based on traditional product liability grounds, such as defective manufacturing, unsafe design, fraudulent product claims, and so forth.[14]

In signing the act, Bush succeeded in ending the lawsuits threatening to bankrupt the industry, but not in ending Cosmopolitan America's claims that firearms manufacturers and distributors could do more to enhance gun safety. Gun control proponents have condemned the PLCAA as a major obstacle to the development of safer firearms and sales procedures. They assert that without the fear of civil liability, gun manufacturers will simply disregard more expensive but safer design choices, and distributors will resist more complicated but more secure sales procedures.[15] For Cosmopolitan America, although the PLCAA had finally made the inclusion of trigger locks mandatory with the sale of handguns, this small increase in gun safety did not offset the greater safety increases potentially stymied by the act.

Additionally, gun control advocates have frequently criticized the act as unfairly preventing gun victims from pursuing legal claims against irresponsible manufacturers and distributors. Referring to the PLCAA in an Iowa 2015 campaign event, Hillary Clinton asserted that "[gun manufacturers] are the only business in America that is wholly protected from any kind of liability. They can sell a gun to someone they know they shouldn't and they won't be sued. There will be no consequences."[16] Similarly, the Giffords Law Center to Prevent Gun Violence stated that "when Congress passed the Protection of Lawful Commerce in Arms Act in 2005, our leaders made the gun industry immune from nearly all lawsuits, leaving families of gun violence without an avenue to seek justice."[17] These criticisms are probably best viewed as hyperbole in Cosmopolitan America's propaganda war with Bedrock America. Clinton's assertion in particular was simply incorrect; the act specifically allows legal action in cases where a retailer knowingly sells a firearm to a prohibited person or is negligent in some manner.[18] Further, as noted, the act offers no protection from lawsuits based on traditional product liability grounds. For Cosmopolitan America, though, the PLCAA represented a major strategic setback, and these dubious assertions offered a basis, and a hope, for eventual repeal.

Supreme Court Appointments and Landmark Cases

In the same year that Congress legislated the PLCAA and Bush signed it into law, equally significant judicial events impacted the country's gun culture. In 2005, Chief Justice William Rehnquist, having served on the Supreme Court for over 30 years, died in office, and Sandra Day O'Connor, the first woman to serve on the Court, announced her impending retirement. These developments gave President Bush the opportunity to influence the Court's judicial orientation with two new justices. He nominated John Roberts as the new chief justice and Samuel Alito as the new associate justice to replace Day O'Connor. Like his mentor Rehnquist, Roberts had a moderately conservative judicial orientation, while Alito's orientation was staunchly conservative.[19] Their confirmations tended to move an already conservative-leaning Court even further to the right, and several years later, the impact of these appointments for Cosmopolitan America would become evident in two historic firearms cases that overturned handgun bans, first in Washington, D.C., and then in the rest of the country. Both cases turned on 5–4 split decisions of the Court, and in both cases, John Roberts and Samuel Alito voted with the majority.[20]

The first of these momentous decisions, *District of Columbia et al. v. Heller* (2008), struck down the District's Firearms Control Regulation Act, a statute dating back to 1975 that forbade residents from owning a handgun (except those registered prior to the law) and mandated that they keep rifles and shotguns unloaded and disassembled or secured by a trigger lock. The Supreme Court concluded that such a sweeping ban on handguns and requirements making other firearms inoperable and virtually useless for home defense infringed on an individual's right to keep and bear arms, violated the Second Amendment, and were unconstitutional. However, the practical significance of the Court's decision did not rest just on the overturning of the District's decades-old gun control regulation; it rested on the explicit and unambiguously stated finding—for the first time in Supreme Court jurisprudence—that the Second Amendment protects an individual's right to possess a firearm unconnected with militia service and to use that firearm for traditionally lawful purposes.[21]

Background and Reactions to the *Parker/Heller* Case

Astonishingly, the *Heller* case almost never made it to the Supreme Court, and the force responsible for nearly roadblocking the process was not Cosmopolitan America but Bedrock America's own NRA. Fearing a potentially unfavorable Supreme Court ruling, the association initially attempted to avoid Supreme Court involvement by supporting legislation—the D.C. Personal Protection Act—that would have repealed the D.C. gun ban. Normally, gun rights activists would have rallied behind such a bill, but passage of this act would have preempted the U.S. Court of Appeals case, *Parker v. District of Columbia* (*Heller*'s precursor), that was already examining the constitutionality of the District's gun control regulations. Regardless of the appeals court's eventual ruling, it was clear that the losing side would surely take the case to the Supreme Court. However, if Congress struck down the D.C. gun ban *legislatively*, Bedrock America did not even have to chance a potential loss in the country's highest court.[22]

As a senior fellow at the Cato Institute, a libertarian think tank focused on public advocacy, Robert Levy had organized and financed the *Parker* case (which became *Heller* after the appeals court ruled that only Dick Heller, of the original six appellants, had standing to sue). He pointedly disagreed with this NRA strategy. Levy believed that a legislative repeal of the D.C. gun ban would not prevent a future, more liberal Congress from simply overturning the repeal and that, in any case, a legislative repeal would have no reach beyond the District. In contrast, an unambiguous Supreme Court decision would reverberate across the country, and he believed that the likelihood of a favorable decision, given the Court's conservative makeup after the addition of Roberts and Alito, seemed high. Levy also worried that a legislative repeal would simply allow some future firearms case to reach the Supreme Court, one with much less sympathetic appellants—perhaps murderers or drug dealers.

For the *Parker* case, Levy had carefully selected and vetted six sympathetic plaintiffs. One of the plaintiffs was Shelly Parker, a software designer and former nurse being threatened by the neighborhood thugs she wanted to banish. Another was Dick Heller, a licensed special police officer for the District who carried a gun on the job but who was still prohibited from having one in his home. In the end, the NRA decided to support the *Parker/Heller* litigation and filed an amicus brief with the Court arguing that the D.C. ban was unconstitutional.[23]

Reactions to the *Heller* decision were swift. Bedrock America rejoiced in the Court's vindication of its "individual rights" view of the Second Amendment and immediately set out to litigate other statutes that were unlikely to withstand a Second Amendment challenge. Shortly after the *Heller* decision, the NRA filed lawsuits against Chicago's ban on handguns, the *McDonald* case, and San Francisco's ban on handguns in public housing, the *Guy Montag Doe* suit.

In contrast, the *Heller* decision filled Cosmopolitan America with disbelief and confusion. The ruling represented a serious setback for gun control advocates, both in the practical matter of determining and crafting acceptable firearms regulations—*Heller* had made it clear that while individuals had the right to keep and bear arms, that right was not completely unfettered—and in the philosophical matter of reconciling Cosmopolitan America's "collectivist-militia" view of the Second Amendment with the Court's seemingly new interpretation of past judicial history. Beginning with Justice John Paul Stevens's dissent, much initial reaction in Cosmopolitan America to the Court's majority opinion bordered on outright rejection, with gun control proponents simply asserting that the Court's adjudication of the *Heller* case was flawed. Others tried to suggest that the ruling was not as significant as it first appeared. Justice Stevens, for example, asserted that the majority opinion, penned by Justice Antonin Scalia, rested on a "strained and unpersuasive reading" of the text and history of the Second Amendment and that the Court's decision, by radically misinterpreting an earlier Supreme Court case (*United States v. Miller*), had produced "a dramatic upheaval in the law."[24] Ten years later, having retired from the Court, Stevens would go even further by calling for the actual repeal of the Second Amendment.[25]

Other gun control advocates followed in a similar vein, with some commentators painting the ruling as "very troubling . . . a complete reversal of the court's previous interpretation of the Second Amendment, set forth 70 years ago in *United States v. Miller*,"[26] or as a questionable reading of the amendment—one that the Founders never intended—derived primarily from long-standing, ongoing NRA political and public opinion campaigns to create an individual right to arms where one did not exist: "There is not a single word about an individual's right to a gun for self-defense or recreation"[27] in the amendment or in Madison's notes from the Constitutional Convention. Another gun control proponent, Saul Cornell, a chaired professor of American history at Fordham University and a specialist in early American constitutional thought, characterized the *Heller* ruling as an "incoherent and historically dishonest" decision that cast aside "more than 75 years of established precedent" in holding that individuals have a right to possess firearms for personal use.[28] Other analysts, while noting the decision's enormous symbolic significance, downplayed its realistic impact on common gun regulations, emphasizing the decision's acknowledgment of several "presumptively lawful" regulatory measures, such as prohibitions on the possession of firearms by felons and the mentally ill.[29]

Clarifying the Second Amendment

Cosmopolitan America's vitriolic reaction to the *Heller* decision, reflecting more than the usual emotional response of a sports team to an unfavorable call, partially explains the origins of the rift separating the two Americas. The rift centers on how a reasonable person should interpret the words of the Second Amendment, given its curious sentence construction, and on how definitively prior legal examinations have already answered this question. The *Heller* decision considered both issues.

Scalia's analysis separated the amendment into two clauses, a prefatory clause noting the necessity of a well-regulated militia for keeping the country secure and a substantive (or "operative") clause denoting the specific right affirmed: the right of the people to keep and bear arms free of government infringement. Scalia argued that the prefatory clause offered a clarifying purpose for the substantive clause, but that such an introductory statement—common in legal documents of the founding era—did *not* limit the scope of the substantive clause. He noted that this interpretation followed a long-standing principle in American law whereby a statute's preamble cannot control the statute's enacting part, if the enacting part is unambiguously expressed. He further argued, using comparative analysis with the Bill of Rights' other amendments, comparisons with contemporary state constitutions, and detailed linguistic analysis, that the meaning of "people" and the "right to keep and bear arms" in the Second Amendment's substantive clause was clear and unambiguous and denoted an individual right to possess and use firearms.[30]

Scalia argued that this interpretation reflected

> the widely understood [notion] that the Second Amendment, like the First and Fourth Amendments, codified a *pre-existing* right. The very text of the Second Amendment implicitly recognizes the pre-existence of the right and declares only that "it shall not be infringed." As [the Court] said in *United States v. Cruikshank*, "This is not a right granted by the Constitution. Neither is it in any manner dependent upon that instrument for its existence. The Second Amendment declares that it shall not be infringed."[31]

Scalia tied this preexisting right to possess and carry weapons to self-defense in case of confrontation. Referencing the eminent English jurist Blackstone's interpretation of the arms provision of the English Bill of Rights—"the natural right of resistance and self-preservation; the right of having and using arms for self-preservation and defense"—Scalia concluded that this description of the right clearly precluded any claims that the right was somehow limited to military service or militia duty.[32]

While Scalia and four other justices (and much of Bedrock America) believed his analysis of the historical evidence plainly showed how a reasonable person should interpret the Second Amendment, four other justices (and much of Cosmopolitan America) found the majority's analysis to be unpersuasive and deeply flawed. In rejecting Scalia's analysis, Justice Stevens argued that the essential issue was not whether the Second Amendment protected a "collective right" or an "individual right," but whether the *scope* of the protected right was narrow or broad. The amendment plainly encompassed a narrow right of individuals to use weapons for military purposes, but did it also protect a broader right to possess and use firearms for nonmilitary purposes, such as for self-defense and hunting? His conclusion was that it did not:

> The Second Amendment was adopted to protect the right of the people to maintain a well-regulated militia. Neither the text of the Amendment nor the arguments advanced by its proponents evidenced the slightest interest in limiting any legislature's authority to regulate private civilian use of firearms. Specifically, there is no indication that the Framers of the Amendment intended to enshrine the common-law right of self-defense in the Constitution.[33]

By placing more weight on the amendment's prefatory clause than Scalia did, and by relegating self-defense to a common-law right rather than a constitutional right, Stevens assailed the underlying logic of Scalia's analysis. Stevens argued that the majority opinion failed to recognize the crucial guidance provided by the prefatory clause in interpreting the substantive clause. Given its "militia" reference and the strong military connotations of "to keep and bear arms," Stevens contended that it was more persuasive to infer that the right the amendment champions centers on bearing arms in state militia service only. Further, on just logical grounds, had the framers of the amendment wanted to protect a personal right to arms, they could have expressed their intentions more clearly.

Stevens also rejected the various historical evidence Scalia used for interpreting the Second Amendment—the wording of state constitutions' firearms clauses, the relevance of Blackstone's *Commentaries*, and so forth—but the sharpest contention between the two involved past judicial rulings. Stevens asserted that these had conclusively settled the "meaning" of the Second Amendment and that the present ruling failed to accord these prior rulings appropriate deference. Focusing specifically on *United States v. Miller*, Stevens noted that the earlier Court's analysis of the Second Amendment in this 1939 case, and its ultimate ruling, convincingly supported a narrow "militia/collective-right" interpretation. It also established a precedent that numerous lower courts had cited and followed in firearms cases for seven decades. Additionally, as federal laws regulating firearms had withstood constitutional challenges since at least the 1930s, Stevens suggested that a reversal of precedent in a case that was essentially no different from past cases was inconsistent and made no sense.

Scalia's analysis of *Miller* differed substantially from the one offered by Stevens. Revolving around Jack Miller and Frank Layton—individuals charged with the interstate transportation of an untaxed and unregistered short-barreled shotgun in violation of the National Firearms Act—the *Miller* case reversed the District court's ruling that parts of the National Firearms Act violated the Second Amendment and were unconstitutional and reinstated the defendants' indictment under the NFA. The issue separating Stevens and Scalia was *why* the indictment did not violate the defendants' Second Amendment rights. In Stevens reading of *Miller*, the Second Amendment "protects the right to keep and bear arms for certain military purposes, but it does not curtail the legislature's power to regulate the nonmilitary use and ownership of weapons."[34] As the defendants were not using the shotgun in a military context, its regulation did not violate the Second Amendment and legitimately fell within the scope of the NFA.

Scalia agreed that the regulation did not violate the Second Amendment, but for an entirely different reason. In Scalia's reading, the *Miller* case had nothing to do with "bearing arms" for nonmilitary purposes. Rather, it was about transporting an unregistered short-barreled shotgun—a type of weapon not eligible for Second Amendment protection.

Scalia quoted *Miller*, "In the absence of any evidence [showing that a short-barreled shotgun] has some reasonable relationship to the preservation or efficiency of a well-regulated militia, we cannot say that the Second Amendment guarantees the right to keep and bear such an instrument."[35]

Stevens repeatedly noted that the heart of *Miller* was not about the difference between assorted kinds of weapons ("between muskets and saw-off shotguns") but between "the military and nonmilitary use and possession of guns."[36] Scalia disagreed, arguing that if the Court believed that the Second Amendment only protected those serving in the militia, it would have simply stated that the two defendants were not militiamen rather than examine the character of the weapon they transported. Further, he observed that the Court could have used *Miller* to explicitly clarify the nature of the Second Amendment, as the solicitor general had even made the argument that the right was a collective one, but that the Court had declined to do so. According to Scalia, the reasonable inference was that the Court saw the Second Amendment as conferring an individual right to bear arms, but only arms having a reasonable relationship to the preservation or efficiency of a well-regulated militia. More concretely, "*Miller* stands only for the proposition that the Second Amendment right, whatever its nature, extends only to certain types of weapons."[37]

Aside from disagreeing about the appropriate interpretation of *Miller*, Scalia and Stevens also disagreed about the thoroughness of the Court's examination of the Second Amendment in the *Miller* case, which was important for gauging the proper degree of deference future Courts should accord the case's ruling. Stevens argued that the historical and legal analysis in *Miller* covered much the same ground that *Heller* examined, thus prompting questions about how the two Courts could arrive at markedly different conclusions. In reply, Scalia rejected the assertion that *Miller* represented a meticulous examination of the Second Amendment. He noted that the Court heard from neither the defendants nor their attorney during oral arguments; one of the defendants had died, and the other had disappeared. Arguing that this fact alone curtailed the Court's consideration of Second Amendment issues, Scalia also noted that the government's own short two-page brief recognized that prior court rulings had offered various interpretations of the Second Amendment. While the brief observed that early English law did not guarantee an unrestricted right to bear arms and that *Aymette v. State* found that the Second Amendment protected the uses of arms only in relation to militia work (not self-defense), the final section acknowledged that "some courts have said that the right to bear arms includes the right of the individual to have them for the protection of his person and property" but that weapons commonly used by criminals—such as sawed-off shotguns—are not protected.[38] Scalia concluded his rejection of *Miller* as a meticulous analysis of the Second Amendment by observing that "the Government's *Miller* brief thus provided scant discussion of the history of the Second Amendment—and the Court was presented with no counterdiscussion."[39]

Scalia then analyzed the types of weapons *Miller* allowed, focusing on the phrase found in Miller: "part of ordinary military equipment." If interpreted to mean that the Second Amendment protects only those weapons that are useful in warfare, the restrictions on machine guns (found in the National Firearms Act) would violate the Second Amendment as unconstitutional infringements.[40] Scalia rejected this interpretation, contending that a more accurate reading required a consideration of what came next: "Ordinarily when called for [militia] service [able-bodied] men were expected to appear bearing arms supplied by themselves and of the kind in common use at the time."[41] In this light, as militiamen used the same weapons for militia service as they used for self-defense and home protection, Scalia concluded that the Second Amendment protected commonly used weapons at any given time.

In making his dissent, Stevens contended that "for most of our history, the invalidity of Second-Amendment-based objections to firearms regulations has been well settled and uncontroversial."[42] Scalia dismissed this assertion succinctly, "For most of our history the question did not present itself." As for the many judges that Stevens claimed relied on *Miller*, Scalia further noted, "If so, they over-read Miller. And their erroneous reliance upon an uncontested and virtually unreasoned case cannot nullify the reliance of millions of Americans (as our historical analysis has shown) upon the true meaning of the right to keep and bear arms."[43]

These exchanges between Stevens and Scalia did not represent all the objections to *Heller* raised by the Court's dissenters. Justice Breyer argued that even if the Second Amendment guaranteed a personal right to own and possess firearms, the District's prohibition still remained valid, given the many historical precedents establishing the government's authority to place restrictions on firearms. Further, because handgun violence represented a uniquely urban problem, Breyer argued that an "interest-balancing" approach (weighing city needs against individual rights) would support the constitutionality of the District's firearms regulation. Scalia rejected these arguments also. He contended that the precedents cited by Breyer imposed minor fines and penalties on those violating the regulations and thus provided little support for the severe restrictions imposed by the District's regulations. As for Breyer's "balancing" approach, Scalia observed that the Court subjected no other enumerated constitutional right to such an analysis and that the very enumeration of the right forbade such an approach. As he put it, even the Judicial Branch cannot "decide on a case-by-case basis whether [an enumerated] right is really worth insisting upon. A constitutional guarantee subject to future judges' assessments of its usefulness is no constitutional guarantee at all."[44]

The *Heller* decision vindicated Bedrock America's interpretation of the Second Amendment and gave gun rights advocates a stunning triumph in their battle with gun control proponents. While not all gun enthusiasts were impressed with *Heller*—some reacted negatively to Scalia's assertion that the amendment was subject to reasonable prohibitions[45]—Cosmopolitan America lambasted the decision and offered the strongest critical reactions. Juliet Leftwich, the legal director of the Legal Community Against Violence, argued that *Heller* created a "new" constitutional right, and in doing so, "wreaked havoc in the courts . . . creating legal uncertainty where there had been none."[46] Jeff Toobin, a senior legal analyst for CNN, asserted that the *Heller* decision represented "a novel interpretation of the Second Amendment" that stemmed from the ongoing machinations of the National Rifle Association.[47] Michael Waldman, the president of the Brennan Center for Justice at the NYU School of Law, claimed that "from 1888, when law review articles were first indexed, through 1959, every single one on the Second Amendment concluded that it did not guarantee an individual right to a gun."[48] Similarly, Saul Cornell, a professor of American history, characterized Scalia's vision of the Constitution and his "theory" of gun rights as "downright radical," one that "would have shocked the framers of the Second Amendment."[49] In the end, though, regardless of these criticisms, Antonin Scalia, Associate Justice of the Supreme Court, had the last word, "The District's ban on handgun possession in the home violates the Second Amendment, [and] the District must permit [Heller] to register his handgun and must issue him a license to carry it in the home."[50]

A Second Landmark Decision: *McDonald v. City of Chicago*

Two years after *Heller*, the country had a new president, the Democrat Barack Obama, and a new case before the Supreme Court with significant implications for gun policies and politics in America. As a retired maintenance engineer living on Chicago's South Side, Otis McDonald had watched his neighborhood deteriorate over the years, taken over by gangsters, thugs, and drug dealers. His house had been broken into three times and his garage twice. McDonald wanted a handgun to carry in the house and to keep in his bedroom at night; the shotguns he owned were simply too unwieldy for nighttime self-defense. He believed that the possibility of confronting homeowners armed with pistols and revolvers might deter thugs and burglars from their lawless activities.[51] However, like Washington, D.C., Chicago had enacted such stringent gun control regulations that it was impossible for Chicagoans to legally own a handgun. Although the city mandated that residents register all firearms, it then refused to accept handgun registrations after passing a 1982 handgun ban. Thus, shortly after *Heller* struck down the District's handgun ban, McDonald joined with three other Chicagoans in challenging Chicago's ban. The Illinois State Rifle Association and the Second Amendment Foundation sponsored the litigation, with Alan Gura, who had successfully argued the *Heller* case, serving as lead counsel on this case also.[52]

At issue was whether *Heller's* Second Amendment findings applied only to federal jurisdictions (like the District of Columbia) or whether they also applied to the states and, by extension, to local governments. McDonald and the other plaintiffs argued that the right guaranteed by the Second Amendment was so fundamental and so deeply rooted in the country's history and traditions that the Court must protect it not just from federal infringement but from state and local government infringement as well; that is, the Court must "incorporate" the Second Amendment, making it as applicable to state and local laws as to federal laws.

In a 5–4 decision, the Supreme Court agreed with the plaintiffs that the Second Amendment warranted incorporation, and Justice Samuel Alito (together with Justices Roberts, Scalia, and Kennedy) ruled that the Due Process Clause of the Fourteenth Amendment incorporated the Second Amendment right that *Heller* recognized. Justice Clarence Thomas also supported incorporation and concurred, but he did so by citing the Privileges and Immunities Clause of the Fourteenth Amendment. Justices Breyer, Ginsburg, and Sotomayor dissented, arguing that, regardless of *Heller*, the Framers of the Constitution did not write the Second Amendment to safeguard a private right of armed self-protection and that no consensus existed establishing such a right as "fundamental." Justice Stevens also dissented, but on the basis that the late 19th-century Court decision in *U.S. v. Cruikshank* correctly settled the question of Second Amendment incorporation—by rejecting it.[53]

This 2010 Court ruling effectively made Chicago's decades-long ban on handguns unconstitutional and forced the city to allow residents to keep pistols and revolvers in their homes for self-defense. In commenting on the decision that carried his name, McDonald noted that his challenge to the Chicago regulation involved more than just a desire for increased personal protection. As a black man, he felt he had a duty to stand up for the rights that slavery had stolen from early African Americans. Referencing the "slave codes" common in Southern states prior to the Civil War and then the "black codes" afterward, McDonald noted that the codes had prohibited slaves from possessing guns and kept guns out of the hands of freed blacks. He observed, "There was a wrong done a long time ago that dates back to slavery time. I could feel the spirit of those people running through me as I sat in the Supreme Court."[54]

As momentous as *Heller* and *McDonald* were, the original fears of gun control advocates that the rulings would create chaos in firearms regulation proved overblown. As Scalia himself noted, the *Heller* decision did not confer an unlimited "right to keep and carry any weapon whatsoever in any manner whatsoever and for whatever purpose."[55] It left intact reasonable, "presumptively lawful" regulations and suggested that analyses and examinations in future courts would continue to clarify the scope of permissible regulation. In the decade since the ruling, legal challenges to gun laws have allowed the courts to do precisely this, offering increasing guidance on when a regulation's severity triggers Second Amendment concerns or on determining the appropriate level of judicial scrutiny— rational basis, intermediate scrutiny, or strict scrutiny—when a statute potentially violates the Second Amendment.

Pragmatically, an examination[56] of over 1,000 lower court cases focused on gun challenges since *Heller* confirmed that the ruling was neither the disaster Cosmopolitan America anticipated nor the silver bullet Bedrock America had hoped for. Covering the period from 2008 through February 2016, the examination categorized every available Second Amendment decision at the state and federal levels in both trial and appellate courts. Of the 1,153 cases in which a litigant challenged a gun regulation as unconstitutional, 108 (about 9 percent) succeeded. Although this low success rate could indicate that courts remain hostile to the Second Amendment—narrowing *Heller* from below—the analysis revealed that, in the majority of unsuccessful cases, the challenges simply failed based on the "long-standing prohibitions" directly discussed in *Heller*. As an example, the investigators noted that 24 percent of the cases involved felon-in-possession laws—gun regulations *Heller* specifically mentions as permissible—and, unsurprisingly, 99 percent of these challenges failed. More generally, about 75 percent of the challenges involved criminal cases, where defendants confronting serious legal charges have strong motivation to take a "kitchen sink" approach and make whatever defense they can, including unlikely-to-succeed gun arguments. In these circumstances, only about 6 percent of Second Amendment claims were upheld.[57]

For Cosmopolitan America, the findings appear reassuring: dire predictions aside, the *Heller* and *McDonald* decisions did not upend decades of gun control regulation in the United States, and they seem unlikely to pose an insurmountable barrier to reasonable—whatever "reasonable" may imply for an individual—regulation in the future. For Bedrock America, the findings may appear disappointing at first: the legal limitations placed by *Heller* and *McDonald* on gun control rulings are not nearly as extensive as desired. But in actuality, the study's results may not justify such disappointment. As the investigators observed, the low success rate of Second Amendment litigation may simply underscore Bedrock America's achievement in blocking strict gun regulations to begin with. For example, the handgun bans of Chicago and Washington, D.C., were the only two such laws in America's major cities.[58] From this perspective, egregious Second Amendment infringements are unusual, and gun rights litigators simply have few gun regulations worth challenging.[59]

Mass Shootings and Classroom Killers

With President Barack Obama's election in 2008, Bedrock America girded itself for an onslaught of gun control initiatives. As an Illinois senator, the new president had a history of supporting gun control legislation, and Democratic administrations traditionally favored anti-gun stances. The NRA had virulently opposed Obama during his first presidential campaign, deriding him as having "a deep-rooted hatred of firearm freedoms,"[60] and in the 2012 election, it advised its members that, should he win a second term, he would "push the most extreme elements of his gun-ban agenda to every corner of America."[61]

Despite these apprehensions, Bedrock America had little to fear from the Obama administration. Although President Obama certainly was fiercely critical of the "gun lobby" and the general availability of firearms, he was unable to drive his agenda through the Congress, which was controlled by the GOP for the last six of his eight years in the White House. His efforts to restrict the size of gun magazines, to expand gun-buyer background checks, to ban gun sales to individuals on "watch" lists, and to reinstate an assault-style weapons ban all failed, and his executive action requiring the Social Security Administration to report mental health disability recipients to the gun-buyer background check system did not survive the next administration. Ironically, the only two major gun laws that Obama signed *expanded* the rights of gun owners—one allowing gun owners to carry firearms in national parks and the other allowing Amtrak passengers to carry firearms in checked baggage.[62] Obama's inability to accomplish "commonsense" gun regulation aside— he once described gun control failure as "the one area where . . . I've been most frustrated and most stymied"—his legacy in this area was unlikely to revolve around gun laws in any case. Obama had to deal with more mass shootings than any of his predecessors, and as president, he had to console the country about such violence over a dozen times.[63]

Mass shootings (typically defined as incidents where a gunman kills four or more victims[64]) have a tragically extensive history in the United States. Such incidents trace back to at least 1949, when Howard Unruh went on his 12-minute "walk of death" through his Camden, New Jersey, community, shooting and killing 13 individuals.[65] They continued through 1966, when Charles Whitman climbed the University of Texas tower, slaying 18 people, and extend past 2007, when Seung-Hui Cho, an undergraduate, wantonly slaughtered 32 students and faculty at the Virginia Polytechnic Institute and State University.[66] So, such heartbreaking violence did not begin with Obama (nor did it end with him), but during his years as president, these horrible massacres roiled the nation on a regular basis.[67]

Murderous mass shooting episodes started early in Obama's tenure as president. In March 2009, Michael McLendon, an angry, depressed misfit harboring grudges against his family and neighbors, used a mix of rifles and a handgun to slay 10 individuals and then himself. McLendon's rampage in Geneva County was the worst mass shooting in Alabama history.[68] A month later, in New York, Jiverly Wong—a naturalized American from Vietnam, feeling disrespected for his poor English, believing himself wronged by the police, depressed, and angry about his employment struggles—entered New York's Binghamton American Civic Association immigration center, where he had taken English-language classes. Wearing a ballistic vest and carrying two Beretta handguns, he shot and killed 13 people before killing himself. Wong's attack was the worst mass shooting in New York State's history.[69] Seven months later, in Fort Hood, Texas, Major Nidal Hasan, an army psychiatrist, decided that he was a "soldier of Allah" and that his religious beliefs obligated him to place the commandments of Islam over any man-made constitution. Determined to act on his religious convictions, Hasan acquired a pair of handguns from a local gun shop (an FN Five-seveN pistol and a Smith & Wesson .357 Magnum revolver), and he fatally shot 13 individuals at the military facility before being severely wounded and apprehended. His shooting rampage was the deadliest mass shooting ever at an American military installation.[70]

The country attempted to understand such bewildering savagery, to find a hidden pattern that might reveal some clarifying insight and perhaps offer a way to prevent more carnage, but none was evident. Comforting the nation on these occasions, President Obama captured the dismal mood of America in describing the shootings as "senseless violence."[71] In the absence of more substantive explanations and solutions, Cosmopolitan America and many of the victims' friends and family vented their anger and sorrow by indicting firearms and the gun laws that enabled the killers.[72] Bedrock America, also angry and grieving, mourned the victims as well but refused to blame inert tools for the murders. Pointing to the killers themselves as the responsible parties, gun rights proponents noted that any solution to violence should necessarily start with restraining violent individuals. In the end, the argument was academic. The nation found no new keys to resolve mass shootings, and in 2012, Obama's first term as president ended as violently has it had begun, with three more spectacularly violent incidents.

In July 2012, the Century 16 multiplex theater in Aurora, Colorado, presented a midnight screening of a then-popular film, *Dark Knight Rising*. James Holmes, who had long suffered from mental illness and had become obsessed with killing,[73] attended the show but slipped out early through an emergency exit. Leaving the exit door ajar, he retrieved from his car a Smith & Wesson AR-15 rifle, a Remington 870 12-gauge shotgun, a .40-caliber Glock pistol, and two tear gas grenades. Upon reentering the theater, Holmes triggered the tear gas canisters and started firing at random individuals. His lethal attack—the second deadliest in Colorado history after the 1999 Columbine High School carnage—left 12 people dead and 70 injured.[74] The following month, motivated by racial hatred, Wade Page—a white supremacist and army veteran who had received a general discharge for misconduct—used a Springfield 9mm pistol to kill six worshippers at the Sikh temple in Oak Creek, Wisconsin. After being wounded by responding police, Page then killed himself.[75] Four months later, in Newtown, Connecticut, Adam Lanza carried out the deadliest grade school/high school shooting in U.S. history. Lanza, who had been diagnosed with a host of physical and mental problems, including Asperger syndrome, obsessive-compulsive disorder, depression, anxiety, and anorexia, first shot and killed his mother, Nancy (a gun enthusiast), thus gaining accessing to her car and firearms. After arming himself with a Bushmaster AR-15 rifle and a 10mm Glock pistol, Lanza then drove to Sandy Hook Elementary School, where he fatally shot 20 children and 6 staff members before killing himself as police arrived.[76]

The country's reactions to these murders largely mirrored responses to earlier shooting incidents. As with other gun-related tragedies, gun sales spiked in Colorado after the Aurora shooting, as well as in California, Georgia, Florida, Oregon, and Washington, as people looked to themselves for self-protection.[77] The tragedy renewed calls from New York mayor Michael Bloomberg to make gun control an election issue and spurred the submission of legislation to ban assault-style rifles and high-capacity magazines.[78] However, the attack in Aurora left Americans' views on gun laws unchanged and did not increase popular support for further gun control—a finding true of previous mass shootings.[79] John Boehner, the Republican Speaker of the House, rejected calls for new gun laws, blaming the murders on a "deranged person," and even the Obama administration declared that the president wanted to work within existing gun laws, not new ones, to prevent dangerous individuals from accessing firearms.[80]

In contrast, the Sandy Hook School massacre, occurring only five months after the mass shooting in Aurora, returned the issue of gun control to center stage and prompted the country to reconsider the efficacy of new legislation. Cosmopolitan America again called for making the background check system universal and urged stringent federal and state restrictions on the manufacture and sale of large-capacity magazines and certain semiautomatic firearms.[81] President Obama, changing his previous stance, promised to make gun control a "central issue" during his second term,[82] and in January 2013, after signing a raft of gun-related executive orders, he also submitted to Congress an additional bundle of firearms proposals. Establishing a task force on gun violence, Obama placed Vice President Joe Biden at its head. At the state level, Andrew Cuomo, the governor of New York, bypassed the normal three-day waiting period and expedited through the New York State legislature the Secure Ammunition and Firearms Enforcement Act (the SAFE Act), described by his administration as the "toughest in the nation."[83] SAFE mandated universal background checks, created a mental health database, closed the gun show loophole, and strengthened the state's ban on assault weapons and high-capacity magazines.

Representing Bedrock America, the NRA challenged the likely effectiveness of these actions. It asserted that gun-free school zones simply made schools attractive targets for deranged murderers and that gun bans offered no protection from such individuals. Instead, the association suggested that schools have an armed police officer on campus, with Congress appropriating funds for such staffing. Wayne LaPierre noted that the NRA would establish a National School Shield Emergency Response Program to foster such efforts. Responding to critics of the plan, he replied, "The only way to stop a monster from killing our kids is to be personally involved and invested in a plan of absolute protection. Would you rather have your 911 call bring a good guy with a gun from a mile away or a minute away?"[84] Cleta Mitchell, an NRA board member, further noted that the Clinton assault weapons ban did not prevent Columbine and that Connecticut's stringent gun laws did not stop the current tragedy: "Gun laws don't stop bad guys with guns from killing people."[85]

The practical impact of these different efforts varied. Federal bills to establish an assault weapons ban and to expand background checks for gun purchases failed in the U.S. Senate due to united Republican opposition, but in Connecticut, a major gun control bill expanding the state's assault weapons ban and limiting magazine capacity passed. Maryland similarly placed new restrictions on firearms, but 10 other states *weakened* restrictions (albeit to a lesser degree than those states that had strengthened restrictions).[86] Gabrielle Giffords (the congress member shot and injured in the 2011 Tucson, Arizona, attack) and her husband, Mark Kelly, formed a gun control advocacy group, Americans for Responsible Solutions, in an attempt to counterbalance NRA influence, while the NRA pointed opponents of its "armed school guards" proposal to the Newtown School Board itself, which voted unanimously in January 2013 to request a police presence in all of its elementary schools.[87] But overall, none of these actions had any discernable impact: mass shootings and appalling tragedy marked President Obama's second term as severely as his first.

The first incident of the second term occurred in September 2013. Aaron Alexis, a delusional man plagued by feelings of persecution and discrimination with a long history of arrests (but no prosecutions), legally obtained a Remington Model 870 shotgun from a Virginia area shooting range and gun shop. Driving to the Washington Navy Yard in Washington, D.C. (where he worked as a civilian subcontractor), he proceeded to kill 12 random individuals working in the Naval Sea Systems Command Building before being shot and killed by police.[88] Seven months later, in April 2014, at Fort Hood, Texas, Army Specialist Ivan Lopez—depressed, anxious, grieving, and in financial trouble—requested leave to attend to some family matters. When denied the leave, he used a Smith & Wesson .45-caliber pistol to kill three soldiers before killing himself.[89] The following month, in Ilsa Vista, California, Eliot Roger—a college dropout with a long history of psychiatric problems, suffering from Asperger syndrome, socially maladjusted and spurned by women—sought retribution for his sexual frustrations and perceived rejections. Using a variety of murder instruments—two knives, a BMW coupe, and three pistols (a Glock 34 and two SIG Sauer P226s)—he killed 6 random individuals and injured 14 others before committing suicide.[90]

As with prior incidents, reactions to these mass shooting ranged along familiar and customary lines. After the Navy Yard killings, Obama ordered public buildings and military installations to fly flags at half-mast and urged Congress to toughen the country's gun laws. Further, gun control activists traveled to Washington to demonstrate their anger over another shooting and to lobby for more stringent gun controls. In contrast, conservative analysts, noting that most military bases prohibit soldiers from carrying guns, argued that gun-free zones fueled the problem and urged Congress and the military to rescind them. The NRA's Wayne LaPierre observed, "When the good guys with guns got there, it stopped."[91] Similarly, after the Fort Hood shooting, a "heartbroken" President Obama declared that the country had to keep firearms out of the hands of the mentally troubled, while gun advocates called for permitting soldiers to carry personal firearms on post.[92] With the Isla Vista shooting, attention centered on both gun control and mental health care, and U.S. Senator Richard Blumenthal of Connecticut hit each theme: "I really, sincerely hope that this tragedy . . . will provide the impetus to bring back measures that would keep guns out of the hands of dangerous people . . . and maybe reconfigure [those measures] to center on mental health."[93] U.S. Senator Dianne Feinstein of California castigated the NRA for its "stranglehold" on gun laws and chided Congress for not passing even "commonsense" gun restrictions.[94] Gun advocates responded by noting that, of all the measures proposed in Congress in the wake of Isla Vista, none would have prevented the shooting.[95]

No new strategies for curtailing mass shootings emerged from any of these reactions, and in the next two years, five more terrible incidents occurred. In June 2015, Dylann Roof, a white supremacist eager to start a race war, used a .45-caliber Glock pistol to murder 9 African American churchgoers in Charleston, South Carolina.[96] The next month, Muhammad Youssef Abdulazeez, a naturalized American citizen with drug and alcohol problems and teroristic leanings, murdered 5 servicemen on two military installations in Chattanooga, Tennessee, using an AK-47 rifle, a 12-gauge shotgun, and a 9mm pistol.[97] In October, an emotionally disturbed man named Christopher Harper-Mercer—mentally unbalanced and afflicted with Asperger syndrome—brought four pistols and a revolver to a community college he attended in Roseburg, Oregon. He proceeded to kill 1 professor and 8 students.[98] Two months later, in San Bernardino, California, Syed Farook and his wife, Tashfeen Malik—homegrown terrorists with a commitment to jihadism and martyrdom—attended a departmental work function/holiday party at the city's Inland Regional Center. There, during the festivities, they shot and murdered 14 of Farook's coworkers using AR-15 rifles and 9mm pistols.[99] Yet, the worst attack was still six months away. That attack occurred in Pulse, a gay nightclub in Orlando, Florida, in June 2016. Omar Mateen, an American Muslim of Afghani heritage seeking vengeance for American airstrikes in Iraq and Syria, armed himself with a Sig Sauer semiautomatic rifle and a Glock 9mm pistol. He obtained his vengeance by killing 49 people and wounding 53 others in the nightclub before being slain by local police.[100]

Forever differing on sources of and solutions to "gun violence," Cosmopolitan and Bedrock America interpreted these violent tragedies differently. Cosmopolitan America, exemplified by President Obama, saw killers who had no trouble obtaining firearms and whose terrible actions "commonsense" gun control might have constrained. Other Democratic Party politicians also viewed the murderous rampages through a gun control lens and demanded that Congress pass tighter gun restrictions, prohibit gun sales to individuals on government watch lists, expand background checks, and use executive orders to limit firearms. Cosmopolitan America's journalistic voice, the *New York Times*, trumpeted the need for more stringent gun control in a front-page editorial—the first in 95 years—as did various media entertainers and celebrities.

For Bedrock America, the tragic shootings had little relevance to weak gun laws or overlooked legislative flaws. Gun violence for this community had never been about the *gun* but about the *violence*—about the angry, deranged, or terroristic shooters who perpetrated the multiple deaths and the mass tragedies. The representatives of Bedrock America—Republican legislators, the NRA, and gun rights activists—focused on the actors in these horrible dramas, noting the recurring roles that mental illness, racial hatred, and violent ideology had in the lives of the murderers. They also emphasized the part unarmed defenselessness played in the deaths of the many victims. Thus, the two Americas were no closer to resolving their differences about the place of firearms in American society than they were in 1911, when New York City passed the original Sullivan Act in the hopes of controlling crime.

Nonetheless, something had indeed changed over the course of a century's time. Bedrock America's judicial triumphs, its victories in stalling new federal legislation even after such horrific incidents, and its growing success in moving attention from the gun to the shooter reflected a considerable reduction in Cosmopolitan America's power to shape the country's attitudes toward firearms. Even worse for gun control proponents, the next presidential election furthered the cultural ascendency of Bedrock America.

CHAPTER NINE

Culture War Assessment:
2017–2018

In November 2016, in an upset election that stunned Cosmopolitan America and overjoyed Bedrock America, Republican Donald Trump defeated Democrat Hillary Clinton to become the 45th president of the United States. His victory was completely unforeseen by all the country's major news outlets and popular political commentators—but not by one advocacy organization. The National Rifle Association early on had endorsed Trump and used its considerable grassroots influence and financial resources to support his campaign. His political triumph was also the association's triumph and the triumph of gun rights proponents across the country. With another gun-friendly president in the White House and Republicans in control of Congress, support for new federal gun restrictions was legislatively improbable, and with the likely appointment of conservative justices to the Supreme Court,[1] past federal restrictions were now even vulnerable to reversal. In the cultural war between the two Americas, Bedrock America was clearly winning.

None of this impacted mass shootings, however. They continued under President Trump much as they had under President Obama. Less than a year into Trump's presidency, Stephen Paddock, for reasons unknown, carried out the deadliest mass shooting ever committed in the United States on October 1, 2017. Firing over 1,100 rounds from his hotel room overlooking a throng of concertgoers in Las Vegas, Nevada, Paddock used an assortment of semiautomatic and bolt-action rifles to murder 58 individuals and wound more than 400 others before killing himself.[2] A month later, in November, Devin Kelley, a social misfit prone to anger and violence, carried out the deadliest mass shooting in Texas history, killing 26 churchgoers in Sutherland Springs, Texas, using an AR-15 rifle.[3] Three months later, in February 2018, Nicholas Cruz, a man with a history of behavioral and mental health problems, including threats to carry out a school shooting, brought a Smith & Wesson AR-15 rifle to the high school that had expelled him and murdered 17 students and staff at the Stoneman Douglas High School in Parkland, Florida.[4]

These recurrent mass shootings, a seemingly permanent feature of life in America, ensured that gun control remained a central political topic across the nation. They also further inflamed passions in both camps of the gun question. Cosmopolitan America's representatives spotlighted and castigated its usual assortment of villains—assault-style rifles, high-capacity magazines, limitations in the federal background check system, the "blood-soaked" NRA—and some new ones: "bump-fire" stocks (a novelty accessory that increases the firing rate of semiautomatic rifles) and age limits thought inappropriately low for rifle purchases.[5] Bedrock America responded with its standard refutation: the problem is not the gun, but the gunman. Commenting on the Sutherland Springs shooting, President Trump observed, "I think that mental health is a problem here. . . . This isn't a guns situation. . . . Fortunately somebody else had a gun [shooting back], otherwise . . . it would have been much worse."[6] After the same shooting, the Texas attorney general noted that such incidents would happen again and called for armed citizens to cut down murderers, whatever their motives, before they had the time to slaughter dozens of innocent victims.[7] But even as Bedrock America's current supremacy in the gun war shifted public attention from the gun to the gunman, Cosmopolitan America did not abandon its faith in gun control as the best solution for eliminating gun violence.[8]

How justifiable is Cosmopolitan America's faith in the efficacy of gun control? Having just explored the country's long, ambivalent relationship with firearms, this question is worth considering. As earlier noted, a person's position on the "gun question" is decidedly value-laden, and surprisingly impervious to rational argument, whether logical, statistical, or philosophical.[9] Thus, the assessment is not aimed at changing personal positions but at examining the strengths and weaknesses of the different rationales that have fueled the gun control debate. The examination may aid individuals in judging which of the two Americas has the stronger case—assuming the person has not already reached a judgment—and in predicting the set of values likely to dominate in the gun culture war in times ahead. For Cosmopolitan America, four main rationales support its gun control orientation: crime prevention, general societal safety, individual personal safety, and an abiding belief that guns have no legitimate place in a truly civilized society. For Bedrock America, four main rationales buttress its gun rights orientation: philosophical, constitutional, political, and pragmatic.

Cosmopolitan America: Crime Prevention

Reducing gun crimes provided the initial impetus for widespread gun regulation in the United States, eventually resulting in New York City's attempt to control easily concealed handguns—the mugger's favorite weapon—through passage of the Sullivan Act in 1911; and in the country's attempt, on the federal level, to control gangster-friendly tommy guns and sawed-off shotguns through passage of the National Firearms Act in 1934. The belief was that the regulations would increase the safety of the average law-abiding citizen, particularly those residing in urban enclaves, by making it difficult for criminals (and other suspect individuals) to obtain these kinds of firearms. Additionally, while acknowledging that gun regulations would also discourage an unknown number of noncriminals from obtaining firearms (due to the fees and increased effort involved), proponents perceived benefit even in this undesirable by-product of regulation: by reducing the overall number of firearms in circulation, burglars and other criminals would find fewer to steal in home break-ins.

For proponents, the link between gun regulations and reduced violent crime is apparent, requiring no further justification. Opponents of gun control regard this presumed link more skeptically, observing that the cities with the most stringent gun laws also appear to have the highest levels of violent crime. President Trump cited Chicago as an example, as did New Jersey governor Chris Christie.[10] But as discussed in chapter 1, establishing the empirical effectiveness (or ineffectiveness) of gun control is extremely complex, and this complexity can create questions about the actual validity of the examined evidence. In this case, even assuming that Chicago has some of the toughest gun laws in the country (an assumption not everyone concedes[11]), drawing the correct inference from Chicago's more than 4,000 shooting victims in 2016 and from its startling large gun homicide rate of 25.1 per 100,000 residents—five times the national average[12]—remains difficult. Do these findings indicate the essential ineffectiveness of gun control, as Bedrock America contends, or do they merely demonstrate, as Cosmopolitan America argues, that Chicago's proximity to Wisconsin and Indiana—states with weaker gun laws—still gives thugs easy access to firearms and thus prevents Chicago's gun laws from working?

Even if this contention is accurate, gun rights advocates note that the contention only offers a reason for *why* Chicago's gun control efforts do not work; it in no way alters the futility of those efforts. Gang members and other criminals are still able to obtain guns and still commit violent crime. Further, these skeptics argue that criminals by definition are not law-abiding: they will ignore firearms regulations as readily as they ignore other criminal statutes. Asserting it is a misplaced belief that gun control legislation can substantially reduce serious crime, such skeptics quote Colin Greenwood, a British chief inspector who studied the effectiveness of British gun control legislation and concluded pessimistically, "The greater danger lies not [just] in the ineffectiveness of such restrictions, but in a belief that they will solve the problem."[13]

Cosmopolitan America might concede that tough gun laws do not dramatically decrease gun violence[14] but still assert that the discussion above sets the bar for judging the effectiveness of gun control legislation unfairly high. From the perspective of many of its members, requiring a verifiably observable decrease in gun crimes is unnecessarily stringent. If gun control efforts succeed in reducing gun violence even a little, stopping some violent incidents but not enough to "move the needle" empirically, would that not justify gun legislation? As a variation of the "if it saves just one life" theme, a satisfactory response to such an argument requires a thoughtful analysis of the likely social benefits the legislation provides relative to the likely social costs entailed. Modest benefits justify only modest costs. Proponents of Bedrock America would assert that much gun control regulation does not pass this test. They believe that regulations interfering with the ability of law-abiding individuals to arm themselves purchase only small gains in gun crime prevention but necessitate large losses in citizen security.

Leaders of Bedrock America often point to the statistics on defensive gun uses (DGUs)—the presentation or use of a firearm to protect oneself or others from harm—to support this assertion. While estimates of the prevalence of DGUs vary widely (due to the different methodologies used to the collect the data and to the sample sizes of groups providing the information), even using the conservative estimate derived from the National Crime Victimization Survey of about 100,000 incidents per year, the frequency of DGUs is substantial. Thus, if gun control regulations discourage law-abiding individuals from obtaining firearms, they potentially inflict a cost in lessened individual security far greater than the small decrease in violent gun crime they achieve. Additionally, if the frequently cited larger estimate of DGU incidents obtained by Gary Kleck, a professor emeritus of criminology at Florida State University, is correct, about 2.5 million DGUs per year,[15] the argument is even more compelling. Research on the inverse relationship between armed citizens and crime by John Lott, the president of the Crime Prevention Research Center, further supports Kleck's larger estimate. His research[16] indicated that simply showing ("brandishing") a firearm stopped an attack in over 90 percent of the cases, and as no one was shot or harmed, these DGUs rarely get reported to the police—explaining why Kleck's estimate of DGU frequency is much larger than estimates gleaned from police reports or hospital gunshot admissions.[17]

As with all analyses of gun-related evidence, the research conducted by Kleck and Lott has its critics. Cosmopolitan America's David Hemenway, a professor of health policy in the Harvard School of Public Health and the director of the Harvard Injury Control Research Center, dismisses Kleck's estimates of DGUs as far too high and argues that the criminal use of guns is more frequent than the defensive use of guns.[18] Similarly, detractors of Lott's work (and of Lott personally) have faulted his methods and analyses and have even questioned his intellectual integrity.[19] Nonetheless, overall, the available evidence does not offer strong support for the efficacy of gun control in reducing violent gun crime. While certain specific regulatory measures may have limited impact—barring criminals and alcoholics from possessing guns appears to reduce robberies, assaults, and homicides—gun control laws generally have no broad effect on crime rates[20] and are highly unlikely to serve as a viable solution to the country's violent crime problem.

General Societal Safety

As violent crimes—homicide, rape, robbery, and aggravated assault—decreased in the mid-1990s from their earlier highs in the 1970s and 1980s, gun control strategists such as Josh Sugarmann recognized that, as society's attention shifted from violent crime to other concerns, justifications for regulating firearms had to broaden. Spotlighting the lethality of guns, and thus the concomitant need for "gun safety," offered such a broadened justification. It was during this period that gun control advocates began to characterize the AR-15 semiautomatic rifle (which had been on the market for over three decades[21]) as an "assault weapon," with features such as rapid-fire capability and large-capacity magazines making them too deadly for civilian ownership. Supporting this characterization, the near universal popularity among American gun enthusiasts of

AR-style rifles[22] ensured that these rifles were often the deranged spree killer's weapon of choice. Cosmopolitan America's editorial writers and popular commentators regularly noted this fact.[23] Arguing that individuals had no need for a military-style rifle whose only purpose was to kill masses of people quickly,[24] gun control proponents successfully lobbied for an assault weapons ban in 1994 to protect society from such firearms.

Although the inherent lethality of "assault weapons" formed the core of Cosmopolitan America's demand for increased societal protection from guns, the argument was multifaceted. Gun control advocates could also link the claimed "easy availability" of firearms to the often unpredictable volatility of human nature, painting speculative pictures of road rage shootouts, drunken bar fights ending in gunplay, disgruntled employees "going postal," and domestic squabbles escalating to homicidal gun violence. While Bedrock America might object that the actual frequency of such incidents was astonishingly small relative to the number of gun owners in the country, the frequency certainly was not zero, and the media voices of Cosmopolitan America ensured that those infrequent instances received prominent attention. Playing on a favorite rejoinder of Bedrock America—"guns don't kill people; people kill people"—gun control advocates countered that "guns don't kill people, but they sure make it easier for people to kill people"[25] and contended that stringent gun regulations offered society some protection from the dangers of lethal tools in the hands of impulsive human beings. "Gun-free" zones strikingly embodied this peculiar belief that society could achieve safety by containing the instrument rather than the instrument's user.

Reinforcing the idea that societal safety actually necessitated gun control was the burgeoning interest in gun violence taken by public health researchers beginning in the 1980s. Coming from an epidemiological orientation, these investigators approached gun deaths and injuries as they would any other disease, noting the people involved but also looking beyond them to examine environmental factors supporting the disease. In the case of gun violence, individuals are the acknowledged source of the violence, but the availability, design, and marketing of firearms represent significant environmental factors supporting gun violence. The researchers accepted that changing people—the actual cause of violence— was preferable, but they also recognized the enormous difficulties involved in changing human behavior. As with certain diseases, they believed that modifying environmental factors supporting gun violence was far less complicated than changing individuals, and done effectively, this could provide almost as great a societal benefit in reduced gun deaths and injuries.[26] Thus, instead of addressing the shooter's personal characteristics—rage, depression, emotional instability, or carelessness—to solve the country's gun problem, these public health researchers asserted that policies focused on the gun and its characteristics offered a better alternative. For example, by concentrating on the design of the firearm—intervening early in the gun violence process, *before* millions of buyers acquire the gun—manufacturers might build in accident-preventing modifications (such as loaded chamber indicators and magazine safety devices) that save lives and reduce injuries without relying on countless end users to always handle the firearm prudently.[27]

Does societal safety actually necessitate gun regulation? Bedrock America and other skeptics reject the arguments above, asserting that they rest on flimsy or dubious claims. In the case of "assault" rifles, for example, these critics point out that the National Institute of Justice's commissioned evaluation of the 10-year ban on such rifles concluded that, despite their high visibility in spree killings, the rifles are infrequently used in "normal" gun crimes and that the ban had a negligible impact in reducing the severity or lethality of gun violence.[28] The same report asserted that a new congressional ban would likely have an insignificant impact on gun violence, perhaps one even too small to measure. Other evaluations reached similar conclusions.[29] Thus, while semiautomatic AR-style rifles in the wrong hands certainly are dangerous and lethal, they are not more deadly than other traditional semiautomatic hunting rifles and pose no greater threat to societal safety than firearms generally.

Accepting the conclusion above, Cosmopolitan America might suggest that this very argument underscores society's need for gun control: given the acknowledged vagaries of human nature, *all* firearms—rifles, pistols, and shotguns—pose a genuine threat to societal safety and thus require close regulation. As the epidemiologists have implied, if society cannot effectively regulate or control human behavior to achieve safety, the only alternative is to carefully regulate firearms. Although such an argument appears eminently sensible to inhabitants of Cosmopolitan America—individuals typically having no personal interest in owning firearms—for Bedrock America, this position encapsulates the essential nature of the gun control debate. *All* regulation is likely to appear eminently sensible to individuals not impacted by the controls. As an illustration, gun rights activists note that most of Cosmopolitan America considered the gun regulations struck down by *Heller* as eminently sensible, although virtually no one in Bedrock America did.

Similarly, gun control advocates' seemingly casual consideration of regulations sure to spark fierce opposition in Bedrock America suggests that regulatory reasonableness is not a major concern for Cosmopolitan America. This is evident in reviewing many of the proposed solutions put forth by advocates having a public health orientation to gun violence. These solutions include regulatory "interventions" at the manufacturing level (such as "smart gun" modifications whereby only authorized users can fire the weapon); interventions at the sales level (such as stringent licensing and registration requirements); interventions in the private sales market (such as mandatory universal background checks); and interventions at the dealer level (such as complete bans on those firearms considered the most dangerous and least useful).[30] The researchers assert that "none of the challenges [in implementing the interventions] are insurmountable,"[31] suggesting a striking unawareness of how incendiary Bedrock America finds these proposals. Whatever their assumed benefits, such politicized solutions to gun violence impose high costs on Bedrock America's core values, and each of these interventions has generated severe resistance in the past. Characterizing the restrictions as "reasonable" or "commonsensical" is unlikely to make them any more palatable than previously. Thus, as their actual future implementation is improbable, their usefulness for enhancing societal safety becomes a moot point.

Individual Personal Safety

For many Americans, even those indifferent to the ownership and regulation of firearms, references to "gun control" prompt vaguely sinister images of faceless government bureaucracies meddling with personal freedom. In their propaganda war with Bedrock America, strategists for Cosmopolitan America have periodically[32] recognized the negative connotations associated with the "gun control" label, and they have attempted to reframe their regulatory agenda into more people-friendly "gun safety" presentations. Concentrating on issues identified by polls and focus groups as ones that resonate with average Americans, these issues include standard gun control fare, such as strengthening the background check system, ensuring that the system contains all relevant mental health records, prosecuting prohibited individuals who attempt to purchase firearms, and stopping terrorists from obtaining weapons.[33] Gun rights advocates deride this repackaging of past regulatory ideas as no more than a marketing ploy,[34] putting a new hat on an old outfit. However, the approach also includes a prominent emphasis on issues that speak directly to the personal safety of anyone, both gun owners and nonowners, inhabiting a firearms-rich environment: gun accidents, gun suicides, and gun carelessness. (Gun homicides also impact personal safety, but the typically unlawful nature of those firearm fatalities place them in a qualitatively different class.)

Gunshot accidents, whether the result of clumsy hunters in the field,[35] unsupervised children at home,[36] or negligent law enforcement officers on the dance floor[37] or the classroom,[38] actually constitute only a small percentage of gun injuries and fatalities. In 2015, of the more than 36,000 shooting deaths in the country, fewer than 500 individuals (less than 2 percent) lost their lives in unintentional shootings.[39] Further, the frequency of such deaths have steadily declined, from almost 2,000 in 1981 to a little more than 800 in 1999 to the 2015 level.[40] Nonetheless, accidental shootings, particularly involving children, provide a compelling argument for some milder forms of gun control (trigger locks; safe-storage gun boxes, mandatory safety classes, and so forth). Additionally, tapping into the fears that all parents have for their children and into the trust they have for their physicians, gun control advocates have successfully enlisted medical professionals to warn families about the dangers inherent in mixing both guns and children, citing statistics meant to underscore these dangers: "There were 77 unintentional firearms deaths in children under the age of 18 in the U.S. in 2015. An additional 948 nonfatal gun and shooting accidents resulted in an estimated 461 children needing to be hospitalized."[41]

Regardless of statistical infrequency, unintentional shootings alarm all rational individuals, pro- or anti-gun, and both Bedrock and Cosmopolitan America typically endorse similar solutions to the issue: both advocate implementing available protections and exploring additional safeguards. Their fierce disagreements arise over *how* to implement these safety measures, with Cosmopolitan America arguing for mandatory implementations enforced with legal penalties and Bedrock America supporting voluntary implementations founded on educational campaigns. The ongoing skirmishes over how to address lax gun storage illustrate these two differing approaches. Both camps agree that safe-storage gun boxes—mechanically or digitally locked boxes that can house a homeowner's pistol while still permitting the gun owner relatively quick access—offer a potential means of protecting curious youngsters from finding a parent's firearm and inadvertently shooting themselves or one of their companions. Cosmopolitan America essentially wants to make such boxes (or their functional equivalent) a mandatory requirement for gun owners through the passage and enforcement of Child Access Prevention (CAP) laws. These laws make adults criminally liable for gun safety lapses endangering children and allow prosecutors to bring charges against parents whose children use the parents' firearms to harm themselves or others.[42]

Bedrock America agrees that safe gun storage is necessary[43] but notes that the gun owner in the end determines whether to use (or not use) any required storage procedure. Rather than mandate a solution the individual may well ignore, gun rights advocates contend that as the owner ultimately remains responsible for the firearms, a better approach than more laws and prosecutions is to provide robust support for gun safety education and training. They also note that education is proactive, while CAP laws are enforceable only after an incident occurs. Even after a deadly tragedy, prosecutors are often reluctant to charge a grieving family member, and when they do, grand juries are often reluctant to indict.[44]

A similar divide separates the two Americas on their approaches to gunshot suicides. Of the roughly 36,000 shooting deaths in 2015, more than 60 percent (about 22,000) were suicides[45]—a percentage far exceeding the number attributable to gun homicides (about 13,000). Both camps agree that individuals intent on harming themselves should not have access to firearms, but as with unintentional shootings, they diverge on how to prevent such access. Following its regulatory instincts, Cosmopolitan America has championed the passage of "red flag laws"—gun violence prevention legislation that allows family members or police to petition a court to order the temporary removal of firearms from an individual presenting a danger to himself or others.[46] Variously known as "extreme risk protection orders," "gun violence restraining orders," "risk warrants," and "risk protection orders," evidence suggests that such orders effectively mitigate some risk posed by suicidal gun owners: "one averted suicide for every ten to eleven gun seizure cases."[47] Additionally, gun control advocates note the mitigating effects that gun lock laws and minimum age purchasing requirements have on teen suicides; as well as the preventive impact that required waiting periods (before collecting a purchased firearm or obtaining a gun license) likely have.[48]

Bedrock America considers this regulatory approach a decidedly mixed blessing. Gun rights proponents assert that the vast majority of millions of Americans wishing to obtain firearms are not suicidal, yet they are equally impacted by these regulatory hurdles. Further, many are not convinced that these laws actually deter suicide. John Lott, a prominent gun rights advocate, asserts that suicidal individuals, in the absence of guns, will simply choose an alternative method to end their lives.[49] In turn, gun control advocates dismiss Lott's substitution hypothesis as overly simplistic.[50] As with most empirically based assertions in the gun debate, the supporting evidence has methodological limitations and is open to multiple interpretations and conflicting assessments.

Bedrock America is wary of red flag laws for related reasons. Many of the medical health professionals who conduct research investigating the effectiveness of these laws—and who embrace the public health approach to gun safety generally—work in institutions and associations with gun control orientations. Although this does not necessarily mean that their research findings are biased, gun rights proponents typically assume they are, and they point to a decades-long battle with the Centers for Disease Control and Prevention (CDC)—a premiere medical research institution with a well-known reputation for supporting gun control—to justify this assumption. In the 1990s, Dr. Arthur Kellermann and his colleagues published research in the *New England Journal of Medicine* concluding that the practice of keeping firearms in the home for personal protection was counterproductive. Their study found that the practice appeared to increase the homeowner's risk of injury or death.[51] Funded by the CDC, the study's findings provided Cosmopolitan America with a major gun control talking point, and the research received frequent citation[52] in gun control debates.

Gun rights proponents attacked the study, noting serious methodological limitations[53] that substantially undermined Kellermann's conclusions. The NRA even characterized the study and associated research as "junk science . . . designed to provide ammunition for the gun control lobby."[54] The association contended that CDC officials supported gun bans and funded research that simply advocated for this result. Quoting a CDC-funded researcher who claimed, "We're going to systematically build the case that owning firearms causes deaths," and another who stated he foresaw a long-term campaign "to convince Americans that guns are, first and foremost, a public health menace," and a third who endorsed "a public health model [that changes] society's attitudes toward guns so that it becomes socially unacceptable for private citizens to have guns," the NRA asserted that it was not opposed to legitimate gun violence research, but it rigorously objected to investigations where the research conclusions were known even before the data were collected.[55]

Three years after the publication of the Kellermann study, the NRA convinced an Arkansas congressman, Jay Dickey, to insert a rider into the 1996 federal omnibus spending bill that curtailed the CDC's ability to provide funding support for research on the impact of firearms in American society. The rider mandated that no CDC funds for injury control and prevention could finance studies advocating or promoting gun control. To ensure that the center received the message, Congress removed

$2.6 million dollars from the CDC's budget, the precise amount the center had allocated for firearms research the prior year.[56] While the amendment did not specifically prevent the CDC from supporting gun research, the difficulties in determining "legitimate" gun research from "advocacy" research effectively discouraged it from financing any investigations in this area. Cosmopolitan America has periodically attempted to get Congress to repeal the Dickey amendment, arguing that reasonable policy decisions concerning firearms are impossible without ongoing research into all the parameters of gun violence.[57] Bedrock America remains unmoved, convinced that the CDC's approach "medicalizes" gun issues in ways that are inherently misleading. Noting that gun control advocates typically *merge* gun crime with gun suicides and gun accidents but *separate* gun crimes from other violent crimes, gun suicides from other suicides, and gun accidents from other accidents, these skeptics fear that such a reduced perspective, even without deliberate advocacy, cannot produce useful solutions to gun issues.[58]

Rather than rely on mandated regulations of limited effectiveness for dealing with gun suicides, Bedrock America gravitates to its accustomed solutions for firearms issues: understanding the individual psychological dynamics driving the problem and then using focused educational interventions and increased training to curtail it. Illustrating the importance of examining the dynamics of the problem, gun rights proponents note that not all gun suicides are impulsive responses to transient conditions. Some suicides occur among individuals who are both self-reliant and who are willing to take definitive action when they believe such action is in their own best interest—including ending one's life when the individual decides the time is appropriate, such as when suffering from a painful terminal illness.[59] Attempts to prevent such incidents—interfering with an autonomous individual's right to self-determination—are morally complex and are qualitatively different from potential suicides sparked by transient episodes of depression or hopelessness.

In cases where fleeting emotions underlie potential suicide, the preventive responses of Bedrock America generally mirror the solutions emphasized by Cosmopolitan America, but they are voluntary rather than mandated. Gun rights proponents see limiting a suicidal individual's access to firearms, at least temporarily, as an effective way to diminish impulse suicide, and they have undertaken educational campaigns alerting gun owners and their families to the value of gun locks and other safe storage methods for combating this problem. For example, both the National Rifle Association and the Second Amendment Foundation, in partnership with Forefront Suicide Prevention, endorse the SAFER Homes educational campaign, an undertaking aimed at increasing suicide awareness and encouraging voluntary implementation of suicide prevention strategies. In the home, these strategies include securing all firearms in locked storage, with only the homeowner and one additional adult having access. For firearm retailers and instructors, the strategies include displaying suicide prevention posters, providing customers with brochures containing prevention tips, and providing online suicide awareness training sessions geared to recognizing suicidal risk indicators and ways to keep someone considering suicide safe.[60] In New Hampshire [61] and Montana,[62] gun rights proponents have initiated similar programs.

From an individual safety perspective, gun carelessness—negligently securing a firearm or handling it in a dangerous or unsafe manner—is often a precursor to unintentional shooting accidents, and Cosmopolitan America has railed against such negligence in its demands for laws to protect children and other innocents from reckless gun owners. Bedrock America's objections to these laws—requiring pistol permits and licenses, mandatory training hours, required storage procedures, firearms liability insurance, and so forth—generally arise not from the substance of these regulations but from their regulatory nature. Responsible gun owners ensure that they are familiar with the operation of their firearms, receive training on their safe use, store them securely against unauthorized users, and accept the legal and financial consequences attendant on their misuse. Owners argue they have no need of such regulation and that these requirements frequently infringe on Second Amendment guarantees. They also note that the regulations are often either unnecessary or ineffective, referencing Emile Durkheim, an eminent French sociologist: when customs and traditions are sufficient, laws are unnecessary; when they are not, laws are ineffective.

Cosmopolitan America rejects these contentions, observing that not all gun owners are responsible—even highly trained law enforcement professionals sometimes get negligent—and submits that legal mandates ensure that gun safety is always a top priority for those carrying firearms. Gun rights proponents turn the argument around. If even highly trained law enforcement professionals are sometimes negligent, more gun laws and gun regulations are unlikely to minimize carelessness, but ongoing gun safety awareness education and training might. As with firearms accidents generally, Bedrock America believes that safety is better achieved through internally motivated preventive awareness education than externally generated post hoc fines and penalties.[63]

In Civilized Societies, Guns Are Illegitimate

A recurring theme in Cosmopolitan America's war on guns is that fire-arms no longer have a legitimate place in a modern country, and enlight-ened societies either stringently regulate civilian possession of firearms or ban guns entirely. To support this assertion, Cosmopolitan America cites the gun orientations found in a number of advanced Western cultures—Great Britain, Canada, and Australia prominent among them—and some Asian cultures as well—Japan and China come to mind. All ban or severely control civilian access to firearms. At first glance, this argument for justifying gun regulation appears less compelling than the other ratio-nales put forth by Cosmopolitan America. This rationale offers no tangi-ble beneficial outcomes. It does not strengthen society by moderating crime or by increasing general or individual safety; it merely suggests that other successful clusters of humanity, facing challenges similar to those faced by America, have determined that firearms in civilian hands create more problems than they solve. Why have we not followed their more enlightened lead?

Bedrock America dismisses this argument with a figurative eye roll, with gun rights proponents simply noting that America is not Great Brit-ain or Australia or Japan. The history and culture of those countries are not the history and culture of the United States, and what works and is appropriate in those nations is not necessarily appropriate and workable in this nation. If they are feeling particularly aggrieved, these gun propo-nents even question the touted successes of these "more advanced" orien-tations to firearms, observing in the case of Australia that reductions in gun homicides and suicides began *before* Australia passed its major gun control law[64] and that the law's drawbacks include homeowners getting harassed and prosecuted for protecting themselves and their families from dangerous intruders.[65] In the case of Great Britain, they point out that the tight restrictions on gun ownership has not stopped firearms crime but has increased knife assaults and violent crime generally,[66] with the United Kingdom currently having the highest crime rate of any West-ern industrialized country, with rapes and murders in the largest cities at record levels.[67] The response of London's mayor, Sadiq Khan, to the crime wave engulfing his city is a campaign calling for additional knife control legislation. Carrying a knife longer than three inches "without good rea-son" (self-protection does not meet this standard[68]) is already illegal, but Khan would ban the carrying of all knives, stating, "No excuses: there is never a reason to carry a knife. Anyone who does will . . . feel the full force of the law."[69]

In arguing about the effectiveness (or ineffectiveness) of other nations' experiences with gun control, Bedrock America likely misses the real significance of Cosmopolitan America's emphasis on other countries' treatment of guns. Although gun control proponents in America would certainly reject Bedrock America's portrayal of other countries' regulatory efforts as unadulterated failures—they have their own set of advocates to show how "remarkably effective" these foreign efforts have been[70]—the argument at heart is not about effectiveness. For Cosmopolitan America, gun control is a value-expressive statement: a society without guns is simply a better society than one with guns, and this is true whether gun control "works" or not. Other nations have recognized this and are willing to bear the associated costs. Why does America insist on remaining so out of line?

Bedrock America: Philosophical Foundations

If a society without guns is value-expressive for Cosmopolitan America, self-reliance and individual independence are value-expressive for Bedrock America, and gun control strikes at both core values. To people who reside in Bedrock America, gun regulations erode self-reliance by demanding that citizens rely on the police for protection against lawbreakers and other varieties of social threats. They also erode individual independence by conceding to the government yet another arena for limiting citizens' rights and lawful behaviors. While Cosmopolitan America may impatiently shrug off such grievances and imply they are overblown—one discussion of the Australian gun ban made sure to note that "Australian independence didn't end. Tyranny didn't come. Australians still hunted and . . . Invaders never arrived."[71]—Bedrock America can cite a long tradition in Western philosophical and legal writings[72] upholding an individual's right to defend himself or herself against violent attack. They also can point to suspicion of central government overreach and abuse of authority dating back to the founding of the nation.

Thus, gun rights advocates view firearms regulations, especially those that prevent law-abiding individuals from acquiring commonly available pistols and rifles, as simply contrary to natural (or God-given) rights and historical understandings. Regardless of whether the actual frequency of defensive gun use is high or low or whether the actual likelihood of government tyranny is great or small, Bedrock America sees no reason to surrender the most potent means for ensuring individual self-protection or for checking potential governmental abuse of power. Humanity has long endorsed both objectives as legitimate and honorable, Cosmopolitan America's contentions notwithstanding.

Constitutional Considerations

Before the *Heller* and *McDonald* Supreme Court cases, much of the gun debate centered on whether the right to keep and bear arms was an individual or a collective/militia right. That controversy existed because, contrary to Cosmopolitan America's numerous assertions that the question was "settled law," the Second Amendment had received only scant and confusing interpretations on the federal level and contradictory interpretations in state courts. Now, with the *Heller* and *McDonald* decisions, the Supreme Court *has* truly settled the controversy by confirming that "the right of the people to keep and bear arms" is indeed an individual right, as are all the rights referencing "people" in the Bill of Rights.

As discussed in chapter 8, gun control proponents consider the *Heller* decision a misreading of the Second Amendment, so it is likely that Cosmopolitan America will continue to support a militia interpretation as the amendment's "true" purpose, keeping the controversy alive. Nonetheless, with *Heller* as an unambiguous precedent, the types of gun regulations that Cosmopolitan America can realistically expect to pass judicial muster, assuming they even clear the legislative hurdles Bedrock America usually erects, will by necessity be much narrower in scope than prior to *Heller*. Further, if the Court's conservative composition during President Trump's tenure becomes even more pronounced and gun-friendly (as expected), High Court adjudications of new gun cases will reference *Heller*'s Second Amendment view, embedding and expanding that perspective even more deeply in the country's judicial system. This will in turn deter lower courts that might otherwise be tempted to ignore or limit *Heller* "from below."[73]

Aside from the unlikely possibility that some future Supreme Court willfully ignores past precedent and overturns the *Heller* decision, Cosmopolitan America's other option for neutralizing Bedrock America's constitutional advantage in the gun debate centers on repealing the Second Amendment. The procedures for repealing a constitutional amendment are arduous, and the criteria are stringent. But they are not impossible to meet—the repeal in 1933 of the Eighteenth Amendment, banning the sale and consumption of alcohol, comes to mind. Further, prominent gun control proponents, including a former Supreme Court justice[74] and popular news[75] and entertainment periodicals,[76] have actually advocated for such a repeal. Despite such support, a Second Amendment repeal is a low-probability event and unlikely to serve Cosmopolitan America's best interests. According to a 2018 Accuracy in Media poll, any attempt at repeal would upset most Americans, with about 80 percent against the effort,[77] and would allow Bedrock America to portray the attempt as further proof that Cosmopolitan America ultimately wants to ban all firearms.

Political Considerations

Even in the face of recurring mass shootings, Bedrock America has been remarkably successful in forestalling significant federal firearms legislation. The 1994 Assault Weapons Ban represents Cosmopolitan America's last and most notable legislative success, and that ban expired 10 years later despite rigorous renewal efforts. Little reason exists to expect that Cosmopolitan America will have any greater legislative success in the next quarter century than in the past quarter century. Bedrock America's main advantage in the political arena is the impassioned commitment of gun rights proponents in defending their "cause" against perceived infringements, whether large or small.[78] Gun control supporters consistently blame legislative failures on the political machinations of an unrepresentative NRA,[79] dismissing the alternative explanation that the NRA accurately conveys the shooting fraternity's orientation to additional gun regulations: adamant rejection.

While Cosmopolitan America portrays its recurring calls for more firearms legislation—"gun law reform"—as just "commonsense" measures,[80] Bedrock America sees little connection between the laws proposed and the problems they presumably solve.[81] Consequently, gun rights supporters mobilize not simply to defend their firearms but to oppose policies perceived as ineffective. And, as a more focused advocacy group than gun control proponents, they can better ensure their votes reward congressional allies and punish congressional foes. The political power of pro-gun advocates comes not just from the money of the NRA but from the sustaining votes of Bedrock America.[82]

Further, given gun control's questionable delivery on promised results, galvanizing past supporters and attracting new recruits is likely more difficult for Cosmopolitan America than Bedrock America. Beginning with Big Tim Sullivan in New York City, politicians have touted gun control as a viable solution to urban brutality and have used firearms regulations as visible and reassuring indicators that violent crime is not intractable. They frame new gun laws as tools capable of containing the scourge of violence. Constituents endorse the approach—at least *something* is being done—and execution is not especially complicated or expensive. Its major drawback—little evidence that it actually reduces violent crime or makes society safer—may not rattle loyal gun control advocates who blame lackluster results on incomplete data, misinterpreted evidence, or extenuating circumstances, but unbiased observers are typically more skeptical.

Pragmatic Considerations

Perhaps inspired by Australia's first national mandatory gun buyback program in the late 1990s, American municipalities have periodically experimented with voluntary buyback programs of their own. These programs offer gun owners incentives, typically cash or gift cards, for turning unwanted firearms into the police, no questions asked.[83] The purpose of such programs is to decrease the number of guns in a local community, presumably reducing violent crime and making the community safer. Depending on the amount of the incentive offered and the overall amount allocated to the effort, buyback programs typically remove from circulation anywhere from a few hundred to a few thousand firearms.[84] With over 300 million firearms in the hands of private citizens (with some estimates putting the figure higher, at over 350 million[85]), voluntary buyback programs, even when they function as conceived,[86] confront a Herculean task in trying to fulfill their sponsors' expectations. Realistically, the vast number of pistols, rifles, and shotguns already in circulation ensure that buyback programs are ineffective. Bedrock America asserts that, similarly, most other regulatory limitations would be just as ineffective. If a prohibited felon wants a gun in America, no degree of government regulation will prevent the individual from obtaining a firearm (although, ironically, such regulation may well prevent a law-abiding citizen from doing so).

Modern digital technology further compounds the regulatory problems created by the sheer availability of firearms. Although the expense and durability of 3D-printed firearms currently make such guns impractical, nonetheless, Defense Distributed—an online, open-source organization dedicated to developing digital firearms files—has created a digital library of files allowing anyone with the motivation and a 3D printer to manufacture functioning versions of many of America's most popular guns. These files include programs for producing the AR-15 and AR-10 rifles and the 1911 M1 and Beretta M9 pistols. In assessing the future of firearms regulation in America, the founder of Defense

Distributed, Cody Wilson, has made his evaluation clear. Outside his office, he has placed a tombstone engraved with the words "American Gun Control."[87]

Even if Wilson's assessment is premature—several Democratic lawmakers and state attorneys general want to prevent Defense Distributed from uploading the files onto the Internet[88]—fabricating metal guns is already easy and cheap with tools common in the garages of many dedicated home machinists. Such homemade firearms are entirely legal, and if made for personal use, with no intention of selling, hobbyists do not even need a license or manufacturing permit.[89] For unscrupulous hobbyists, severe restrictions on legal firearms merely create a lucrative black market catering to criminals and gang members wanting firepower,[90] supplementing the roughly quarter of a million stolen firearms feeding the black market annually.[91] Thus, despite Cosmopolitan America's perennial hope that just one more gun law will tamp down gun violence, the practical reality is that regulatory efforts are mostly powerless in reducing the number of firearms "on the street" or in keeping them out of the hands of a person determined to procure one. Bedrock America recognizes the inability of gun laws to prevent gun violence and chafes at the unnecessary limitations such laws impose on peaceable individuals simply wanting a gun for self-protection. As one film character observes, "Better to have a gun and not need it, than need a gun and not have it."[92] For gun rights proponents, this sentiment precisely sums up their position on arms.

Some Concluding Thoughts

What does the future hold for America's great gun debate? Prognostication is always a perilous undertaking, but one prediction seems fairly safe: regardless of the particular strengths or the specific weaknesses of one side or the other, a cease-fire in the culture war between Cosmopolitan and Bedrock America is unlikely. In 1975, Lee Kennett and James Anderson, in their generally benevolent treatment of gun rights, nevertheless concluded that the inexorable urbanization of the United States ultimately favored the cultural dominance of Cosmopolitan America.[93] Almost a half-century later, that assessment appears strikingly incorrect. The enduring capacity of Bedrock America to stave off Cosmopolitan America's assaults on gun rights, even in the face of national tragedies, has astonished virtually everyone. A half-century from now, perhaps another commentator will reach an identical conclusion about the pessimistic assessment of gun control's continuing viability found here.

In the meantime, the war of values between the two Americas will undoubtedly persist. The challenge facing the gun control advocates of Cosmopolitan America is that, despite the media attention garnered after a mass shooting, firearms may not be that important an issue for the majority of Americans. In a Gallup poll taken in September 2018, only 2 percent of Americans mentioned gun control as the most important problem facing the country today, and a recent informal Internet poll of political issues that matter most to people ranked gun control 15th on a list of 35 issues.[94] Further, strict gun control proposals represent a major change in the status quo, a prospect that typically makes individuals uncomfortable. Judged in Overton window terms—the "window" classifies the range of ideas tolerated in public discourse[95]—Cosmopolitan America needs to find ways to shift gun control's fairly marginal location in the window to a more central position, moving public discourse about gun regulation from possibly "acceptable" to "popular" and, eventually, to "policy." One general technique for adjusting the window and accomplishing movement is the deliberate promotion of more radical positions (such as calling for the repeal of the Second Amendment or demanding the complete confiscation of even legal firearms) in the hopes of making less-radical stances appear acceptable.[96] Using this strategy is risky, however, as it would allow Bedrock America to portray gun control advocates as wild fanatics. Of course, Bedrock America will aggressively attempt to counter whatever new communication strategies Cosmopolitan America employs in any event.

Bedrock America's present ascendency in the culture war means that gun rights proponents have a realistic opportunity to dismantle gun regulations it considers particularly egregious: gun-free zones; high-capacity magazine bans, "may-issue" licensing schemes, "cooling-off" waiting periods for purchasers already possessing firearms, interstate sales restrictions despite the availability of the National Instant Criminal Background Check System (NICS), and other questionable gun laws. It also foreshadows an aggressive expansion of new gun rights, such as national concealed carry reciprocity, which would require all states to recognize the concealed carry permits granted by other states.[97] Such legislation stalled in Congress in 2017, but the byzantine maze of different state firearm laws and their unreasonable application ensure that this issue will surface again.[98]

Of course, speculations of this nature are only relevant for determining which of the two Americas is "winning" the culture war at a specific point in time, admittedly a crucial question for the pro- and anti-gun frontline participants in the war and for their supporting organizations. Prevailing in the legal skirmishes over bills to support and bills to block, influencing the interpretation of crime statistics and the calculation of defensive gun uses, triumphing in the appointment of federal judges and Supreme Court nominations, and succeeding in all the other contested battlegrounds of the war are essential outcomes for keeping morale and motivation high and for demonstrating (to those who believe that culture wars are winnable) that the right side—"our side"—is winning. But for those who want to *understand* the war, a central focus on these details misleads more than it informs.

At heart, the conflict between the two Americas is not about gun control. The struggle over guns and gun regulations is merely the external manifestation of a much deeper struggle around sharply different national visions for the country and two distinct value systems. For Bedrock America, independence, individual responsibility, and self-determination are values that have served America well in the past and will surely continue to serve the country well in the future. Should anyone demand proof of the worth of these principles—why these values should continue to guide the country—the answer is self-evident: under these banners, the country became, and is, a beacon to the world. For Cosmopolitan America, the complexities of modern society have destroyed the ability of the old traditional values—captured by the iconic rugged individual—to effectively cope with contemporary social dilemmas and political issues. Values emphasizing the interconnectedness of individuals and the mutual responsibilities and shared obligations between the individual and the group, communitarian values, are the principles now necessary if the nation is to continue to thrive and prosper.

On this level, the divergence between the two Americas' value orientations spills over into issues of appropriate governance far more thorny than just gun regulation and its effectiveness. What type of society do citizens want, and what type of risks are they willing to accept, and to impose on others, to create that society? The gun culture war is a proxy war fought around fundamental philosophical, social, and political beliefs, and it offers tantalizing insights into the country America might become. For involved citizens, understanding the fight over gun culture, thought-provoking in its own right, is perhaps even more fascinating for the preview it provides into the nation's ongoing political and social evolutions.

Notes

Chapter 1

1. Sharpe, P. (1938). *The Rifle in America*. New York: William Morrow. Cited in Kennett, L. & Anderson, J. (1975). *The Gun in America: The Origins of a National Dilemma*. Westport, CT: Greenwood Press, p. 36.

2. John Browning's design contributions to iconic American firearms have made him a giant in the pantheon of firearm designers. It was his genius that resulted in the world-recognized .45-caliber M1911 pistol, the Browning Auto-5 semiautomatic shotgun, and the well-known and highly regarded Browning Automatic Rifle (BAR).

3. Because of the gun's significance in daily life, the gunsmith was one of the first trained professionals in American society and was found throughout the colonies at least since the early 1600s. See Kennett, L. & Anderson, J. (1975). *The Gun in America: The Origins of a National Dilemma*. Westport, CT: Greenwood Press, pp. 38–40.

4. Ibid., pp. 85–93.

5. Rose, A. (2008). *American Rifle*. New York: Delacorte Press, p. 105.

6. Kennett & Anderson, *Gun in America*, p. 42.

7. See Nisbet, L. (ed.). (2001). *The Gun Control Debate*. Amherst, NY: Prometheus Press, pp. 23–90, in particular, pp. 42–43; also, Tonso, W. (ed.). (1990). *The Gun Culture and Its Enemies*. Bellevue, WA: Second Amendment Foundation.

8. Hansen, G. (1976). The History of Gun Control in America. *Dissertations and Theses*. Paper 2281. Master of Arts in History, Portland State University, pp. 12–13.

9. See Celinska, K. (2007). Individualism and Collectivism in America: The Case of Gun Ownership and Attitudes toward Gun Control. *Sociological Perspectives, 50*(2), pp. 229–247.

10. Bruce-Briggs, B. (1976). The Great American Gun War. *Public Interest, 45*(Fall), p. 37.

11. Nisbet, *Gun Control Debate*, pp. 23–94.

12. Street, C. (2016). *Gun Control: Guns in America, the Full Debate*. New York: CreateSpace Independent Publishing Platform, pp. 6–7.

13. Celinska, Individualism and Collectivism.

14. Ibid.

15. See Tonso, W. Social Problems and Sagecraft: Gun Control as a Case in Point. In Nisbet, L. (ed.), *Gun Control Debate*, pp. 42–43.

16. See, for example, Mencken, F. C. & Froese, P. (2017). Gun Culture in Action. *Social Problems*, spx040. https://doi.org/10.1093/socpro/spx040; Cook, C. & Puddifoot, P. (2000). Gun Culture and Symbolism among U.K. and U.S. Women. *Journal of Social Psychology, 140*(4), pp. 423–433; Felson, R. & Pare, P. (2010). Gun Cultures or Honor Cultures? Explaining Regional and Race Differences in Weapon Carrying. *Social Forces, 88*(3), pp. 1357–1378; Kohn, A. (2004). *Shooters: Myths, Realities, and America's Gun Cultures*. New York: Oxford University Press.

17. Ibid., pp. 42–43. See also Kennett & Anderson, *Gun in America*, p. 254, citing the *Wall Street Journal*, June 7, 1972, p. 14.

18. Exploring such alternative avenues goes beyond the scope of this book, but possibilities might include a revision of the country's drug laws. By legalizing, regulating, and taxing many of the illegal narcotics fueling criminal activities, the government could remove much of the profit currently associated with the drug trade and substantially lessen the gun violence and homicides perpetrated by criminal gangs. Similarly, channeling increased resources into mental health, and the understanding of depression and alienation might lessen the toll inflicted by those who use firearms to harm themselves and others. Governmental and community efforts to increase employment and reduce poverty might also limit the attractiveness of gun-related crimes (such as robbery) by individuals who currently see themselves as having no other options. Certainly, many other violence-alleviating approaches are possible and likely to have an impact on societal violence in general, and not just on gun violence.

19. Bruce-Briggs, Great American Gun War, p. 39.

20. See NRA-ILA Report. (2000). Firearms Registration: New York City's Lesson. January 27. Available at https://www.nraila.org/articles/20000127/firearms -registration-new-york-city-s.

21. For a representative recent illustration of this mind-set, see Knighton, T. (2017). No, HuffPo, Compromise Will Not Happen on Gun Control. December 8. Available at https://bearingarms.com/tom-k/2017/12/08/no-huffpo-compromise -will-not-happen-gun-control. This column is a response to an opinion piece in the *Huffington Post* that suggests a current gun control bill wending its way through the Senate (i.e., S.2009, the Murphy-Cornyn bill) offers an attractive legislative compromise on gun issues that even strong pro-gun advocates could support.

Knighton had this to say:

And here we see what compromise really means to the anti-gun crusader. "Compromise with me" really means "shut up and do what I tell you." . . . Compromise is the word they use to pretend that they're being reasonable for those who have no opinion on the subject. . . . But compromise isn't really on the agenda. It's just a means to an end, and that end being the eventual dismantling of our Second Amendment rights.

Chapter 2

1. See Malcolm, J. L. (1994). *To Keep and Bear Arms: The Origins of an Anglo-American Right.* Cambridge, MA: Harvard University Press, pp. ix–13. This section relies on Malcolm's analysis of English developments, but events occurring in France during the same period suggest that America's French emigrants would have experienced remarkably similar struggles with their French kings. See Kennett, L. & Anderson, J. (1975). *The Gun in America: The Origins of a National Dilemma.* Westport, CT: Greenwood Press, pp. 8–16.

2. See Henderson, H. (2005). *Gun Control.* New York: Facts On File, Inc., p. 95; also, Kruschke, E. (1995). *Gun Control: A Reference Handbook.* Santa Barbara, CA: ABC-CLIO, pp. 61–62.

3. Malcolm, *To Keep and Bear Arms*, pp. 4–10.

4. Ibid., pp. 12–15.

5. Ibid., pp. 17–22.

6. Ibid., p. 23.

7. Ibid., pp. 28–35.

8. Ibid., pp. 42–50.

9. Ibid., pp. 64–76.

10. Ibid., p. ix.

11. Ibid., pp. 8–9, 79.

12. Even earlier, non-Englishmen, such as Machiavelli in his *Discourses*, had advanced similar arguments regarding the necessity of an armed citizenry for maintaining freedom from political abuse. Educated Englishmen would also be familiar with these writers.

13. In modern times, Malcolm has observed that the right to own and keep firearms (and perhaps the right of self-defense generally) appears to have been "a casualty of benign neglect." Malcolm, *To Keep and Bear Arms*, p. ix.

14. Kopel, D. (2002). What State Constitutions Teach about the Second Amendment. *Northern Kentucky Law Review, 29*(4), pp. 823–847.

15. Currently, the constitutions of only six states—California, Iowa, Maryland, Minnesota, New Jersey, and New York—do not include a right to keep and bear arms clause. Of these, the constitutions of both Iowa and New Jersey contain a general defense of life and liberty self-protection clause.

16. Quoted in Elliot's *Debates*. See Quotes on the Second Amendment. Available at www.madisonbrigade.com/p_henry.htm.

17. First Annual Message to Congress, Federal Hall, NYC, January 8, 1790. Available at Avalon.law.yale.edu/18th_century/washs01.asp.

18. From his opening remarks defending the British Redcoats tried for the Boston Massacre. Found in Wroth, L. & Zobel, H. (1965). *Legal Papers of John Adams*. Available at https://www.azquotes.com/quote/1308685.

19. From Adams, J. (1788). *A Defense of the Constitutions of the Government of the United States of America*. See Quotes on the Second Amendment. Available at www.madisonbrigade.com/j_adams.htm.

20. Adams, S. (1772). *The Rights of the Colonists*. Report of the Committee of Correspondence to the Boston Town Meeting, November 20. Available at https://history.hanover.edu/texts/adamss.html.

21. Adams, S. (1788). *Debates and Proceedings in the Convention of the Commonwealth of Massachusetts*. February 6. See Quotes on the Second Amendment. Available at www.madisonbrigade.com/s_adams.htm.

22. Beccaria, C. (1764). *Essay on Crimes and Punishments*. Available at https://www.monticello.org/site/jefferson/laws-forbid-carrying-armsquotation.

23. Jefferson, T. (1776). *Virginia Constitution of 1776*. First draft, June 13. Available at https://www.monticello.org/site/jefferson/no-freeman-shall-be-debarred-use-of-arms-spurious-quotation.

24. Lee, R. (1788). *Letters from the Federal Farmer to the Republican*. #18, January 25. Available at press-pubs.uchicago.edu/founders/documents/a1_8_15s11.html.

25. Webster, N. (1787). *An Examination of the Leading Principles of the Federal Constitution*. October 17. See Quotes on the Second Amendment. Available at www.madisonbrigade.com/n_webster.htm.

26. Coxe, T., writing as An American Citizen. (1788). *Pennsylvania Gazette*. February 20. See Quotes on the Second Amendment. Available at www.madisonbrigade.com/t_coxer.htm. See also Halbrook, S. & Kopel, D. (1999). Tench Coxe and the Right to Keep and Bear Arms, 1787–1823. *William and Mary Bill of Rights Journal*, 7(3), pp. 347–399.

27. Kennett, L. & Anderson, J. (1975). *The Gun in America: The Origins of a National Dilemma*. Westport, CT: Greenwood Press, p. 69.

28. Ibid., p. 76.

29. Ibid., p. 99.

30. Ibid., pp. 98–100. Regarding the use of firearms as loss-leaders, Kennett and Anderson include an amusing anecdote regarding Winchester's tussle with Sears over this practice. When Sears continued to ignore the factory price, Winchester eventually refused to fill orders from Sears. Sears then responded by placing orders through dummy firms, and the tussle continued for a number of years.

31. Ibid., p. 105.

32. Ibid., p. 153.

33. Ibid., p. 50.

34. Ibid, pp. 116–117. The authors note that these rifles were often "trade" muskets, which were inferior to rifles in use at the time. This would change later in the century, and by 1876, many of the warriors at Little Big Horn would have rifles superior to those of General Custer's troopers.

35. Franz, J. & Choate, J. (1955). *The American Cowboy: The Myth and the Reality*. Norman, OK: University of Oklahoma Press, p. 85.

36. See Winkler, A. (2011). *Gunfight: The Battle over the Right to Bear Arms in America*. New York: W. W. Norton & Company. His book includes a photograph of Dodge City's main street taken in 1879. In the middle of the street is a huge billboard with the notice "The Carrying of Firearms Strictly Prohibited" written large. Later, in 1882, Ordinance 67 made it unlawful for anyone to "carry concealed or otherwise about his or her person any pistol, bowie knife, slung shot or other dangerous or deadly weapons." Similarly, Tombstone's Ordinance No. 9 stated, "It is hereby declared to be unlawful for any person to carry deadly weapons concealed or otherwise." Fort Worth had a comparable ban on carrying guns in the city. Winkler has asserted that many of these gun control ordinances were more severe than today's regulations.

37. Winkler, A. (2011). Did the Wild West Have More Gun Control Than We Do Today? *Huffpost, the Blog*, September 9. Available at www.huffingtonpost.com/adam-winkler/did-the-wild-west-have-mo_b_956035.html.

38. Cottrol, R. (1994). *Gun Control and the Constitution*. New York: Garland Publishing, p. xix.

39. Ibid., p. xx.

40. Ibid., pp. xxii–xxiii.

41. Ibid., p. xxiii.

42. Garrett, B. (2018). The Start of Restricted Gun Rights in America. Available at https://www.thoughtco.com/the-first-gun-ban-in-american-history-721341.

The *Nunn v Georgia* case represents the first use of the Second Amendment to overturn a gun control law.

43. Kennett & Anderson, *The Gun in America*, pp. 110, 123–124. See also Cottrol, *Gun Control*, p. xxiv.

44. Rodengen, J. (2002). *NRA: An American Legend*. Ft. Lauderdale, FL: Write Stuff Enterprises, Inc., p. 18.

45. Ibid., p. 20.

46. Ibid., pp. 23–28.

47. Ibid., p. 20.

48. Rose, A. (2008). *American Rifle*. New York: Delacorte Press, p. 196.

49. Ibid., p. 201.

50. Ibid., pp. 200–202.

51. Ibid., p. 101. Rose actually states that Crockett ran against Jackson, but I believe this is simply shorthand for running against Jackson's policies.

52. Ibid., p. 345.

53. Schreier, P. (2002). Personally, I prefer the Winchester. *American Rifleman* (January). Available at dailycaller.com/2012/05/02/personally-i-prefer-the -winchester.

Chapter 3

1. For example, although New York City had passed an ordinance in 1877 requiring a permit to carry a concealed handgun, permits were liberally granted. Even so, a substantial number of residents did not bother to acquire a permit, and the police had little interest in enforcing the ordinance. Further, the maximum fine for noncompliance was small. See Kennett, L. & Anderson, J. (1975). *The Gun in America: The Origins of a National Dilemma*. Westport, CT: Greenwood Press, pp. 169–170.

2. Welch, R. (2009). *King of the Bowery: Big Tim Sullivan, Tammany Hall, and New York City from the Gilded Age to the Progressive Era*. New York: State University of New York Press.

3. *New York Tribune* (1911). May 11, p. 1; a shortened version of this quote appears in the *New York Times* (1911). Bar Hidden Weapons on Sullivan's Plea. May 11. Special to the *New York Times*. Available at https://cityroom.blogs .nytimes.com/2011/01/23/100-years-ago-the-shot-that-spurred-new-yorks-gun -control-law.

4. Duffy, P. (2011). 100 Years Ago, the Shot That Spurred New York's Gun Control Law. *New York Times*, January 23. Available at https://cityroom.blogs .nytimes.com/2011/01/23/100-years-ago-the-shot-that-spurred-new-yorks -gun-control-law.

5. Ibid.; also, Krajicek, D. (2013). How Author's Death over 100 Years Ago Helped Shape NY Gun Laws. *New York Daily News*, January 20. Available at www.dailynews.com/news/justice-story/1911-shooting-led-ny-gun-law-article -1.1240721.

6. Lankevich, G. (2002). *New York City: A Short History*. New York: NYU Press, p. 140; also, Walsh, M. (2012). The Strange Birth of NY's Gun Laws. *New York Post*, January 16. Available at https://nypost.com/2012/01/16/the-strange -birth-of-nys-gun-laws.

7. Hansen, G. (1976). The History of Gun Control in America. *Dissertations and Theses*. Paper 2281. Master's thesis, Portland State University, p. 10.

8. Roberts, S. (1992). Metro Matters; 50 Years of Crime and Stereotypes. *New York Times*, March 2. Available At https://www.nytimes.com/1992/03/02 /nyregion/metro-matters-50-years-of-crime-and-stereotypes.html.

9. Ibid.

10. Welch, op. cit.

11. Hansen, History of Gun Control, pp. 8–11.

12. Kennett & Anderson, *The Gun in America*, p. 175.

13. Turner, F. (1921). *The Frontier in American History*. New York: Henry Holt & Co.

14. Billington, R. (1975). *America's Frontier Heritage*. Albuquerque: University of New Mexico Press.

15. Hansen, History of Gun Control, p. 4.

16. U.S. Census Bureau. History: Urban and Rural Areas. Available at https:// www.census.gov/history/www/programs/geography/urban_and_rural_areas.html.

17. EyeWitness to History. (2000). Immigration in the Early 1900s. Available at www.eyewitnesstohistory.com/snpim1.htm. See also Library of Congress. (n.d.). Progressive Era to New Era, 1900–1929. *Immigrants in the Progressive Era.* Available at http://www.loc.gov/teachers/classroommaterials/presentationsan dactivities/presentations/timeline/progress/immigrnt. This source notes that by 1910, three-fourths of New York City's population were either immigrants or the sons and daughters of immigrants.

18. Hansen, History of Gun Control, p. 21.

19. Illustrated and quoted in *Literary Digest* (1925). Closing the Mails to Murder. January 10, pp. 33–34. Available at www.unz.org/Pub/LiteraryDigest -1925jan10-00033.

20. Ibid., pp. 33–34.

21. Kennett & Anderson, *The Gun in America*, p. 191.

22. Quoted in *Literary Digest* (1921). The Necessity of Pistol Toting. August 6, pp. 33–34. Available at www.unz.org/Pub/LiteraryDigest-1921aug6-00033.

23. Ibid., p. 33.

24. All quoted in *Literary Digest* (1924). A Spike for the One-Hand Gun. December 13, p. 34. Available at www.unz.org/Pub/LiteraryDigest-1924dec13 -00034.

25. See Kennett & Anderson, *The Gun in America*, pp. 187–188.

26. Ibid., p.188. See also *People v. Camperlingo*, 231 P. 601 (Cal/Ct. App. 466 1924). Available at https://www.courtlistener.com/opinion/3282008/people -v-camperlingo.

27. See Hansen, History of Gun Control, pp. 29–31; also, Kennett & Anderson, *The Gun in America*, pp. 192–193 and 196–197.

28. Ibid., p. 196.

29. See Kennert & Anderson, *The Gun in America*, p. 196. See also The Right to Keep and Bear Arms. *New York Times*, May 3, 1923, p. 18. Available at https:// www.nytimes.com/1923/05/03/archives/the-right-to-keep-and-bear-arms.html.

30. Kennert & Anderson, *The Gun in America*, p. 193.

31. Quoted in *Literary Digest* (1921). For Pocket Disarmament. June 25, p. 30. Available at www.unz.org/Pub/LiteraryDigest-1921jun25-00030. See also Hansen, History of Gun Control, p. 20.

32. Kennett & Anderson, *The Gun in America*, pp. 188, 199–204.

33. Ibid., pp. 206–207, 210–211.

34. Ibid., p. 205. See also Rodengen, J. (2002). *NRA: An American Legend.* Ft. Lauderdale, FL: Write Stuff Enterprises, Inc., pp. 96–97, 120–121.

35. National Firearms Act, Hearings before the Committee on Ways and Means, House of Representatives, 73rd Congress, 2nd sess. on H.R. 9066, 1934, pp. 124–125. Available at www.alternatewars.com/Politics/Firearms/NFA _Hearings_HR-9066_Complete.htm.

36. Kennett & Anderson, *The Gun in America*, pp. 206, 210–211.

37. Ibid., p. 210. Although dismissed as virtually useless for practical crime solving during the hearings, both ideas periodically resurface in current gun control debates.

38. Ibid., p. 207, 209–212. See also Rodengen, J., *NRA*, p. 101.

39. Hansen, History of Gun Control, p. 9.

40. See, for example, Cramer, C. (1995) The Racist Roots of Gun Control. *Kansas Journal of Law and Public Policy* (Winter), p. 17. See also Winkler, A. (2011). *Gunfight*. New York: W. W. Norton & Co., pp. 205–206.

41. See Malcolm, J. L. (1994). *To Keep and Bear Arms. The Origins of an Anglo-American Right*. Cambridge, MA: Harvard University Press, p. xx.

42. Quoted in Kennett & Anderson, *The Gun in America*, p. 214.

43. Ibid., pp. 212–214.

44. Ibid., p. 213.

Chapter 4

1. Kennett, L. & Anderson, J. (1975). *The Gun in America: The Origins of a National Dilemma*. Westport, CT: Greenwood Press, p. 223.

2. Ibid., pp. 218–219.

3. Hansen, G. (1976). The History of Gun Control in America. *Dissertations and Theses*. Paper 2281. Master's thesis, Portland State University, p. 42.

4. See Halbrook, S. (2001). Registration: The Nazi Paradigm. *American Rifleman, 149*(6), p. 52. Available at www.stephenhalbrook.com/registration_article/registration.html; also, Hansen, History of Gun Control, pp. 42–43.

5. See Latzer, B. (2016). *The Rise and Fall of Violent Crime in America*. New York: Encounter Books, pp. 18–19.

6. See Kennett & Anderson, *The Gun in America*, p. 222.

7. George-Warren, H. (2002). *Cowboy: How Hollywood Invented the Wild West*. Pleasantville, NY: Reader's Digest Association, Inc., pp. 85–141.

8. Ibid., pp. 132–135.

9. See Kennett & Anderson, *The Gun in America*, pp. 215, 218.

10. Ibid., p. 219.

11. O'Meara, R. (2005) *Colt's Single Action Army Revolver*. New York: Gun Digest Books, p. 5.

12. Kennett & Anderson, *The Gun in America*, p. 217.

13. Ibid., pp. 220–221.

14. O'Meara, *Colt's Single Action*, pp. 41–46. Although fast draw only lasted through the 1950s, the activity evolved into cowboy action shooting in many clubs, a pursuit that even today lures curious but still uncommitted individuals into the shooting sports.

15. Kennett & Anderson, *The Gun in America*, p. 219.

16. Gallager, S. (1959). Fad Brings Boom to Handguns. *Popular Science* (October), p. 136 ff. Available at https//:books.google.com/books?rview=1&lr=&id=sCkDA AAAMBAJ&q=fad+with+handguns#v=snippet&q=fad%20with%20handguns&f =false.

17. Ibid., pp. 136 ff.

18. Kennett & Anderson, *The Gun in America*, pp. 218, 221.

19. Hansen, History of Gun Control, pp. 43–44. President Truman's letter, dated November 14, 1945, appeared in the December 1945 issue of *American Rifleman*.

20. O'Meara, *Colt's Single Action*, p. 41.

21. Kennett & Anderson, *The Gun in America*, p. 223.

22. Ibid., p. 224.

23. Ibid., pp. 224–228.

24. Hansen, History of Gun Control, p. 48. See also *American Rifleman* (1960). Legislative Activity in 1960. July, p. 20.

25. Kennett & Anderson, *The Gun in America*, p. 223.

26. Hansen, History of Gun Control, pp. 47–48; also, Kennett & Anderson, *The Gun in America*, p. 225.

27. Kennett & Anderson, *The Gun in America*, pp. 225–226.

28. Ibid., p. 222.

29. *New Republic* (1956). Sale of Firearms. June 18, p. 2; cited in Hansen, History of Gun Control, p. 48.

Chapter 5

1. Kennett, L. & Anderson, J. (1975). *The Gun in America: The Origins of a National Dilemma*. Westport, CT: Greenwood Press, p. 229.

2. Ibid., pp. 228–231; also, Hansen, G. (1976). The History of Gun Control in America. *Dissertations and Theses*. Paper 2281. Master's thesis, Portland State University, pp. 52–53.

3. Ibid., pp. 232–232.

4. Hansen, History of Gun Control, pp. 52–53.

5. Kennett & Anderson, *The Gun in America*, pp. 231–232.

6. Hansen, History of Gun Control, pp. 53–54.

7. *Newsweek* (1963). Right to Bear Arms. December 9, pp. 71–72.

8. Ibid., p. 72.

9. Robert Spitzer has rejected this aspect of the Second Amendment, arguing that the amendment does not confer an innate "right of revolution" (thus calling into question an individual right to keep and bear arms). He bases his argument on the idea that, as a revolution is carried out against the government, it must also be carried out against the government's constitution, that is, the Bill of Rights and the Second Amendment. He concludes that one cannot revolt against the government and then point to that government's constitution for justification or protection. This reasoning seems to ignore the philosophical underpinnings of the Bill of Rights, which presumes that certain rights are natural and innate, neither conferred by nor dependent on the government for their existence. (Indeed, the very origins of the Bill of Rights implies that when these rights need protection, they typically need it from government intrusion.) See Spritzer, R. (2008). *The Politics of Gun Control*. Washington, D.C.: CQ Press, pp. 38–41.

10. Kennett & Anderson, *The Gun in America*, p. 233.

11. Ibid., p. 233.

12. Ibid., pp. 232–233.

13. Ibid., pp. 234–235.

14. See Hansen, History of Gun Control, pp. 56–57.

15. Shapiro, F. & Sullivan, J. (1964). *Race Riots, New York, 1964*. New York: Crowell, p. 65.

16. Ibid., p. 67.

17. See Threadcraft, S. (2007). *New York City Riot of 1964*. In Rucker, W. & Upton, J. (eds.). *Encyclopedia of American Race Riots*. Vol. 2. Westport, CT: Greenwood Press, pp. 478–480.

18. See BlackPast.org. (n.d.). Rochester Rebellion (July 1964). Available at https://blackpast.org./aah/Rochester-rebellion-july-1964.

19. See Encyclopedias.biz. (n.d.). Jersey City (New Jersey) Riot of 1964. Available at www.encyclopedias.biz/encyclopedia-of-american-race-riots/16172-jersey-city-riot-of-1964.html. See also Dat boy Monty. (n.d.). 1964 Jersey City Race Riots. Available at https://datboymonty.wordpress.com/2017/09/20/1964-jersey-city-race-riots.

20. See Mack, W. (n.d.). 1964 Paterson, New Jersey Uprising (1964). Available at www.blackpast.org/aah/1964-paterson-new-jersey-uprising-1964.

21. See Mack, W. (n.d.). Elizabeth, New Jersey Uprising (1964). *BlackPast.org*. Available at www.blackpast.org/aah/elizabeth-new-jersey-uprising-1964.

22. See Rodriguez Candeaux, S. (n.d.). Philadelphia Race Riot (1964). *BlackPast.org*. Available at www.blackpast.org/aah/philadelphia-race-riot-1964. Different sources give different estimates for the numbers arrested, injured, and killed. I list those reported by Rodriguez Candeaux.

23. Hansen, History of Gun Control, p. 57.

24. Knox, N. (2009). *The Gun Rights War*. Phoenix, AZ: MacFarlane Press, pp. 52–53.

25. Kennett & Anderson, *The Gun in America*, pp. 235–236.

26. See Hearings Held on Administration Gun Control Bill. In CQ Almanac 1965, 21st ed., 640–645. Washington, D.C.: Congressional Quarterly, 1966. Available at https://library.cqpress.com/cqalmanac/document.php?id=cqal65-1259893.

27. Knox, *Gun Rights War*, pp. 55–57.

28. Kennett & Anderson, *The Gun in America*, p. 232.

29. See Marable, M. (2011). *Malcolm X: A Life of Reinvention*. New York: Viking, pp. 132–135.

30. See *New York Times* (1963). Malcolm X Scores U.S. and Kennedy. December 2, p. 21.

31. West, C. (1984). The Paradox of the Afro-American Rebellion. In Sayres, S., Stephanson, A., Aronowitz, S., and Jameson, F. (eds.). *The 60s without Apology*. Minneapolis: University of Minnesota Press, p. 51.

32. Kondo, Z. (1993). *Conspiracys: Unravelling the Assassination of Malcolm X*. Washington, D.C.: Nubia Press, p. 170.

33. Carson, C. (1991). *Malcolm X: The FBI File*. New York: Carroll & Graf, p. 473.

34. Massaquoi, H. (1964). Mystery of Malcolm X. *Ebony* (September), p. 38 ff.

35. See Marable, *Malcolm X*, pp. 436–437.

36. *New York Times*, Malcolm X.

37. See Malcolm X (1992). *By Any Means Necessary* (Malcolm X Speeches and Writings). New York: Pathfinder Press, pp. 57–96.

38. See Az Quotes. (n.d.). Malcolm X. Available at www.azquotes.com /author/9322-Malcolm_X/tag/gun; also, Winkler, A. (2011). The Secret History of Guns. *The Atlantic* (September). Available at https://www.theatlantic.com/magazine /archive/2011/09/the-secret-history-of-guns/308608.

39. See The Disaster Center. (n.d.). United States Crime Rates 1960–2016. Available at www.disastercenter.com/crime/uscrime.htm.

40. See Kleck, G. (2005). *Point Blank*. New York: Taylor & Francis, p. 306, table 7.1.

41. See Hoenisch, S. (2004). Crime Policy of the Republican Party. Available at www.criticism.com/policy/republicans-crime-policy.php. Reprinted from *The Encyclopedia of the American Democratic and Republican Parties*.

42. See *The Challenge of Crime in a Free Society* (1968). A Report by the President's Commission on Law Enforcement and Administration of Justice. New York: Avon Books. See also Hoenisch, Crime Policy.

43. See Vorenberg, J. (1972). The War on Crime: The First Five Years. *The Atlantic Online*. Available at www.theatlantic.com/past/docs/politics/crime /crimewar.htm.

44. Barnhill, J. (2011) Watts Riots (1965). In Danver, S. (ed.). (2011). *Revolts, Protests, Demonstrations, and Rebellions in American History*. Vol. 3. Santa Barbara, CA: ABC-CLIO, pp. 965–976.

45. Ibid.

46. Hinton, E. (2016). *From the War on Poverty to the War on Crime: The Making of Mass Incarceration in America*. Boston: Harvard University Press, pp. 68–72.

47. Ibid., pp. 68–72.

48. Barnhill, Watts Riots.

49. Lavergne, G. (1997). *A Sniper in the Tower*. Denton: University of North Texas Press, p. 223.

50. Hansen, History of Gun Control, p. 59. See also Buckley, W. (1966). On the Right. *National Review*, August 23, p. 821.

51. Rosenfeld, S. (2013). The Surprising Unknown History of the NRA. Available at https://www.alternet.org/surprising-unknown-history-nra.

52. Winkler, Secret History of Guns.

53. Ibid.

54. Ibid.

55. Ibid.

56. Ibid.

57. Sitkoff, H. (2000). *Postwar America*. New York: Oxford University Press, p. 85.

58. See BlackPast.org. (n.d.). Detroit Race Riot (1967). Available at https:// blackpast.org/aah/detroit-race-riot-1967.

59. Ibid.

60. Fine, S. (1989). *Violence in the Model City: The Cavanagh Administration, Race Relations, and the Detroit Riot of 1967.* Ann Arbor: University of Michigan Press, p. 371.

61. See BlackPast.org. (n.d.). Newark Riot (1967). Available at https://blackpast .org/aahnewark-riot-1967.

62. BlackPast.org, Detroit Race Riot.

63. Winkler, A. Secret History of Guns. See also the *Report of the National Advisory Commission on Civil Disorders* (1968). New York: Bantam Books.

64. See Music, Marsha. (2008). Joe Von Battle—Requiem for a Record Shop Man. Available at https://marshamusic.wordpress.com/page-joe-von-battle-requiem -for-a-record-shop-man.

65. See Gun Control Bills Stalled by Stiff Opposition (1968). *CQ Almanac 1967* (23rd ed.), 08-859-863. Washington, D.C.: Congressional Quarterly. Available at http://library.cqpress.com/cqalmanac/cqal67-1313024.

66. Kukla, R. (1973). *Gun Control.* Harrisburg, PA: Stackpole Books, p. 342. See also Risen, C. (2009). *A Nation on Fire: America in the Wake of the King Assassination.* New York: John Wiley & Sons.

67. Ibid., p. 344.

68. Ibid.

69. Ibid., pp. 344–345.

70. *Time* (1968). The Gun Under Fire. June 21, pp. 14–18; also, Hansen, History of Gun Control, p. 61.

71. *Newsweek* (1968). A Question of Guns. June 24, pp. 81–85; also, Hansen, History of Gun Control, p, 62.

72. Ridgeway, J. (1968). The Kind of Gun Control We Need. *New Republic,* June 22, pp. 10–11; also, Hansen, History of Gun Control, p. 63.

73. Ibid.

74. Kukla, *Gun Control,* pp. 345–346, 352.

75. Kennett & Anderson, *The Gun in America,* p. 237.

76. Ibid., p. 238.

77. Hansen, History of Gun Control, pp. 64–65.

78. Ibid., pp. 66–67.

79. Ibid., p. 67. Also, Kennett & Anderson, *The Gun in America,* pp. 243–244.

Chapter 6

1. Kennett, L. & Anderson, J. (1975). *The Gun in America: The Origins of a National Dilemma.* Westport, CT: Greenwood Press, p. 244; also, *American Rifleman* (1968). New U.S. Law Limits All Gun Sales. December, p. 17.

2. Hansen, G. (1976). The History of Gun Control in America. *Dissertations and Theses.* Paper 2281. Master's thesis, Portland State University, pp. 71–72.

3. Ibid., pp. 68–69.

4. Ibid., pp. 75–76.

5. Ibid., p. 75.

6. *New York Times* (1972). The Gun Menace. May 18, p. 46. Available at https://www.nytimes.com/1972/05/18/archives/the-gun-menace.html.

7. *New York Times* (1972). Daley Asks Handgun Curb. May 17, p. 26. Available at https://www.nytimes.com/1972/05/17/archives/daley-asks-handgun-curb.html.

8. Hansen, History of Gun Control, p. 77.

9. Ibid., p. 77.

10. Kennett & Anderson, *The Gun in America*, pp. 242–243.

11. Hansen, History of Gun Control, p. 80.

12. See Ghosts of DC. (n.d.). Senator John Stennis Mugged and Shot in Front of Cleveland Park Home. Available at https://ghostsofdc.org/2012/05/08/senator-stennis-shot-1973, quoting the *Washington Post*.

13. Hansen, History of Gun Control, p. 80.

14. See History of ATF from Oxford University Press, Inc. 1789–1998 U.S. Available at http://www.arrowsmithweb.com/2014/09/history-of-the-atf. The name of the agency continues to evolve; currently, it is often abbreviated to BATFE, recognizing its additional responsibility for the regulation of explosives.

15. Ibid.

16. Hansen, History of Gun Control, pp. 78–79.

17. Moore, J. (2001). *Very Special Agents*. Urbana-Champaign: University of Illinois Press, p. 144. Mr. Moore, a retired ATF agent, presents an account of the incident much less sympathetic to Mr. Ballew than Hansen does. See also *American Rifleman* (1971). How the 1968 Gun Act Caused a Shooting. August, p. 46.

18. Moore, *Very Special Agents*, p. 146.

19. See Reimann, M. (2017). When the Cops Shot This Man in a Weapons Raid, the Entire Conversation on Guns in America Changed. Available at https://timeline.com/ballew-raid-nra-guns-3c60344f56c3.

20. See This Day in Quotes (2016). Wayne LaPierre's (In)famous "Jack-Booted Government Thugs" Quote . . . April 13. Available at www.thisdayinquotes.com/2012/04/wayne-lapierre-vs-jack-booted.html. Mr. LaPierre later apologized for the remark, saying he did not intend to paint all federal law enforcement officials with the same broad brush.

21. See Brown, A. (2016). America Should Regulate Bullets. *Washington Post*, January 6. Available at https://www.washingtonpost.com/opinions/we-should-regulate-bullets/2016/01/0662de9322-b3dc-11e5-a76a-0b5145e8679a_story.html; also, Hansen, History of Gun Control, p. 81.

22. See Wheeler, T. (2004). Guns vs. Teddy Bears. *National Review*, January 13. Available at https://www.nationalreview.com/2004/01/guns-vs-teddy-bears-tim-wheeler-dave-kopel; also, Halsey, A. (1975). Attempt to Ban Handgun Ammo Seen as Attack on All Guns. *American Rifleman* (March), p. 14.

23. See Brown, America Should Regulate Bullets.

24. See Robinson, M. (2016). The Robinson Report # 24: Let Us Make Guns Safer. Available at https://leadership.cpsc.gov/robinson/2016/07/12/the-robinson-report-24-let-us-make-guns-safer.

25. Wheeler, Guns vs. Teddy Bears.

26. See History on the NET. (n.d.). Samuel Byck: Would-Be Nixon Assassin. Available at https://www.historyonthenet.com/samuel-byck.

27. Carroll, W. (2012). Borinsky, Mark (1945–). In Carter, G. (ed.). *Guns in American Society*. Santa Barbara, CA: ABC-CLIO, p. 94.

28. Ibid.

29. See Spitzer, R. (2012). *The Politics of Gun Control*. Seattle, WA: Paradigm Press, pp. 111–112.

30. Ibid.

31. Kennett & Anderson, *The Gun in America*, pp. 240–241.

32. See Achenbach, J., Higham, S. & Horwitz, S. (2013). How NRA's True Believers Converted a Marksmanship Group into a Mighty Gun Lobby. *Washington Post*, January 12. Available at https://www.washingtonpost.com/politics/how-nras-true-believers-converted-a-marksmanship-group-into-a-mighty-gun-lobby/2013/01/12/51c62288-59b9-11e2-88d0c4cf65c3ad15_story.html?utm_term=.d6df3945dc5a.

33. See Winkler, A. (2011). The Secret History of Guns. *The Atlantic* (September). Available at https://www.theatlantic.com/magazine/archive/2011/09/the-secret-history-of-guns/308608.

34. See Lambert, B. (1991). Harlan B. Carter, Longtime Head of Rifle Association Dies at 78. New York Times (November 22). Available at https://www.nytimes.com/1991/11/22/us/harlon-b-carter-longtime-head-of-rifle-association-dies-at-78.html.

35. Crewdson, J. (1981). Hard Line Opponent of Gun Laws Wins New Term at Helm of Rifle Association. *New York Times*, p. a1. Available at www.nytimes.com/1981/05/04/us/hard-line-opponent-of-gun-laws-wins-new-term-at-helm-of-rifle.html.

36. Rosenfeld, Surprising Unknown History. The quote was taken from Winkler, A. (2011). *Gunfight: The Battle over the Right to Bear Arms in America*. New York: W. W. Norton & Company.

37. See Naughton, J. (1975). Two Feet Away. *New York Times*, September 6. Available at https://www.nytimes.com/1975/09/06/archives/front-page-1-no-title-ford-safe-as-guard-seizes-a-gun-woman-pointed,html.

38. See CourtTVNews. (n.d.). SLA: The Shootout. Available at https://web.archive.org/20070815204928/http://www.courttv.com/trials/soliah/slahistory5_ctv.html.

39. See United States Secret Service. Public Report of the White House Security Review. Department of the Treasury. Available at https://fas.org/irp/agency/ustreas/usss/t1pubrpt.html.

40. See Laskow, S. (2015). A 45-year-old Mom and a Manson Girl Both Tried to Kill Gerald Ford. *Atlas Obscura*, June 3. Available at https://www.atlasobscura.com/articles/female-assassins-sara-jane-moore-and-lynette-fromme-gerald-ford.

41. See Biography. (n.d.). Sara Jane Moore. Available at https://www.biography.com/people/sara-jane-moore-21155825.

42. See *New York Times*. (1975). Gov. Brown Signs Bills Tightening 2 Gun Laws. September 24. Available at https://www.nytimes.com/1975/09/24/archives/gov-brown-signs-bills-tightening-2-gun-laws-html.

43. *Time* (1975). Protecting the President. October 6, p. 7.

44. Ibid., p. 16.

45. See Hansen, History of Gun Control, pp. 82–83.

46. See Schultz, L. (n.d.). March 4th,1966: The Beginning of the End for John Lennon? Available at https://web.archive.org/web/20070927/000251/http://www .secweb.org/index.aspx?action=viewAsset&id=73.

47. Ibid.

48. See Spitzer, R. (2012). *The Politics of Gun Control.* Seattle, WA: Paradigm Press.

49. See *New York Times.* (1981). Tape by Hinckley Is Said to Reveal Obsession with Slaying of Lennon. May 15. Available at www.nytimes.com/1981/05/15/us /tape-by-hinckley-is-said-to-reveal-obsession-with-slaying-of-lennon.html.

50. See Feaver, D. (1981). Three Men Shot at the Side of Their President. *Washington Post,* March 31; also, Hunter, M. (1981). Two in Reagan Security Detail Are Wounded Outside Hotel. *New York Times,* March 31.

51. See CNN Library. (2018). John Hinckley Jr Fast Facts, September 3. Available at https://www.cnn.com/2013/03/20/us/john-hinckley-jr-fast-facts/index.html.

52. See *Delahanty v Hinckley,* 564 A.2d 758 (D.C. App. 1989).

53. See Armed Career Criminal Act, 18 U.S.C. 924(e).

54. See S. 49 (99th). Firearm Owners Protection Act. Available at https:// www.govtrack.us/congress/bills/99/s49/text.

55. See *Time.* (1989). Slaughter in a School Yard. January 30. Available at content.time.com/time/magazine/article/0,9171,151105,00.html.

56. Ibid.

57. See Assault Weapons Identification Guide. California Department of Justice. Available at https://oag.ca.gov/sites/all/files/agweb/pdfs/firearms/forms /awguide.pdf.

Chapter 7

1. See Ball, M. (2013). How the Gun Control Movement Got Smart. *The Atlantic,* February 7. Available at https://www.theatlantic.com/politics/archive /2013/02/how-the-gun-control-movement-got-smart/272934.

2. See Sugarmann, J. (1988). Assault Weapons and Accessories in America. Violence Poverty Center. Available at www.vpc.org/studies/awamarkt.htm.

3. See Blake, A. (2013). Is It Fair to Call Them "Assault Weapons"? *Washington Post,* January 17. Available at www.washingtonpost.com/news/the-fix/wp/2013/01 /17/is-it-fair-to-call-them-assault-weapons/?utm_term=.699992d5f5a7.

4. See Violence Policy Center. Available at vpc.org/about-the-vpc.

5. Sugarmann, Assault Weapons, Conclusions.

6. Blake, Is It Fair.

7. See Assault Weapons Identification Guide. Available at https://oag.ca.gov /sites/all/files/agweb/pdfs/firearms/forms/awguide.pdf.

8. See Mohr, C. (1989). U.S. Bans Imports of Assault Rifles in Shift by Bush. *New York Times,* March 15. Available at https://www.nytimes.com/1989/03/15 /us/us-bans-assault-rifles-in-shift-by-bush.html.

9. Ibid.

10. Ibid.

11. See Rasky, S. (1989). Import Ban on Assault Rifles Becomes Permanent. *New York Times*, July 8. Available at https://www.nytimes.com/1989/07/08/us /import-ban-on-assault-rifles-becomes-permanent.html.

12. Ibid.

13. Ibid.

14. Ibid.

15. See Encyclopædia Britannica. (n.d.). Ruby Ridge Incident. Available at https://www.britannica.com/event/ruby-ridge-incident.

16. See Senate Subcommittee on Terrorism, Technology and Government Information. (1996). *Ruby Ridge: Report of the Subcommittee on Terrorism, Technology and Government Information of the Senate Committee on the Judiciary*. Darby, PA: DIANE Publishing.

17. Ibid.

18. See Wright, S. (1995). *Armageddon in Waco: Critical Perspectives in the Branch Davidian Conflict*. Chicago: University of Chicago Press.

19. Ibid.

20. Ibid.

21. Ibid. See also *Waco: Rules of Engagement* (1997). A documentary film directed by W. Gazecki and produced by M. McNulty.

22. Wright, *Armageddon in Waco*. See also U.S. Dept. of Justice. (1999). *Operation Megiddo: A Strategic Assessment of the Potential for Domestic Terrorism in the United States Undertaken in Anticipation of, or Response to, the Arrival of the New Millennium*. FBI report. See also Stone, A. (1993). *Report and Recommendations Concerning the Handling of Incidents Such as the Branch Davidian Standoff in Waco Texas*. Available at https://www.pbs.org/wgbh/pages/frontline/waco /stonerpt.html.

23. Wright, *Armageddon in Waco*.

24. Ibid.

25. See Siegler, K. (2017). How What Happened 25 Years Ago at Ruby Ridge Still Matters Today. *NPR*, August 18. Available at https://www.npr.org/2017/08/18 /544523302/how-what-happened-25-years-ago-at-ruby-ridge-still-matters-today.

26. See Encyclopædia Britannica. (2018). Brady Law. Available at https:// www.britannica.com/topic/Brady-Law.

27. At least one analyst attributes the death of the comprehensive crime bill to Bush's unwillingness to see the Brady Bill become law. See Dickenson, M. (1992). Bush's Assassination of the Brady Bill. *Washington Post*, November 2. Available at https:// www.washingtonpost.com/archive/opinions/1992/11/02/bush-assassination -of-the brady-bill/ed6ec050-fda2-4d5e-b886-99fc445da84a/?utm_term= .557fc850ed1a.

28. Encyclopædia Britannica, Brady Law.

29. Ibid.

30. See Garrett, B. (2018). Gun Show Laws By State. *ThoughtCo*, September 9. Available at https://www.thoughtco.com/gun-shows-laws-by-state-721345.

31. Ibid.

32. Federal bills aimed at closing the "gun show loophole" have been introduced in Congress from at least 2001 through 2017. None have passed. However, some states require unlicensed private sellers to conduct background checks. See *Washington Post*. (n.d.). History of Gun-Control Legislation. Available at http://www .washingtonpost.com/national/history-of-gun-control-legislation/2012/12/22 /80c8d624-4ad3-11e2-9a42-d1ce6d0ed278_story.html.

33. See Steiner, M. (n.d.). The Federal Assault Weapons Ban. Criminal Defense Lawyer. Available at https://www.criminaldefenselawyer.com/resources/the-federal -assault-weapons-ban.htm.

34. See Lott, J. (2010). *More Guns, Less Crime*. Chicago: University of Chicago Press.

35. See Brady Center to Prevent Gun Violence Report. (2004). *On Target: The Impact of the 1994 Federal Assault Weapons Act*. Washington, D.C.: author.

36. See Garrett, B. (2017). Gun Rights under President Bill Clinton. *ThoughtCo*, March 17. Available at https://www.thoughtco.com/gun-rights-under-president -bill-clinton-721330.

37. See Lytton. T. (2009). *Suing the Gun Industry*. Ann Arbor: University of Michigan Press, p. 23.

38. See Levin, M. (1998). New Orleans Is Expected to Sue Gun Manufacturers. *Los Angeles Times*, October 30. Available at articles.latimes.com/1998/oct/30 /business/fi-37548.

39. See Levin, M. (1998). Chicago Sues Gun Makers and Sellers. *Los Angeles Times*, November 13. Available at articles.latimes.com/1998/nov/13/news/mn -42399; also, Jeter, J. (1998). Chicago Files Suit against Gun Makers, dealers. *Washington Post*, November 13. Available at http://www.washingtonpost.com /archive/politics/1998/11/13/chicago-files-suit-against-gun-makers-dealers.

40. See Butterfield, F. (1998). Chicago Is Suing over Guns from Suburbs. *New York Times*, November 13. Available at https://www.nytimes.com/1998/11/13/us /chicago-is-suing-over-guns-from-suburbs.html.

41. Levin, Chicago Sues.

42. Ibid.

43. See Lytton, *Suing the Gun Industry*.

44. See Appleson, G. (1999). Two More Cities Sue Gun Makers. *Washington Post*, January 28. Available at http://www.washingtonpost.com/archive/politics /1999/01/28/two-more-cities-sue-gun-makers/1346a9b6-8638-424a-86c4-55c 224a35c56/?utm_term=8597953635fa.

45. Ibid.

46. Butterfield, Chicago Is Suing.

47. Levin, Chicago Sues.

48. See Franks, A. (1999). Two More Cities Sue Gun Manufacturers. *CNN .com*, January 27. Available at www.cnn.com/US/9901/27/gun.lawsuits.

49. Jeter, Chicago Files Suit.

50. See Lighty, T. (1999). Two Lawsuits against Gunmakers Tossed Out. *Chicago Tribune*, December 14. Available at articles.chicagotribune.com/1999-12-14 /news/9912140098_1_gun-violence-gun-manufacturers-and-dealers.

51. See CNN.com/LAWCENTER. (2001). Louisiana High Court Shoots Down New Orleans Gun Lawsuit. *CNN.com*, April 3. Available at edition.cnn.com/2001 /LAW/04/03/gun.lawsuit/index.html?_s=PM:LAW.

52. See NRA-ILA. (2004). Illinois Supreme Court Dismisses Chicago Suit against Gun Manufacturers: Legal Cause "Not Found." November 18. Available at https://www.nraila.org/articles/20041118/illinois-supreme-court-dismisses -chicag.

53. CNN.com/LAWCENTER, Louisiana High Court.

54. NRA-ILA, Illinois Supreme Court.

55. Lighty, Two Lawsuits.

56. Levin, Chicago Sues.

57. See NRA-ILA. (1999). Mandatory Storage/Trigger Lock Legislation. July 29. Available at https://www.nraila.org/articles/19990729/mandatory-storagetrigger -lock-legislat.

58. See Bennett, J. (1997). Gun Makers Agree on Safety Locks. *New York Times*, October 9. Available at https://www.nytimes.com/1997/10/09/us/gun-makers -agree-on-safety-locks.html.

59. See Tribune News Services. (1997). Gunmakers, Clinton Forge Pact over Childproof Locks on Triggers. Available at articles.chicagotribune.com/1997-10-10 /news/9710100305_1_gunmakers-american-shooting-sports-council-brady-law.

60. Ibid.; Bennet, Gun Makers Agree.

61. Violence Policy Center (1997). President's Trigger Lock Deal with Gun Industry Protects Industry—Not Children. October 9. Available at www.vpc .org/press/press-release-archives/presidents-trigger-lock-deal-with-gun -industry-protects-industry-not-children.

62. Fiore, F. & Peterson, J. (1997). 8 Gun Makers Agree to Provide Trigger Locks. *Los Angeles Times*, October 10. Available at articles.latimes.com/1997/oct/10 /news/mn-41270.

63. See Associated Press. (1998). NRA Hails Senate Rejection of Mandatory Trigger Locks. *Deseret News*, July 22. Available at www.deseretnews.com/article/642769 /NRA-hails-Senate-rejection-of-mandatory-trigger-locks.html; also, Longley, R. (2017). See a Timeline of Gun Control in the United States. *ThoughtCo*, November 3. Available at https://www.thoughtco.com/us-gun-control-timeline-3963620.

64. See Biography. (n.d.). Dylan Klebold. Available at https://www.biography .com/people/dylan-klebold-235979.

65. Ibid.

66. Allpolitics.com. (1999). Senate Passes Juvenile Crime Bill. May 21. Available at edition.cnn.com/ALLPOLITICS/stories/1999/05/20/gun.control.

67. See Pianin, E. & Eilperin, J. (1999). House Defeats Gun Control Bill. *Washington Post*, June 19. Available at http://www.washingtonpost.com/archive /politics/1999/06/19/house-defeats-gun-control-bill/9b903285-1339-4379 -a209-49ffb41af509/?utm_term=.e7fcdd930da8.

68. NRA-ILA, Mandatory Storage/Trigger Lock Legislation.

69. See S.2070. Gun-Free School Zones Act of 1990. Available at https://www .congress.gov/bill/101st-congress/senate-bill/207070.

70. Ibid.

71. See Letter to Mr. Tim Gillespie from Ashan Benedict (2013). Available at www.handgunlaw.us/documents/BATFletterONGFSZ2013.pdf.

Chapter 8

1. See Garrett, B. (2017). Gun Rights under President George W. Bush. *ThoughtCo*, March 6. Available at https://www.thoughtco.com/gun-rights-under -president-george-w-bush-721332.

2. Ibid. Comment of Angel Shamaya, publisher of keepandbeararms.com, to the *New York Times*.

3. Ibid. Comment of Senator John Kerry, the Democratic nominee in the 2004 election.

4. Ibid.

5. Gorman, M. (2016). Democratic Lawmakers Seek Repeal of Protections for Gun Manufacturers. *Newsweek*, January 27. Available at www.newsweek. com/democracts-seek-repeal-protections-gun-manufacturers-420361; also, Zillman, C. (2015). Hillary Clinton Takes Aim at Gun Makers' Best Legal Defense. *Fortune*, October 5. Available at fortune.com/2015/10/05/hillary-clinton-gun.

6. See NRA-ILA. (2000). The Smith & Wesson Sellout. March 20. Available at https://www.nraila.org/articles/20000320/the-smith-wesson-sellout.

7. Ibid.

8. See Wayne, L. & Butterfield, F. (2000) Gun Makers See Betrayal in Decision by Smith and Wesson. *New York Times*, March 18. Available at https://www .nytimes.com/2000/03/18/us/gun-makers-see-betrayal-in-decision-by-smith -wesson.html.

9. Selk, A. (2018). A Gunmaker Once Tried to Reform Itself. The NRA nearly destroyed it. *Washington Post*, February 27. Available at https://www .washingtonpost.com/news/retropolis/wp/2018/02/27/a-gunmaker-once-tried-to -reform-itself-the-nra-nearly-destroyed-it/?noredirect=on&utm_term+795041 94c89a.

10. Dao, J. (2000). Under Siege, Gun Maker Agrees to Accept Curbs. *New York Times*, March 18. Available at https://www.nytimes.com/2000/03/18/us/under-siege -gun-maker-agrees-to-accept-curbs.html.

11. See Wayne & Butterfield, Gun Makers See Betrayal.

12. Selk, Gunmaker Once Tried.

13. Garrett, Gun Rights.

14. See Protection of Lawful Commerce in Arms Act. Available at https:// www.govinfo.gov/content/pkg/PLAW-109publ92/html/PLAW-109publ92.htm.

15. See Zillman, Hillary Clinton Takes Aim.

16. See Carroll, L. (2015). Clinton: Gun Industry Is "Wholly Protected" from All Lawsuits. *POLITIFACT*, October 16. Available at www.politifact.com/truth -o-meter/statements/2015/Oct/16/hillary-clinton/clinton-gun-industry -wholly-protected-all-lawsuits.

17. See Giffords Law Center. (2017). Gun Industry Immunity. Available at https://lawcenter.giffords.org/gun-laws/policy-areas//other-laws-policies/gun -industry-immunity/#state.

18. See Carroll, Clinton. See also the six exceptions to blanket civil immunity in Giffords Law Center, Gun Industry Immunity.

19. See Encyclopædia Britannica. (2018). Samuel A. Alito, Jr. Available at https://www.britannica.com/biography/Samuel-A-Alito-Jr.

20. Garrett, Gun Rights.

21. *District of Columbia et al. v. Heller.* (2008). Available at https://www .supremecourt.gov/opinions/07pdf/07-290.pdf.

22. Levy, R. (2007). Should Congress or the Courts Decide D.C. Gun Ban's Fate? *DC Examiner,* April 3. Available at https://www.cato.org/publications /commentary/should-congress-or-courts-decide-dc-gun-bans-fate.

23. Ibid.

24. See Greenhouse, L. (2008). Justices, Ruling 5–4, Endorse Personal Right to Own Gun. *New York Times,* June 27. Available at https://www.nytimes.com /2008/06/27/washington/27scotuscnd.html?pagewanted=1&_r1&hp&adxnnlx= 1214566644-y9NRsbBuErVPCyegbU0ryg. See also *District of Columbia et al. v. Heller.*

25. Stevens, J. (2018). John Paul Stevens: Repeal the Second Amendment. *New York Times,* March 27. Available at https://www.nytimes.com/2018/03/27 /opinion/john-paul-stevens-repeal-second-amendment.html.

26. Leftwich, J. (2009). Heller's Wake. *Los Angeles Daily Journal,* June 26. Available at lawcenter.giffords.org/wp-content/uploads/2012/05/Op_Ed_Hellers _Wake.0626.2009.pdf.

27. Waldman, M. (2014). How the NRA Rewrote the Second Amendment. *Politico,* May 19. Available at https://www.politco.com/magazine/story/2014/05/nra -guns-second-amendment-106856. See also Toobin, J. (2012). So You Think You Know the Second Amendment? *New Yorker,* December 17. Available at https:// www.newyorker.com/news/daily-comments/so-you-thin-you-know-the-second -amendment.

28. Cornell, S. (2015). Guns Have Always Been Regulated. *The Atlantic,* December 17. Available at https://www.theatlantic.com/politics/archive/2015/12 /guns-have-always-been-regulated/420531.

29. See Greenhouse, Justices, Ruling 5–.

30. *District of Columbia et al. v. Heller,* pp. 3–27.

31. Ibid., p. 19.

32. Ibid., p. 20.

33. Ibid., Stevens, J. dissenting, pp. 1–2.

34. *District of Columbia et al. v. Heller,* p. 49.

35. Ibid., pp. 49–50.

36. Ibid., p. 50.

37. Ibid., p. 50.

38. Ibid., p. 51.

39. Ibid., p. 51.

40. In fact, many extremists in the gun rights camp continue to argue that this is the most appropriate interpretation of the Second Amendment's phrase "shall not be infringed."

41. *District of Columbia et al. v. Heller*, p. 52.

42. Ibid., p. 54.

43. Ibid., p. 52, footnote.

44. Ibid., pp. 59–63, quotation, p. 63.

45. See Farago, R. (2015). Supreme Court Got It Wrong on *Heller*. The Truth about Guns, November 2. Available at https://www.thetruthaboutguns.com/author /robert-farago.

46. Leftwich, Heller's Wake.

47. Toobin, So You Think You Know.

48. Waldman, How the NRA Rewrote.

49. Cornell, Guns Have Always.

50. *District of Columbia et al. v. Heller*, p. 64.

51. See Tanaka, J. (2009). On Otis McDonald and His Lawsuit Challenging Chicago's 1982 Handgun Ban. *Politics & City Life*, December 30. Available at www.chicagomag.com/Chicago-Magazine/January-2010/In-Their-Sights -Lawsuit-challenging-Chicagos-1982-handgun-ban-to-be-heard-by-Supreme -Court.

52. *McDonald v. City of Chicago*, 561 U.S. 742 (2010). Available at https:// supreme.justia.com/cases/federal/us/561/742.

53. Ibid.

54. See Glanton, D. (2014). Otis McDonald, 1933–2014: Fought Chicago's Gun Ban. *Chicago Tribune*, April 6. Available at articles.chicagotribune.com /2014-04-06/news/ct-otis-mcdonald-obituary-met-20140406_1_gun-ban-illinois -state-rifle-association-gun-rights.

55. *District of Columbia et al. v. Heller*, p. 54.

56. See Blocher, J. & Ruben, E. (2018). The Second Amendment Allows for More Gun Control Than You Think. *Vox*, May 23. Available at https://www.vox .com/the-big-idea/2018/5/23/17383644/second-2nd-amendment-gun-control -debate-santa-fe-parkland-heller-anniversary-constitution.

57. Ibid.

58. Not everyone in Bedrock America would agree that these were the only cities with significant prohibitions infringing the Second Amendment. For example, in June 2015, Justice Clarence Thomas dissented from the Court's denial of certiorari in the case of *Espanola Jackson, et al. v. City of and County of San Francisco, California, et al.* That case centered on the city's regulation that prohibited residents from hav- ing a handgun in the home unless the firearm was "carried on the person" or stored in a locked container. Because the law required firearm owners to lock up their pistols and revolvers while sleeping, Jackson argued that the law burdened their ability to defend themselves—a gun owner needing the firearm to ward off an intruder might have to spend critical seconds unlocking and retrieving the firearm.

Justice Thomas contended that the case was substantially identical to *Heller*, and by denying certiorari, the Court missed an opportunity to reiterate the reasoning of *Heller*—reasoning that Thomas felt lower courts had been "narrowing" with their rulings. See Re, R. (2015). Is Heller Being Narrowed from Below? *PrawfsBlawg*, June 14. Available at prawfsblawg.blogs.com/prawfsblawg/2015/06 /is-heller-being-narrowed-from-below.html. See also *Espanola Jackson, et al. v. City of and County of San Francisco, California, et al.* Thomas, C. dissenting (June 8, 2015). Available at https://www.supremecourt.gov/opinions/14pdf/14-704_jiel.pdf.

59. Blocher & Ruben, Second Amendment Allows.

60. See Garrett, B. (2017). President Barack Obama and Gun Rights. *ThoughtCo*, October 7. Available at https://www.thoughtco.com/president-barack -obama-and-gun-rights-721329.

61. See Murse, T. (2018). List of Obama Gun Control Measures. *ThoughtCo*, February 21. Available at https://www.thoughtco.com/obama-gun-laws-passed-by -congress-336759.

62. Ibid.

63. Garrett, President Barack Obama.

64. See. Follman, M. (2012). What Exactly Is a Mass Shooting? *Mother Jones*, August 24. Available at https://www.motherjones.com/crime-justice/2012/08 /what-is-a-mass-shooting/.

65. See Berger, M. (1949). Veteran Kills 12 in Mad Rampage on Camden Street. *New York Times*, September 7. Available at https://archive.nytimes.com /www.nytimes.com/library/national/090749nj-shoot.html?module=inline.

66. See Virginia Tech Shootings Fast Facts. Available at https://www.cnn .com/2013/10/31/us/virginia-tech-shootings-fast-facts/index.html.

67. See. Troy, T. (2018). Presidents and Mass Shootings. *National Affairs* (Spring). Available at https://www.nationalaffairs.com/publications/detail/presidents -and-mass-shootings.

68. See Robinson, C. (2016). Alabama's Most Notorious Mass Murders: 64 People Killed in 12 Massacres. *AL.com*, August 28. Available at https://www.al.com/news /birmingham/index.ssf/2016/08/alabama_mass_murders_56_killed.html.

69. See McFadden, R. (2009). 13 Shot Dead during a Class on Citizenship. *New York Times*, April 3. Available at https://www.nytimes.com/2009/04/04nyre gion/04hostage.html?_r=1&partner=MOREOVERNEWS&ei=5040.

70. See Gay, E. (2011). Army Reprimands 9 Officers in Fort Hood Shooting. *USA Today*, March 11. Available at https://usatoday30.usatoday.com/news /military/2011-03-10-fort-hood-shooting_N.htm.

71. See Central NY News. (2009). Obama Calls Binghamton Shooting Act of "Senseless Violence. *Syracuse.com*, April 3. Available at https://www.syracuse .com/news/index.ssf/2009/04/obama_calls_binghamton_shootin.html.

72. See Brady Campaign to Prevent Gun Violence (2009). Assault Weapons, Weak Gun Laws Enable Dangerous People Like the Alabama Man Who Killed 10." March 11.

73. See CNN Library. (2018). Colorado Theater Shooting Fast Facts. *CNN*, July 16. Available at https://www.cnn.com/2013/07/19/us/colorado-theater-shooting -fast-facts/index.html.

74. Ibid.

75. See CNN Wire Staff. (2012). Police Identify Army Veteran as Wisconsin Temple Shooting Gunman. *CNN*, August 7. Available at https://www.cnn.com /2012/08/06/us/wisconsin-temple-shooting/index.html.

76. See Pilkington, Ed. (2013). Sandy Hook Report—Shooter Adam Lanza Was Obsessed with Mass Murder. *The Guardian*, November 25. Available at https: //www.theguardian.com/world/2013/nov/25/sandy-hook-shooter-adam-lanza -report.

77. Post Staff Report. (2012). Gun Sales Surging in Wake of *Dark Knight Rises* Shooting. *New York Post*, July 25. Available at https://nypost.com/2012/07/25/gun -sales-surging-in-wake-of-dark-knight-rises-shooting.

78. Jervis, R. & McAuliff, J. (2012). Colo. Rampage Adds Fuel to Gun-Control Debate. *USA Today*, July 25. Available at https://usatoday30.usatoday.com/news /nation/story/2012-07-24/aurora-gun-control-debate/56465980/1.

79. Pew Research Center. (2012). Views on Gun Laws Unchanged after Aurora Shooting. U.S. Politics & Policy section, July 30. Available at www.people-press .org/2012/07/30/views-on-gun-laws-unchanged-after-aurora-shooting.

80. Jervis & McAuliff, Colo. Rampage.

81. See CNN. (2013). Obama Announces 23 Executive Actions, Asks Congress to Pass Gun Laws. January 16. Available at news.blogs.cnn.com/2013/01/16 /obama-to-announce-gun–control-proposals-shortly.

82. Shear, M. (2012). Obama Vows Fast Action in New Push for Gun Control. *New York Times*, December 19. Available at https://www.nytimes.com/2012/12/20 /us/politics/obama-to-give-congress-plan-on-gun-control-within-weeks.html.

83. Walshe, S. (2013). New York Passes Nation's Toughest Gun-Control Law. *ABC News*, January 15. Available at https://abcnews.go.com/Politics/york-state -passes-toughest-gun-control-law-nation/story?id=18224091.

84. Nakamura, D. & Hamburger, T. (2012). Put Armed Police in Every School, NRA Urges. *Washington Post*, December 21. Available at https://www.washington post.com/politics/put-armed-police-officers-in-every-school-nra-head-says/2012 /12/21/9ac7d4ae-4b8b-11e2-9a42-d1ce6d0ed278_story.html?utm_term=.100 d4c7f248b.

85. Ibid.

86. Hartmann, M. (2013). Post-Newtown, States Passed More Gun-Rights Laws, Not Restrictions. *New York Magazine*, April 4. Available at nymag.com /daily/intelligencer/2013/04/post-newtown-states-loosen-gun-restrictions.html.

87. See Dewey, C. (2013). Newtown Board Requests Armed Guards for Elementary Schools. *Washington Post*, February 1. Available at https://www.washingtonpost .com/national/newtown-board-requests-armed-guards-for-elementary-schools /2013/02/01/762b8e04-6cb2-11e2-8740-9b58f43c191a_story.html?noredirect.

88. See Shear, M. & Schmidt, M. (2013). Gunman and 12 Victims Killed in Shooting at D.C. Navy Yard. *New York Times*, September 16. Available at https://www .nytimes.com/2013/09/17/us/shooting-reported-at-washington-navy-yard.html.

89. See Fernandez, M. & Blinder, A. (2014). Army Releases Detailed Account of Base Rampage. *New York Times,* April 7. Available at https://www.nytimes .com/2014/04/08/us/officials-give-account-of-fort-hood-shooting.html.

90. See Serna, J. (2015). Elliot Roger Meticulously Planned Isla Vista Rampage, Report Says. *Los Angeles Times*, February 19. Available at www.latimes.com /local/lanow/la-me-in-santa-barbara-isla-vista-rampage-investigation-20150219 -story.html.

91. See Curry, T. (2013). NRA's LaPierre Calls for More Armed Personnel after Navy Yard Shooting. *NBC News*, September 22. Available at presspass.nbcnews .com/_news/2013/09/22/20636650-nras-lapierre-calls-for-more-armed-personnel -after-navy-yard-shooting?lite.

92. See Langford, T. (2014). Fort Hood Shooting Sparks Debate on Concealed Guns. *Texas Tribune*, April 16. Available at https://www.chron.com/news/houston-texas/article/Fort-Hood-shooting-sparks-debate-on concealed-guns-5406551.php.

93. Bordelon, B. (2014). Dem Senator Uses Santa Barbara Shooting to Urge Stricter Gun Laws. *Daily Caller*, May 25. Available at dailycaller.com/2014/05/25 /dem-senator-uses-santa-barbara-shooting-to-urge-stricter-gun-laws.

94. Dennis, S. (2014). Elliot Rodger Shooting Prompts Feinstein to Blame NRA "Stranglehold" on Guns. *Roll Call*, May 25. Available at www.rollcall.com /wgdb/elliot-rodger-guns-feinstein-nra-stranglehold.

95. See, for example, Bordelon, Dem Senator.

96. See Horowitz, J., Corasaniti, N. & Southall, A. (2015). Nine Killed in Shooting at Black Church in Charleston. *New York Times*, June 17. Available at https://www.nytimes.com/2016/06/18/us/church-attacked-in-charleston-south -carolina.html.

97. See Shoichet, C. & Tuchman, G. (2015). Chattanooga Shooting: 4 Marines Killed, a Dead Suspect and Questions of Motive. *CNN*, July 17. Available at https:// www.cnn.com/2015/07/16/us/tennessee-naval-reserve-shooting/index.html.

98. See Ford, D. & Payne, E. (2015). Oregon Shooting: Gunman Dead after College Rampage. *CNN*, October 2. Available at https://www.cnn.com/2015 /10/01/us/oregon-college-shooting/index.html.

99. See Schmidt, M. & Perez-Pena, R. (2015). F.B.I. Treating San Bernardino Attack as Terrorism Case. *New York Times*, December 4. Available at https://www .nytimes.com/2015/12/05/us/tashfeen-malik-islamic-state.html.

100. See Ellis, R., Fantz, A., Karimi, F. & McLaughlin, E. (2016). Orlando Shooting: 49 Killed, Shooter Pledged ISIS Allegiance. *CNN*, June 13. Available at https://www.cnn.com/2016/06/12/us/orlando-nightclub-shooting/index.html.

Chapter 9

1. President Trump appointed Neil Gorsuch, a conservative jurist and gun rights supporter, to the Supreme Court to succeed Antonin Scalia in April 2017, and Brett Kavanaugh, his nominee to replace retiring Justice Anthony Kennedy, was narrowly confirmed in October 2018.

2. See History.com. (2018). 2017 Las Vegas Shooting. Available at https:// www.history.com/this-day-in-history/2017-las-vegas-shooting.

3. See Hanna, J. & Yan, H. (2017). Sutherland Springs Church Shooting: What We Know. Available at https://www.cnn.com/2017/11/05/us/texas-church-shooting-what-we-know/index.html.

4. See Sanchez, R. (2018). "My School Is Being Shot Up." *CNN*, February 18. Available at https://www.cnn.com/2018/02/18/us/parkland-florida-school-shooting-accounts/index.html.

5. See Astor, M. (2018). Florida Gun Bill: What's In It and What Isn't. *New York Times*, March 8. Available at https://www.nytimes.com/2018/03/08/us/florida-gun-bill.html.

6. See McCurry, J. Beckett, L. & Dart, T. (2017). "This Isn't a Guns Situation," Says Trump after Texas Church Shooting. *The Guardian,* November 6. Available at https://www.theguardian.com/us-news/2017/nov/06/this-isn't-a-guns-situation-says-trump-after-texas-church-shooting.

7. Ibid.

8. For example, right after the Las Vegas shooting, Senator Dianne Feinstein of California introduced the Automatic Gunfire Prevention Act in an effort to ban devices that increase a rifle's firing rate and the Background Check Completion Act that blocked an individual's gun purchase until the background check cleared, even if the check exceeded the current 72-hour time limit.

9. See Kahan, D. (2003). More Statistics, Less Persuasion: A Cultural Theory of Gun-Risk Perceptions. *Faculty Scholarship Series*, Paper 106, Yale Law School, for an intriguing analysis of why rational arguments are not likely to work.

10. See Kurtzleben, D. (2017). Fact Check: Is Chicago Proof That Gun Laws Don't Work? NPR Politics, October 5. Available at https://www.npr.org/2017/10/05/5555805598/fact-check-is-chicago-proof-that-gun-laws-don-t-work.

11. Ibid.

12. Ibid. In comparison to Chicago's homicide rate of 25.1/100,000 residents, the rate for the whole country in 2016 was 5.3/100,000.

13. See Greenwood, C. (1972). *Firearms Control*. London: Routledge & Kegan Paul, Ltd., p. 254.

14. See Lewis, N. (2017). Do Tougher Gun Laws Lead to Dramatically Lower Rates of Gun Violence? *Washington Post*, October 17. Available at https://www.washingtonpost.com/news/fact-checker/wp/2017/10/17/do-tougher-gun-laws-lead-todramatically-lower-rates-of-gun-violence/?utm_term=.8aa1c0e61872.

15. See Kleck, G. & Gertz, M. (1995). Armed Resistance to Crime: The Prevalence and Nature of Self-Defense with a Gun. *Journal of Criminal Law and Criminology, 86,* 150–187. Available at https://scholarlycommons.law.northwestern.edu/cgi/viewcontent.cgi?article=6853&content=jclc.

16. See Lott, J. (2010). *More Guns, Less Crime: Understanding Crime and Gun Control Laws*. 3rd ed. Chicago: University of Chicago Press.

17. Ibid.

18. Hemenway, D. (2000). Gun Use in the United States: Results from Two National surveys. *Injury Prevention, 6*, pp. 263–267.

19. DeFilippis, E. & Hughes, D. (2016). The GOP's Favorite Gun "Academic" Is a Fraud. *ThinkProgress*, August 12. Available at https://thinkprogress.org /debunking-john-lott-5456e83cf326.

20. See Kleck, G., Kovandzic, T. & Bellows, J. (2016). Does Gun Control Reduce Violent Crime? *Criminal Justice Review, 4*, pp. 488–513.

21. See Sweeney, P. (2016). *Gunsmithing the AR-15: The Bench Manual*. Iola, WI: F+W Media, Inc.

22. "AR" stands for "Armalite," the small arms engineering company that originally developed the firearm, rather than "assault rifle."

23. See, for example, Feuer, A. (2016). AR-15 Rifles Are Beloved, Reviled and a Common Element in Mass Shootings. *New York Times*, June 13. Available at https://www.nytimes.com/2016/06/04/nyregion/ar-15-rifles-are-beloved -reviled-and-a-common-element-in mass-shootings.html.

24. See, for example, Moore, E. (2018). The Parkland Shooter's AR-15 Was Designed to Kill as Efficiently as Possible. Available at https://www.nbcnews .com/think/opinion/parkland-shooter-s-ar-15-was-designed-kill-efficiently -possible-ncna848346.

25. This quote is often attributed to Philip J. Cook, the ITT/Terry Sanford Professor Emeritus of Public Policy Studies at Duke University and a respected gun violence researcher.

26. See Mair, J., Teret, S. & Frattaroli, S. (n.d.). A Public Health Perspective on Gun Violence Prevention. Available at https://www.press.umich.edu/pdf /0472115103-ch1.pdf.

27. Ibid.

28. Koper, C., Woods, D. & Roth, J. (2004). An Updated Assessment of the Federal Assault Weapons Ban: Impact on Gun Markets and Gun Violence, 1994–2003. Report to the National Institute of Justice, United States Department of Justice.

29. See Lott, *More Guns, Less Crime*.

30. See Mair et al., Public Health Perspective.

31. Ibid., p. 55.

32. See Crane, D. (2011). "Newsweek" Attempts to Rebrand Gun Control Scheme as "Gun Safety" Cause: Tina Brown Gets Cute, Right out of the Gate. *DefenseReview*, April 24. Available at www.defensereview.com/newsweek -attempts-to-rebrand-gun-control-scheme-as-gun-safety-cause-tina-brown-gets -cute-right-out-of-the-gate; also, McGough, M. (2015). Sorry, Rebranding Gun Control as "Gun Safety" Won't Work. *Los Angeles Times*, October 9. Available at www.latimes.com/opinion/opinion-la/la-ol-guns-obama-safety-20151009-story. html; also, Cox, C. (2017). Political Report: Gun Control Rebranded. *NRA-ILA*, December 19. Available at https://www.nraila.org/articles/20171219/political-report -gun-control-rebranded.

33. See, for example, Wheaton, S. (2016). Dems Urged to Retool Their Guns Message. *Politico*, July 19. Available at https://www.politico.com/story/2016/07 /democrats-gun-messaging-225722.

34. See, for example, Cox, Political Report and Edwards, C. (2015). Cam's Corner: The Rebranding of the Gun Control Movement. *America's 1st Freedom*, November 4. Available at https://www.americas1stfreedom.org/articles/2015/11/4/cams-corner-the-rebranding-of-the-gun-control-movement.

35. For example, Bash, D. (2006). Cheney Accidently Shoots Fellow Hunter. *CNN Politics*, February 13. Available at www.cnn.com/2006/POLITICS/02/12/cheney.

36. See Foley, R., Fenn, L. & Penzenstadler, N. (2016). Chronicle of Agony: Gun Accidents Kill at Least 1 Kid Every Other Day. *USA Today*, October 14. Available at https://www.usatoday.com/story/news/2016/10/14/ap-usa-today-gun-accidents-children-91906700.

37. See Yan, H. & Moshtaghain, A. (2018). FBI Agent Loses His Gun during Dance-Floor Backflip, Accidently Shoots Bar Patron. *CNN*, June 4. Available at https://www.cnn.com/2018/06/03/us/dancing-fbi-agent-gun-discharge/index.html.

38. See Snopes. (2005). Safety First. March 22. Available at https://www.snopes.com/fact-check/safety-first.

39. See Lee, K. (2018). Amid Rising Gun Violence, Accidental Shooting Deaths Have Plummeted. Why? *Los Angeles Times*, January 1. Available at www.latimes.com/nation/la-na-accidental-gun-deaths-20180101-story.html.

40. Ibid.

41. Iannelli, V., MD. (2018). Preventing Childhood Gun and Shooting Accidents. Verywell Family, July 7. Available at https://www.verywellfamily.com/gun-and-shooting-accidents-2634213.

42. Foley et al., Chronicle of Agony.

43. See, for example, Horman, B. (2016). 6 Ways to Safely Store Your Firearms. NRA Family, April 14. Available at https://wwwnrafamily.org/articles/2016/4/14/6-ways-tosafely-store-your-firearms.

44. Foley et al., Chronicle of Agony.

45. See Centers for Disease Control and Prevention, National Center for Health Statistics. (2015). Suicide and Self-Inflicted Injury. Available at https://www.cdc.gov/nchs/fastats/suicide.htm.

46. See Gaudiano, N. (2018). "Red Flag" Laws That Allow for Temporary Restrictions on Access to Guns Gain Momentum across Nation. *USA Today*, March 25. Available at https://www.usatoday.com/story/news/politics/2018/03/25/red-flag-laws-allow-temporary-restrictions-access-guns-gain-momentum-across-nation/454395002.

47. Ibid.

48. Soffen, K. (2016). To Reduce Suicides, Look at Guns. *Washington Post*, July 13. Available at https://www.washingtonpost.com/graphics/business/wonkblog/suicide-rates.

49. Ibid.

50. See, for example, Sarchiapone, M., Mandelli, L., Iosue, M., Andrisano, C. & Roy, A. (2011). Controlling Access to Suicide Means. *International Journal of Environmental Research and Public Health*, 8, 4550–4562. Available at https://www.ncbi.nim.nih.gov/pmc/articles/PMC3290984.

51. Kellermann, A., Rivara, F., Rushforth, N., Banton, J., Reay, D., Francisco, J., Locci, A., Prodzinski, J., Hackman, B., & Somes, G. (1993). Gun ownership as a risk factor for homicide in the home. *New England Journal of Medicine, 329*, pp. 1084–1091. Available at https://www.nejm.org/doi/full/10.1056/NEJM 199310073291506.

52. For example, APA PsycNET indicates that the study has garnered about 750 citations in academic and scholarly journals alone.

53. See, for example, Schaffer, H. (1993). Serious Flaws in Kellermann, et al. (1993) NEJM. Available at www.firearmsandliberty.com/kellermann-schaffer .html.

54. See Union of Concerned Scientists (n.d.). How the NRA Suppressed Gun Violence Research. Available at https://www.ucsusa.org/suppressing-research -effects-gun-violence.

55. See Cox, C. (2015). Why We Can't Trust the CDC with Gun Research. *Politico*, December 9. Available at https://www.politico.com/agenda/story/2015 /12/why-we-cant-trust-the-cdc-with-gun-research-000340.

56. See Jamieson, C. (2013). Gun Violence Research: History of the Federal Funding Freeze. American Psychological Association, February. Available at https://www.apa.org/science/about/psa/2013/02/gun-violence.aspx.

57. Union of Concerned Scientists, How the NRA Suppressed.

58. McLaughlin, D. (2018). There's No Ban on Studying Gun Violence. *National Review*, April 2. Available at https://www.nationalreview.com/2018/04 /no-ban-on-gun-violence-studies-gun-control-public-health-argument.

59. See NRA-ILA. (1999). Suicide and Firearms. November 6. Available at https://www.nraila.org/articles/19991106/suicide-and-firearms.

60. See Safer Homes Coalition. (n.d.). What Is a Safer Home? Available at depts.washington.edu./saferwa/what-is-a-safer-home.

61. See Suicide Prevention Resource Center. (n.d.). Suicide Prevention: A Role for Firearm Dealers and Range Owners (New Hampshire Gun Shop Project). Available at https://www.sprc.org/resources-programs/suicide-prevention-role -firearm-dealers-range-owners-new-hampshire-gun-shop.

62. See Bryan, Z. (2018). What Gun Shops Can Do to Help Prevent Suicide. *High Country News*, July 17. Available at https://www.hcn.org/articles/the-montana -gap-gun-sellers-on-the-front-line-of-suicide-prevention.

63. See, for example, Beekman, D. (2018). Gun Owners Face Fines of up to $10,000 for Not Locking Up Their Guns under New Seattle Law. *Seattle Times*, July 9. Available at www.seattletimes.com/seattle-news/politics/gun-owners-face -fines-up-to-10000-for-not-locking-up-their-guns-under-new-seattle-law.

Although this particular law may not survive the State of Washington's preemption regulations that forbid cities from passing gun regulations more severe than state regulations, Seattle's punitive approach for achieving gun safety is representative of Cosmopolitan America's general orientation in this arena.

64. See Kiely, E. (2017). Gun Control in Australia, Updated. *FactCheck.org*, October 6. Available at https://www.factcheck.org/2017/10/gun-control-australia -updated.

65. See, for example, Cox, C. (2017). Despite Little Evidence of Success, Australia Continues to Expand Gun Control. NRA-ILA, November 20. Available at https://www.nraila.org/articles/20171120/despite-little-evidence-of-success-australia-continues-to-expand-gun-control.

66. See Burnett, D. (2017). Britain Is Bleeding: Violent Crime Rises in England Despite Gun Control. America's 1st Freedom, October 27. Available at https://www.americas1stfreedom.org/2017/10/27/britain-is-bleeding-violent-crime-rises-in-england-despite-gun-control.

67. See McPherson, S. (2018). Gun Control in Britain Has Failed. Future of Freedom Foundation, April 16. Available at https://www.fff.org/explore-freedom/article/gun-control-britain-failed.

68. See Swearer, A. (2018). Amid Push for Knife Control, UK Shows Gun Control Doesn't Increase Safety. *Daily Signal*, April 12. Available at https://www.dailysignal.com/2018/04/12/london-mayor-imposes-knife-control-because-gun-control-hasn't-worked.

69. See Cummings, W. (2018). After Murder Rate Passes NYC, London Mayor Sadiq Khan Calls for Sharper Knife Control. *USA Today*, April 9. Available at https://www.usatoday.com/story/news/world/2018/04/09/london-mayor-knife-control/500328002.

70. See Frum, D. (2017). What Trump Doesn't Understand about Gun Control in Great Britain. *The Atlantic*, June 4. Available at https://www.theatlantic.com/international/archive/2017/06/london-bridge/529107.

Also, Leaf, C. (2018). How Australia All but Ended Gun Violence. *Fortune*, February 20. Available at fortune.com/2018/02/20/Australia-gun-control-success.

71. Ibid.

72. John Locke's *Two Treatises on Government* and the *Commentaries* of William Blackstone are representative of this tradition. See Cherry, R. (2013). Locke and Self-Defense. *American Thinker*, February 5. Available at https://www.americanthinker.com/blog/2013/02/locke-and-self-defense.html; also, Pratt, E. (n.d.). Self-Government and the Unalienable Right of Self-Defense: Restoring the Second Amendment. Available at https://lonang.com/commentaries/conlaw/bill-of-rights/unalienable-right-of-self-defense.

73. See Re, R. (2015). Is *Heller* Being Narrowed from Below? *PrawfsBlawg*, June 14. Available at prawfsblawg.blogs.com/prawfsblawg/2015/06/is-heller-being-narrowed-from-below.html.

74. Stevens, J. (2018). John Paul Stevens: Repeal the Second Amendment. *New York Times*, March 27. Available at https://www.nytimes.com/2018/03/27/opinion/john-paul-stevens-repeal-second-amendment.html.

75. See Turley, J. (2018). Repealing the Second Amendment Isn't Easy but It's What March for Our Lives Students Need. *USA Today*, March 28. Available at https://www.usatoday.com/story/opinion/2018/03/28/repealing-second-amendment-march-our-lives-students/463644002.

76. See Cohen, D. (2016). Why It's Time to Repeal the Second Amendment. *Rolling Stone*, June 13. Available at https://www.rollingstone.com/culture/culture-news/why-its-time-to-repeal-the-second-amendment-95622; also, Eichenwald,

E. (2013). Kurt Eichenwald: Let's Repeal the Second Amendment. *Vanity Fair*, January 3. Available at https://www.vanityfair.com/news/politics/2013/01 /kurt-eichenwald-lets-repeal-second-amendment.

77. See Accuracy In Media (2018). Media Mostly Silent on 2nd Amendment Repeal Poll Results. *Accuracy in Media*, April 3. Available at https://www.aim.org /on-target-blog/media-mostly-silent-on-2nd-amendment-repeal-poll-results.

78. The shooting fraternity's defense of "bump stocks" is a good illustration. Such stocks are a novelty accessory that increase a rifle's rate of fire at the cost of severely degraded accuracy. Owners typically use them once or twice at the range, note how they function, have some fun burning through hundreds of rounds of pricey ammunition, and then retire them to the back of the gun closet, never to be seen again. If bump stocks were banned, few shooters would miss them. Nonetheless, Bedrock America fiercely fights any attempt at such a ban. See, for example, McCullagh, D. (2018). ATF Flips on Bump Stock Ban, Some Gun Rights Groups Are Mad. *Reason*, June 17. Available at https://reason.com /archives/2018/06/27/atf-flips-on-bump-stock-ban-some-gun-rig.

79. See Novak, J. (2018). Stop Blaming the NRA for Failed Gun Control Efforts. *CNBC*, February 16. Available at https://www.cnbc.com/2018/02/16 /nra-money-isnt-why-gun-control-efforts-are-failing-commentary.html.

80. See, for example, Murillo, M. (2018). "Common-Sense Gun Laws" Urged by Democratic Attorneys General. *WTOP News*, February 26. Available at https:// wtop.com/government/2018/02/gun-laws-democratic-attorneys-general.

81. See Elder, L. (2018). Where's the Common Sense in "Common Sense" Gun Laws? *Townhall*, March 29. Available at https://townhall.com/columnists /larryelder/2018/03/29/where-is-the-common-sense-in-common-sense-gun -laws-n2465644.

82. See Novak, Stop Blaming the NRA.

83. See Parry, R. (1974). Guns of Baltimore: Why Did Bounty Stop? *Toledo Blade*, December 8. Available at https://news.google.com/newspapers?nid=1350.

84. Ibid.

85. See Ingraham, C. (2015). There Are Now More Guns Than People in the United States. *Washington Post*, October 5. Available at https://www.washingtonpost .com/news/wonk/wp/2015/10/05/guns-in-the-united-states-one-for-every -man-woman-and-child-and-then-some/?utm_term=6eca7cea5270.

86. Issues with buyback programs are numerous. Critics contend that a large proportion of the guns netted are not the truly dangerous weapons envisioned, but inoperable, rusted, and otherwise useless specimens unlikely to buttress criminal activity. The typical "no-questions-asked" provision of the programs also allows criminals to safely dispose of otherwise valuable legal evidence: guns used in prior crimes. The programs sometimes attract gun owners and entrepreneurs who offer participants higher rewards for their functioning firearms, turning the event into an open-air gun bazaar. Most discouragingly, the programs' effectiveness in lowering gun crime is not just unproven but sometimes counterintuitive. After spending almost $700,000 in a gun buyback program,

the Baltimore Police Department reported that the city's gun homicide and assault rates actually increased during the program. See Parry, Guns of Baltimore.

87. CBS News. (2018). 3D-Printed Gun Blueprint Maker Cody Wilson Says "the Debate Is Over." *CBS This Morning*, August 1. Available at https://www.cbsnews.com/news/3d-printed-gun-cody-wilson-says-gun-access-fundamental-human-right.

88. Barrett, B. (2018). DIY Gun Blueprints Have Been Taken Offline—For Now. *Wired*, August 1. Available at https://www.wired.com/story/3d-gun-blueprints-injunction-cody-wilson-defense-distributed.

89. See French, D. (2018). The 3D-Gun Debate: Separating Truth from Fiction. *National Review*, July 31. Available at https://www.nationalreview.com/2018/07/3d-printed-guns-truth-from-fiction.

90. The British experience with severe gun restrictions illustrates this. See Webb, S. (2013). Gangland Armourer Who Was Caught with Improvised Single-Shot Handgun, a Revolver and Hundreds of Bullets Is Jailed for Nine Years. *Daily Mail*, October 7. Available at www.dailymail.co.uk/news/article-24449078/Gangland-armourer-Thomas-Keatly-caught-handgun-jailed-9-years.html.

For an American example, see Gartrell, N. (2018). California Man Sentenced for Selling Guns He Made with YouTube Tutorial. *East Bay Times*, July 30. Available at https://www.eastbaytimes.com/2018/07/30/california-man-sentenced-for-selling-guns-he-made-with-youtube-tutorial.

91. See Weiss, B. (2017). Criminals Steal More Than 237,000 Guns from Legal American Gun Owners Every Year. *Business Insider*, November 20. Available at https://www.businessinsider.com/criminals-steal-guns-from-legal-gun-owners-2017-11.

92. This is a paraphrase of a line spoken by Christian Slater's character, Clarence Worley, in the 1993 film *True Romance*.

93. Kennett, L. & Anderson, J. (1975). *The Gun in America: The Origins of a National Dilemma*. Westport, CT: Greenwood Press.

94. See Gallup. (n.d.). Most Important Problem. Available at https://news.gallup.com/poll/1675/most-important-problem.aspx. See also Rothschild, M. (n.d.). Political Issues That Matter the Most Right Now. Available at https://www.ranker.com/list/political-issues-that-matter-the-most/mike-rothschild.

95. See Russell, N. (2006). An Introduction to the Overton Window of Political Possibilities. MacKinac Center for Public Policies. Available at https://www.mackinac.org/750496.

96. Ibid.

97. See Concealed Carry Reciprocity Act of 2017. Available at https://www.congress.gov/bill/115th-congress/house-bill/38.

98. Consider the illustrative case of Shaneen Allen, a Pennsylvania resident licensed to carry a concealed firearm in Pennsylvania. Not realizing her permit was invalid in New Jersey, she told the New Jersey police officer stopping her for a routine traffic violation that she had a pistol and her permit in her purse. The

officer immediately arrested her for unlawful possession of a handgun. She faced a mandatory three-year prison sentence for her error. See Napoliello, A. (2014). Woman with Pa. Handgun Permit Faces Prison Sentence for Carrying in New Jersey. *NJ.com*, August 4. Available at https://www.nj.com/atlantic/index.ssf /2014/08/philadelphia_mom_who_legally_purchased_gun_in_pa_arrested_in _new_jersey_faces_three_years_in_prison.html.

Index

About the Author

Donald J. Campbell, PhD, is professor emeritus of leadership and management at the U.S. Military Academy at West Point, New York. He received his graduate degree in psychology from Purdue University, West Lafayette, Indiana. During his academic career, Don served on the faculties of nationally and internationally renowned universities, including Duke University, the U.S. Air Force Academy, and the National University of Singapore. He is a certified pistol instructor and currently spends his time in Colorado Springs and Westcliffe, Colorado.

DISCARD